US $
$5.95 — Paper
$7.95 — Wire Spiral
$11.95 — Vinyl Ring Binder

LET'S COOK

469 - 7487
465 - 2005

MICROWAVE!™

by BARBARA HARRIS

4th EDITION

Adjustments may be needed since microwave ovens vary in wattage and power output. Our recipes were tested in ovens with 600-700 watts. To adjust cooking times for **400-500 watts,** consult charts on p. 13, 14, and 15. Under many recipes you will note **"maxi-time"**. This gives you the variable power advantage. The recipe will say if minimum or maximum time is needed for best results. In low wattage ovens, the recipe may not be suitable for large volumes serving more than 4. If the dish size won't fit in the oven, cook half the recipe at a time in a smaller dish. For reheating, reduce energy to medium-high (70%) or high for low wattage ovens.

If you don't know the wattage-write your manufacturer with model number or call 1-800-555-1212 to see if they have a toll-free number.

Barbara Harris

MICROWAVE
COOKING SERVICES
P.O. Box 2992
Portland, Oregon 97208

D0954648

Brand names mentioned in this book are used to indicate consumer products which I have personally tested and with which I am pleased. I am not subsidized by anyone and there may be other products that are comparable or even better of which I am not aware.

THE COOK'S SAD RECIPE

I didn't have potatoes, so I substituted rice
I didn't have paprika, so I used another spice.
I didn't have tomato sauce, I used tomato paste. . .
A whole can, not a half can. . .
I can't believe in waste.
A friend gave me the recipe,
she said, "you couldn't beat it!"
There must be something wrong with her,
I couldn't even eat it!

For Braille copy write:
NBA Reader-Transcriber Registry
5300 Hamilton Ave. #1404
Cincinnati, Ohio 45224
Attn: Mrs. Lawrence M. Levine, Chm.

27th Printing
Library of Congress Catalog Card Number 79-84435
ISBN #0-9601060-0-6, paper; #0-9601060-1-4, wire spiral; #0-9601060-2-2, 3-ring vinyl

Table of Contents

LITTLE HANDS like to cook with microwaves as well as big. I frequently receive requests for recipes children can prepare and have taught several children's classes. Small children may need help preparing ingredients but can easily assemble recipes. These are also easy to try as you learn to use the microwave. Several will become family favorites! 135 recipes have been selected.

 Most frequently used time-tables are identified by this clock symbol, making it easier for you to find times on the pages. 44 tables are located in the book.

 ELEGANT BUT EASY recipes are great for entertaining and special dinners — not always everyday fare. More steps may be required for preparation; ingredients may be more costly; others are not costly or difficult but accommodate elegant occasions. 69 recipes were selected.

MICROWAVE MAGIC: gives other uses of your microwave that don't fit in a recipe category (p. 189-197).

The **How? and Why? Chapter** includes repeatedly asked questions about microwave cooking. Other questions are answered throughout the book. Beginners find it helpful to read cover to cover for a better understanding of the many uses of your microwave. It reads like a novel or going to a class — not a traditional cookbook. It is written to be used as an everyday handbook. The bright pink cover makes it easy to locate in a drawer or cookbook shelf (p. 185-189).

Think Time — Not Heat!!

Think Microwave!

Dear Microwave Friend,

Welcome to convenience — cooking in a MICROWAVE OVEN! You are among the many who will seek as much information as possible to best utilize this time and energy-saving appliance in your home. You are a pioneer of cooking methods of the future! I hope you will use your microwave every day — for every meal — not just heating and defrosting.

Let's Cook Microwave! will give you many basics to answer important questions: Why is my food tough? How can I cook a meal? Can I cook everything at once? Why does my food cook unevenly? And on and on . . . ! Information was compiled through seminars, workshops, classes, correspondence and literally thousands of phone calls. Possibly you are experiencing many of the same concerns:
  — My husband and I are getting tired of "charcoal briquets!"
  — I'm in desperate need of help — what an expensive dust catcher!
  — My oven's cookbook leaves many questions unanswered!
  — I am much more interested in how to use the oven for every-day foods than how to cook snails, for instance!
and even . . .
  — I'm currently using my "Brand X" oven for a breadbox!

Initially you will probably experience "microwave frustrations," but that is true of most new experiences . . . driving a car, hanging wallpaper, sewing, and even conventional cooking! If you have a failure with conventional cooking, it is usually blamed on the recipe. If you have a failure in the microwave, it is the oven's fault. (Seldom is it our failure to read and follow directions!!) With this new appliance, you must read the recipe completely before you begin your preparation. Timing and methods are just as important as ingredients. And the techniques for most foods will be easy to master after you have a basic understanding of HOW the oven cooks various foods. Many techniques may seem unusual to you in the beginning, but with more experience you will learn the WHYS. You are learning to cook all over.

Walk before you run! To begin your new adventure, try a few things at every meal and between meals if you have time (for reheating later). When beginning to cook breakfasts, you'll have to read recipes and directions for everything — eggs, bacon, hot cereal, rolls, etc! What an experience! Especially when the "kids" are in a hurry to catch the bus, and Dad is rushing off to work, and maybe you work, too! If you have to deliver little ones at the babysitter, you'll have even more on your mind and a new microwave could be very frustrating! Do your experimenting leisurely at first. As you gain experience, you will learn to use your microwave for complete meals. You'll get many ideas for use by browsing through our pages. Remember, you didn't learn to cook conventionally overnight!

You may not like microwave cooking for all foods. Not all foods will be the same color, texture and flavor. Cakes, cookies and bread are good examples. You may frequently "trade-off" quality for speed. Many foods, however, will taste better. If you prefer a dry, crusty skin on your baked potato, for example, cook it conventionally. It just won't happen in the microwave. But, if you like instant sauces, fast baked potatoes, fluffy scrambled eggs, tasty meats, wonderful casseroles that are not dried out, vegetables that are garden-fresh in color, flavor and nutrition, and roasts cooked in less than one-fourth conventional cooking time — the microwave is the way for you to cook! You **cannot** cook deep-fried foods, angel food and sponge cakes, popovers, or hard or soft-cooked eggs in the shell, so don't try these. USE YOUR MICROWAVE FOR THE FOODS IT COOKS BEST!! AND IT WILL BECOME YOUR BEST FRIEND!

Recipes in this book have been tested in 30 brands of microwave ovens. In addition to testing of recipes and techniques at microwave classes and workshops, I have answered many questions daily at seminars on microwave cooking throughout the United States. Recipe testing for many food companies has been a daily activity at our test kitchen.

Consumer (as opposed to commercial) countertop ovens vary in wattage from 400 to 720 watts. Recipe times in this book are based on ovens ranging from 600 to 650 watts. If your oven is more or less than average, you will have to adjust your cooking time. Lower wattage units will require more cooking time (page 15 .) Make a note of the time by the recipe. If you do not know the wattage output of your oven, test it using the formula on page 197. Countertop ovens operate on a frequency of 2450 MHz. If your microwave is the Super Stove-Microwave Cooking Center or Versatronic by General Electric or Hotpoint, it operates on a frequency of 915 MHz and will require longer cooking time, but may be used in combination with conventional cooking. Combination microwave ranges require about twice as long for a microwave recipe for short cooking foods (1-10 minutes). For those requiring 20 minutes or more, the times will be about the same. Use the manual with these ovens to make adjustments.

All recipes were tested as you would use the foods at home. Some foods are taken directly from the refrigerator and others were room temperature. It should not be necessary for you to make adjustments because of the starting temperature when cooking.

The microwave oven should make cooking fun! Information is included in the first chapter to give you the BASIC knowledge you will need.   Tips are also included with recipes and in each chapter to give you a better understanding about your new adventure. You may wonder initially why there are so many "dos and don'ts." It is because some cooking principles change and others remain the same. Refer to the "Why and How" chapter for answers to some of the most commonly asked questions. If you have suggestions or ideas, please share them with us so they can be included in future additions. You will note many are included in this book.

Continue to use many of your home appliances to supplement and complement your microwave. I still use my toaster, egg cooker, waffle iron and occasionally an oven for a quantity of food. And let your family participate in the action. Teach the basics and you may be relieved of some of your duties!!

Let's Cook Microwave! would not have been possible without the encouragement, comments and suggestions I have received from students and co-workers! Thanks to all of you! Your letters help to keep me informed of information needed to make microwave cooking more successful! It's fun to share new tips as we find them. I can't promise to personally answer all letters but I do try. Information is also emphasized at classes.

Thanks to the many manufacturers, distributors and dealers who have shared information about their microwave ovens. Special thanks to Tammy Lawrence and Jan Thiesen for their encouragement and the many hours they have spent sharing ideas and information. Special thanks also to Arlene Christianson Pickard for her friendship and the many hours and helpful suggestions pouring over reams of copy! Many special thanks to my husband and daughter who have spent most of their non-working or non-school hours discussing ideas, testing recipes, going to the store, answering the telephone, proof-reading, and on and on . . . ! They are a great team! Leonard chops and April cooks! (And they both think we would starve without our microwave oven!)

Happy microwaving!

Barbara Harris

Basics of Microwave Cooking

You are embarking on a fun, new experience! The microwave oven is an appliance that lends itself to today's lifestyle. Use it often to meet many of your needs — time-saving, energy-saving, economy and convenience. The microwave will cook about 75% of your foods. You will need other appliances to supplement cooking and your family may prefer the results of some conventionally cooked foods.

Use it for what it does best! The microwave will add to the flavor, appearance, and ease of cooking and will produce excellent results if you will take time to read and follow directions. Since you bought it primarily for speed and convenience, we cook most foods on high power. You will also see suggestions for using less power if time is not a factor (**Maxi-Time** under recipes).

You will change many of your traditional **meal planning** steps but will gain satisfaction as your family dines on an elegant microwave prepared meal! "Gourmet" is serving as well as cooking and doesn't necessarily mean long hours in the kitchen. Because microwave cooking is fast, your first change may be setting your table before you begin meal preparation. If you don't, the dinner may be waiting for you. Review your menu to determine which foods are best prepared in the microwave. Begin cooking the food with the longest cooking time and cook in sequence to the shortest time (meat or main dish, potatoes, vegetable, gravy or sauce, and bread). "Carry-over cooking" will keep most food warm until serving. If it cools, quickly reheat in the microwave at serving time.

Relate your PREPARATION TECHNIQUE to **conventional cooking** — what do you want to happen to your food? Bake? Steam? Fry? Roast? Many of the same techniques will apply — such as cover to steam and uncover and place on a rack to bake or dry-roast, or add fat and oil and heat to fry. Cooking happens a different way because you are timing foods and not adding temperature (heat), so the correct use of the timer is very important! Make it fun, not work and confusion, as you cook your foods with new convenience and simplicity. Try a few foods in the beginning and add to these as you become more familiar with techniques. Microwave accessories will also make your job easier. Consult the utensil chapter for a complete review. I have only recommended those you really need for better cooking results.

The purpose of this book is to give you the "HOWS" AND WHYS." Refer to the manual you received with your oven for technical information about microwaves, the operation of your oven, and other specifics. This sampling of recipes is small but add to these with your favorite conventional recipes as you learn to convert them. Discuss microwave cooking with friends who can share many valuable ideas.

Locate your oven in the most convenient spot in your kitchen! You will be using it often, so it should be in the main traffic pattern. Plug the oven into a grounded electrical outlet on its **own circuit**. This is very important because the oven will not operate efficiently without the correct amount of energy. It also influences the amount of time required to cook your food.

To test: 1 cup tap water should boil in 2½-3 minutes.

If it does not, your foods will require longer to cook than recipes indicate. If you have other appliances on the same circuit, you can blow fuses. If water doesn't boil in 3 minutes, the oven may not be on its own circuit and should be relocated. If convenient, the oven can be plugged into the outlet on the range. This is an independent circuit and would work well for this purpose. If the oven cannot be moved, avoid using other appliances when operating the microwave.

As you use your oven for cooking different foods you will need to learn to "**THINK MICROWAVE**" as you now unconsciously "think conventional." What do I want to happen? Which technique should I use to obtain the best results? Does the food need special handling? Which container should I use? These will need to be conscious thoughts but will become unconscious with a little microwave experience.

I feel one of the main difficulties in learning to use your microwave is learning to **cook foods evenly**. Just as you may have had to "turn the heat down" on the range — several alternatives in the microwave are important:
— Rotating and stirring or rearranging.
— Using a ring shaped container or placing a glass in the center of a dish.
— Selecting round containers instead of square.
— Reducing power to distribute energy more efficiently.
All of these must be considered as you learn to "think microwave." Recipes have already taken the above into consideration in their recommendations for utensils and methods. Some recipes you may see are incomplete so you must remember. Cakes and brownies are classic examples of foods that will either be great or awful depending on your use of microwave techniques. Carry-over cooking allows the heat to transfer from the outside to the center for perfection and

should be considered as part of the cooking time. If you ever have any trouble (after you learn not to overcook) it will be getting the center of the food cooked. The following "basics" are important for good results.

Two very important techniques to consciously keep in mind as you learn to use the microwave are **ROTATING OR STIRRING** AND **CARRY-OVER COOKING.** If both of these are used properly, they will solve many of your questions (or complaints) about microwave cooking! I hear questions such as: "Why does my food cook unevenly?" or "Why do I have a raw streak in my food?" Answer — the food must be rotated ¼ turn or stirred to mix ingredients half-way through the cooking time at least once. "When I removed my food from the oven it was perfect. Why was it tough when we ate it?" "Why does my food get dry and tough when I cook it?" "I added more cooking time to get the food done, but why does it get so hard when it cools?" Answer — the microwave energy is stopped when the cooking time is over, but the heat within the food will continue to transfer and increase while the food rests before serving. There is no way to stop this heat transfer so microwave cooking times include resting time in the recipe's total cooking time. You will note a rest time at the end of most microwave recipes.

More specifically — **ROTATING OR STIRRING** — Microwaves are directed into the oven by a specific system. This could be a stirrer fan, carousel tray, baffle or a beam diffuser, as described in your oven manual. It has not been possible to date to distribute microwaves in all places in the oven at equal strength and intensity, just as it is impossible to find the same temperature in all corners of your conventional oven or in foods cooked on the surface unit. Conventionally we make adjustments in the placement of food or by adjusting the heat, or stirring. We make adjustments in the micro-wave by changing the position of the food, or by stirring if we want the food to be mixed or scrambled. **To cook the food evenly, rotate the dish one-fourth turn, halfway through cooking time; or if the food can be mixed, such as liquids, stir halfway through cooking time.** Some recipes may require rotating or stirring more than once, but this will be directed in the recipe. If you are using a microwave recipe that does not tell you to stir or rotate, you must remember to include this technique. Some manufacturers claim this is not necessary with their ovens. If you find this in yours, omit turning the food. Some ovens are built with a turntable. Again, omit turning if not necessary.

To **test the cooking pattern** in your oven, cook an egg (p. 93). If there is an uncooked strip through your food after cooking 15 seconds, you must rotate the dish ¼ turn to finish cooking evenly. You will notice this pattern in other foods — cakes, scrambled eggs, etc. It takes very little effort to turn or stir. Usually when you cook conventionally, you peek in the oven at least once, lift the lid to check cooking, or stir many foods at least once (and some constantly!) Caution: you can stir or rotate too often! The last half of the cooking time will need the most attention, unless you are cooking a very small quantity of food. You may want to set your timer for one-half of the cooking and reset after turning or stirring for convenience.

CARRY-OVER COOKING — Always select the shortest time in a recipe. Some cooking will continue within the food after the energy source is turned off, even when the food is removed from oven cavity. **Rest the food after the cooking time to allow for extra cooking**. The amount of time will vary depending on the size, volume, moisture content and density of the food. Approximate times are:

1-3   minutes for small or many individual items
5   minutes for most vegetables, cakes, sauces, etc.
10   minutes for main dishes and foods that are more dense
15   minutes for large items such as roasts, turkey, etc.

Avoid adding any extra cooking time until you have "carry-over cooked" your food. Then add extra time cooking only 1-2 minutes at each interval to avoid overcooking! You can always add more time but when it is overcooked, it's tough and dry forever! You might want to cover foods that will be held for long periods of time to keep heat in. Foods will stay hot longer than you think in a meal sequence. They cool quickly only when transferred to a cool container.

Each of the following suggestions will affect your cooking results. Many are given in recipes for specific foods but it is important to keep these in mind for more success!

READ through all of the recipe before you begin your preparation! Note specific directions, such as melt, scald, etc. Note the total preparation time and when you will prepare it in your meal sequence.

Evenly **SHAPED** foods cook best. If your foods are not evenly shaped, you must give special attention to uneven corners because they will overcook before the food is done. When possible, use round containers and evenly shaped food; if this is not possible, **SHIELD** uneven corners before cooking foods such as meats — turkey, roast, etc. with a **small, even smooth** piece of aluminum foil. Cover only those areas you wish to keep from exposure to energy. If necessary, hold the foil in place with a toothpick. Remove halfway through cooking time. This will not harm your oven and is necessary to prevent overcooking. **Do not** allow foil to touch the sides of your oven during cooking!

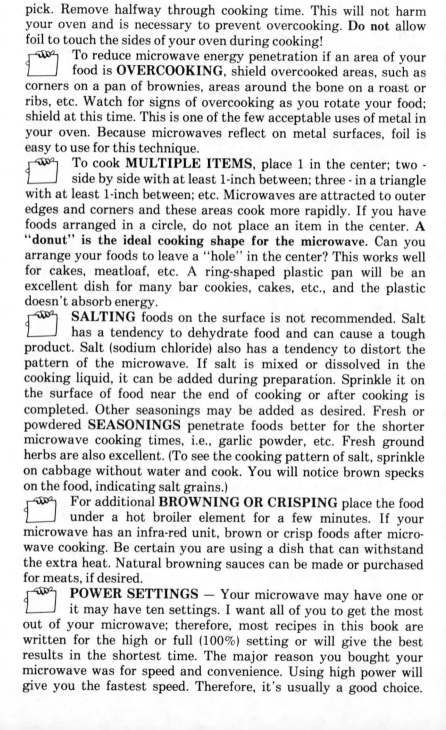 To reduce microwave energy penetration if an area of your food is **OVERCOOKING**, shield overcooked areas, such as corners on a pan of brownies, areas around the bone on a roast or ribs, etc. Watch for signs of overcooking as you rotate your food; shield at this time. This is one of the few acceptable uses of metal in your oven. Because microwaves reflect on metal surfaces, foil is easy to use for this technique.

To cook **MULTIPLE ITEMS**, place 1 in the center; two - side by side with at least 1-inch between; three - in a triangle with at least 1-inch between; etc. Microwaves are attracted to outer edges and corners and these areas cook more rapidly. If you have foods arranged in a circle, do not place an item in the center. **A "donut" is the ideal cooking shape for the microwave.** Can you arrange your foods to leave a "hole" in the center? This works well for cakes, meatloaf, etc. A ring-shaped plastic pan will be an excellent dish for many bar cookies, cakes, etc., and the plastic doesn't absorb energy.

SALTING foods on the surface is not recommended. Salt has a tendency to dehydrate food and can cause a tough product. Salt (sodium chloride) also has a tendency to distort the pattern of the microwave. If salt is mixed or dissolved in the cooking liquid, it can be added during preparation. Sprinkle it on the surface of food near the end of cooking or after cooking is completed. Other seasonings may be added as desired. Fresh or powdered **SEASONINGS** penetrate foods better for the shorter microwave cooking times, i.e., garlic powder, etc. Fresh ground herbs are also excellent. (To see the cooking pattern of salt, sprinkle on cabbage without water and cook. You will notice brown specks on the food, indicating salt grains.)

For additional **BROWNING OR CRISPING** place the food under a hot broiler element for a few minutes. If your microwave has an infra-red unit, brown or crisp foods after microwave cooking. Be certain you are using a dish that can withstand the extra heat. Natural browning sauces can be made or purchased for meats, if desired.

POWER SETTINGS — Your microwave may have one or it may have ten settings. I want all of you to get the most out of your microwave; therefore, most recipes in this book are written for the high or full (100%) setting or will give the best results in the shortest time. The major reason you bought your microwave was for speed and convenience. Using high power will give you the fastest speed. Therefore, it's usually a good choice.

For porous and delicate foods, you may want to reduce the energy a little for better cooking. We have recommended lower settings where this applies. You will also have a choice on some recipes (**Maxi-Time**) — depending on how fast you need foods cooked, the results you prefer, and where it's practical. Someone told me their book said to melt 3 Tbsp. butter on medium (50%) 1½-2 minutes. I think that's ridiculous when 15-30 seconds (high) will do the same thing. In my recipes I have used the most **practical** choice — in this case high, without mention of an alternate. I don't select slower speed unless it really helps a recipe. With a CPA husband working 7 days/week, 5 months of the year, a teenage daughter and my busy schedule, I'm usually in a hurry to fix dinner and would rather spend extra lingering time after dinner for relaxing and conversation. A good example is scrambled eggs:

- 2 eggs may be cooked on high in 2 minutes
or • 2 eggs may be cooked on medium (50%) in 4 minutes.

For the extra 2 minutes you will get a fluffier egg with less attention, even though stirring will be necessary. If you are careful not to overcook on high power, you can have the same fluffy eggs in less time. Try it both ways and decide your own preference.

For some foods, such as cakes and slow cooking meats, we use a combination which may start on a low or high power setting. This will be increased or reduced partway through cooking. Cakes can also be cooked on high power as I did for 7 years before there were several power levels. Again, it's your choice.

Our recipes are **Mini-Time** or minimum time.
Our alternates are **Maxi-Time** or maximum time.

Power settings used in recipes in this book are:

High or full	100% power	600-650 watts
Medium-High	70% power	425-475 watts
Medium	50% power	300-350 watts
Medium-Low	30% power	175-225 watts
Low	10% power	75-125 watts

Adjust the settings as you adjust the amount of heat in your conventional range. We can, however, cook more foods on high since we are cooking the entire surface of the food at the same time and not just the bottom or the outside. If you find a sauce, such as spaghetti, is boiling too fast, reduce the energy so it simmers as with your range.

600-650 WATT RECIPES can be adjusted by using the following times for the selected power levels:

High Power 100%	Medium-High 70%	Medium 50%	Medium-Low 30%
1 minutes	1½ minutes	2 minutes	2½ minutes
2 minutes	3 minutes	4 minutes	5 minutes
3 minutes	4½ minutes	6 minutes	7½ minutes
4 minutes	6 minutes	8 minutes	10 minutes
5 minutes	7½ minutes	10 minutes	12½ minutes
6 minutes	9 minutes	12 minutes	15 minutes
7 minutes	10½ minutes	14 minutes	17½ minutes
8 minutes	12 minutes	16 minutes	20 minutes
9 minutes	13½ minutes	18 minutes	22½ minutes
10 minutes	15 minutes	20 minutes	25 minutes
12 minutes	18 minutes	24 minutes	30 minutes

Find the high power time and follow the same line across the page to reduce energy. 6 minutes on high will take 9 minutes on medium-high (70%), or 12 minutes on medium (50%), or 15 minutes on medium-low (30%). This chart will be most helpful if you want to reduce the energy for part of the cooking time **or** to decrease energy because you like the results with less energy **or** to increase energy if you are now using a recipe written for a lower power than you have time to cook. This may seem technical but it's not — adjust as you change heat on your range. For instance:

- A cake cooked on high power takes 5-6 minutes. Using a combination of powers it will take 5 minutes on medium (half the time) and 2½ minutes on high (last half the time.)

- With a 4 lb. roast, 4x7 (minutes/lb., medium done) = 28 minutes cooking time. Half the time you might want to cook on high (14 minutes). For the last half, cook 21 minutes on medium-high. This was figured by adding the difference between the high and the medium-high times on the chart.

For a Power Identification Chart including all brands of microwave ovens, please send 25¢ and a self-addressed, stamped envelope to address on the cover.

If you are using an oven with less wattage, you will note a 400-500 watt microwave would be about the same as the medium-high setting on a 600-650 watt oven. Therefore you will have to add about 35% to the total cooking time. A 500-600 watt microwave will need an additional 20% cooking time. Use the following table for easy conversion:

600-650 WATTS	500-600 WATTS (add 20%)	400-500 WATTS (add 35%)
15 seconds	18 seconds	21 seconds
30 seconds	36 seconds	42 seconds
45 seconds	54 seconds	1 minute
1 minute	1 min., 10 sec.	1 min., 25 sec.
2 minutes	2 min., 30 sec.	2 min., 45 sec.
3 minutes	3 min., 30 sec.	4 minutes
4 minutes	4 min., 45 sec.	5 min., 30 sec.
5 minutes	6 minutes	7 minutes
6 minutes	7 min., 15 sec.	8 min., 25 sec.
7 minutes	8 min., 25 sec.	9 min., 45 sec.
8 minutes	9 min., 30 sec.	11 minutes
9 minutes	10 min., 45 sec.	12 min., 30 sec.
10 minutes	12 minutes	14 minutes
15 minutes	18 minutes	20 minutes
20 minutes	24 minutes	27 minutes
25 minutes	30 minutes	34 minutes
30 minutes	36 minutes	41 minutes

For an oven with less than 600 watts, you may want to paste this chart on your microwave so it will be an easy conversion. If you have a 700 watt microwave, be careful not to overcook. Always start with a little less time and add more if you need it. With lower powers, the resting time is not as important as on high, since more heat has equalized during cooking.

An easy way to **DETERMINE COOKING TIME** for some foods is to weigh and cook it 6 to 7 minutes/lb. (high). This is very accurate for most vegetables, meats and many other foods. For meats, cook 6-7 minutes/lb. (high) for rare; 7-8 minutes/lb. (high) for medium; and 8-9 minutes/lb. (high) for well. The Micro-Weigh(TM) is a scale that will do this for you. It is also one of the easiest ways to teach kids to cook. When asked how long to cook something, have them weigh it and you'll always have accurate times.

Avoid cooking any food with a sealed skin or covering unless the skin is **PIERCED**. If not pierced, pressure will accumulate within the skin or container and the item could burst or explode. Always pierce baked potatoes, squash, and plastic vegetable or meat containers.

TEMPERATURE PROBES are another feature available on some microwave ovens. I feel the best use of the probe is for heating or reheating foods. They can be used to measure internal temperature of meats but I feel cooking by weight is more reliable for meats than the probe. Foods will need rotating and stirring when using the probe. The oven will turn off at the temperature you have set for the internal temperature of the food. Some ovens also have a holding feature to maintain this temperature if the rest of your dinner isn't ready or you are interrupted at mealtime. Follow manufacturers recommendations for using the probe. Place it in the center of the dish where you have the least amount of cooking. The following temperatures and powers are recommended with the probe:

Beverages	High	180-190°F.
(milk base)	Medium-high	170-180°F.
Canned foods	High or Medium-High	160-180°F.
Casseroles	High or Medium-High	150-170°F.
Dips	High or Medium-High	150°F.
Fish (whole)	High	170°F.
Cooked Ham	High	115-125°F.
Uncooked Ham	High	150-160°F.
Lamb, Pork	High	165-175°F.
Meat		
loaf	High or Medium-High	150-170°F.
roasts rare	High or Medium-High	120-125°F.
medium	High or Medium-High	130-140°F.
well	High or Medium-High	155-165°F.
Reheating	High or Medium-High	140-160°F.
Soup	High	180°F.
(milk base)	High or Medium-High	160-180°F.
Warming	High or Medium	110°F.

A frequent question about using your microwave is whether all foods can be cooked at once. Several microwave ovens come with **MEAL RACKS** that allow you to do this. The main advantage is to put the food in and forget it until it is done. The main disadvantage is that you have to get everything ready before cooking which will be new to most of us. We also must learn which combinations cook well together and their timing. Most microwave cooking is done in sequence and we use the carry-over cooking time to prepare other foods for the meal. Combining foods on the rack will require almost the same time as sequence cooking. Some applications of total meal cooking are good. I feel it is an ideal way to cook breakfast. Rearrangement and stirring of the food is usually necessary anyway and the meal doesn't take much longer than sequence cooking. With other foods it may take longer.

Positioning food requiring the most cooking near the energy source is important. Foods don't have the same efficiency as one dish at a time. Energy in each is reduced. Usually the main dish must be started ahead of time for meals. An open arrangement of foods is important to allow those on the bottom shelf to cook and not be shadowed by those on the upper shelf. One of the best uses of the rack is to elevate those foods that don't cook well in the middle, such as cakes, pies, and thin foods such as appetizers. It does increase the oven capacity for cooking several foods and is ideal when reheating several dishes of leftovers at once. It is faster, however, to heat individual plates of food. Stagger dishes so those on the bottom will cook. Be certain that all dishes you are using at once will fit together on the rack in the oven. Use high power with meal rack.

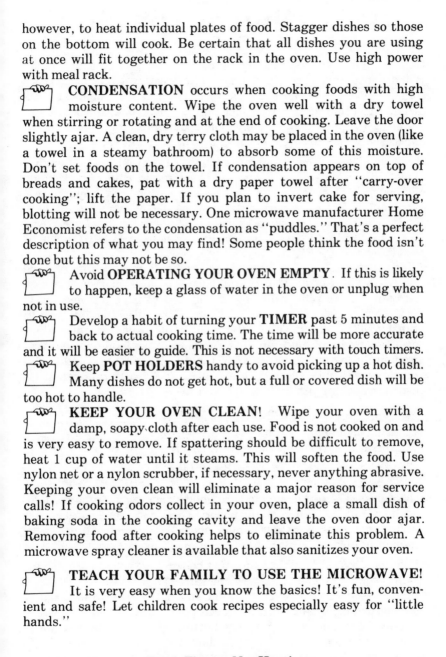 **CONDENSATION** occurs when cooking foods with high moisture content. Wipe the oven well with a dry towel when stirring or rotating and at the end of cooking. Leave the door slightly ajar. A clean, dry terry cloth may be placed in the oven (like a towel in a steamy bathroom) to absorb some of this moisture. Don't set foods on the towel. If condensation appears on top of breads and cakes, pat with a dry paper towel after "carry-over cooking"; lift the paper. If you plan to invert cake for serving, blotting will not be necessary. One microwave manufacturer Home Economist refers to the condensation as "puddles." That's a perfect description of what you may find! Some people think the food isn't done but this may not be so.

Avoid **OPERATING YOUR OVEN EMPTY**. If this is likely to happen, keep a glass of water in the oven or unplug when not in use.

Develop a habit of turning your **TIMER** past 5 minutes and back to actual cooking time. The time will be more accurate and it will be easier to guide. This is not necessary with touch timers.

Keep **POT HOLDERS** handy to avoid picking up a hot dish. Many dishes do not get hot, but a full or covered dish will be too hot to handle.

KEEP YOUR OVEN CLEAN! Wipe your oven with a damp, soapy cloth after each use. Food is not cooked on and is very easy to remove. If spattering should be difficult to remove, heat 1 cup of water until it steams. This will soften the food. Use nylon net or a nylon scrubber, if necessary, never anything abrasive. Keeping your oven clean will eliminate a major reason for service calls! If cooking odors collect in your oven, place a small dish of baking soda in the cooking cavity and leave the oven door ajar. Removing food after cooking helps to eliminate this problem. A microwave spray cleaner is available that also sanitizes your oven.

TEACH YOUR FAMILY TO USE THE MICROWAVE! It is very easy when you know the basics! It's fun, convenient and safe! Let children cook recipes especially easy for "little hands."

Think Time — Not Heat!
Think Microwave!

Defrosting or Thawing

All frozen foods except vegetables must be thawed before cooking. Defrosting foods becomes a regular part of meal preparation timing. When defrosting, a combination cooking-resting cycle is used to transfer heat to the center of the food. High density foods require careful attention so outer surfaces do not overcook. Porous foods defrost very quickly and evenly. The cooking-resting cycle may be unnecessary. Some defrost settings do this automatically.

If possible, rearrange or remove portions of thawed foods. Remove food from insulated containers, as these retain cold even though microwave safe. Shield outer surfaces of bulk foods as they indicate overcooking. Rotate ¼ turn during defrosting. Wax paper makes a good cover. As outer surfaces begin to defrost, the cover traps steam to distribute heat more evenly. To defrost **WITHOUT AN AUTOMATIC DEFROST SETTING:**

Set timer on microwave allowing 2 minutes/lb. of food (high). Rotate ¼ turn and turn food over halfway through defrosting time. When rotating, shield outer surfaces if necessary. At the end of defrosting time, rest food 20 minutes to allow heat to transfer to the center. Test center and if still frozen, set timer allowing 1 minute/lb. of food. Rotate ¼ turn and turn food over halfway through defrosting time. Rest 15 minutes. Test center, and if still frozen, repeat until center is thawed. After defrosting is complete, begin the cooking time.

Two types of **AUTOMATIC** defrost features are:

• **Cycling on and off at full cook power:** Various time cycles are used to automatically cycle cooking on and off for the cooking-resting time. Food may need rotating or turning over halfway through defrosting time. Allow 4 minutes/lb. of food on defrost setting.

• **Medium (50%) to Medium-low (30%):** Microwave energy is reduced by about ½-⅓ of full cooking power. Food may need rotating or turning over halfway. Allow 4 minutes/lb. of food. Defrosting can be interrupted to allow a standing time if overcooking appears. This is more important near the end of the time. It's best to package large amounts of food in small containers so they thaw more evenly.

• One steak thaws unevenly; stack several to achieve an even shape (or shield around circumference).

• Allow 1-2 minutes/lb. for ground meat (high), 2-4 minutes/lb. on medium (50%).

• To serve a 5 lb. roast for dinner, remove from freezer at 5 p.m. Cook 10 minutes (high), rotating halfway through cooking time. Rest 20 minutes. At 5:30 p.m. place on rack in microwave.

Cook 35 minutes (high) for medium roast (7 minutes/lb.), turning over and rotating halfway through cooking. At 6:05 p.m., remove from microwave and "carry-over cook" 15 minutes. Carve and serve at 6:30 p.m. You have a roast for dinner in 1½ hours.If you prefer a lower energy setting for the roast, increase time accordingly (p. 14).

- All frozen foods must be thawed in one step and cooked as the second step. Vegetables are the only frozen foods that may be thawed and cooked in the same step.

TO THAW FROZEN CASSEROLES: Package foods in containers appropriate to freeze and thaw evenly. (Shallow containers defrost faster than deep; however, the outside may need shielding if stirring isn't possible during defrosting.) It is best to package 8 cups of food in 2 containers for faster defrosting than 1 big container. Cover with wax paper during defrosting. Stir or rotate dish ¼ turn halfway. Purchase small reusable containers with lids for 1-2 serving to store in freezer and reheat in microwave for convenience.

AMOUNT	POWER	TIME
1 cup	High	3-4 minutes
2 cups	Medium-high (70%)	5-6 minutes
3 cups	Medium-high (70%)	6-8 minutes
4 cups (1 qt)	Medium (50%)	8-10 minutes
8 cups (2 qts)	Medium (50%)	14-16 minutes

Heating or Reheating

Heating or reheating is one of the oven's greatest virtues. Dinner can be served in literally a "moment's notice." Leftovers can be reheated several times with the same fresh-cooked taste of the first meal. Leftovers should be considered "planned-overs" because of the ease of serving at another meal. The freezer becomes an integral part of meal planning. Entire meals can be prepared in advance and reheated at serving time. Or leftovers can be arranged on a serving plate and reheated when someone arrives late for dinner. To reheat leftovers in serving containers, allow about ¼ the original cooking time (high) at room temperature and 3-4 minutes/lb. if refrigerated. One cup of food takes 2-3 minutes (high) to heat. If you prefer to heat on medium-high (70%) add extra time since you have decreased the energy. Remember, if you are reheating less food, reduce time accordingly. Foods must be stirred or rotated during reheating time. Shield corners that could overcook. I prefer to heat most foods on the medium-high (70%) setting. Cover to trap steam.

- To reheat **frozen foods**, use a combination cooking-resting time for even transfer of heat to thaw; then heat. For small amounts of food, this may be unnecessary. Heat in serving container when possible. (Foods cool faster when transferred from one container to another.) If rice, noodles, mashed potatoes, etc. are frozen in 1-cup containers, they can easily be heated for serving later.

• Foods high in **fat and sugar** heat very rapidly. To reheat meat slices, cover with gravy to increase density and moisture content for more even heating, or arrange surrounded by dense foods on the same plate.

Arrange foods as evenly as possible on a plate for reheating. Place dense foods near outer edges and small, porous foods near the center. Cover with a napkin or wax paper to heat evenly. **TV DINNERS** — pop the frozen food from the tray onto a glass dish and cook 4-5 minutes (high). It will have a far superior quality to those steamed in the metal tray in the carton, even though your manufacturer may allow you to use metal for this purpose. You also avoid the possibility of not having enough food in the oven (2 cups), and of placing the tray too close to the sides! **Reheat a dinner plate of food** ¾-1½ minutes (high) if room temperature; longer if chilled.

Heating **BABY FOOD** can be a real joy! One (4½ oz.) jar of refrigerated food requires ¾-1 minute (with lid off, of course!) To heat a bottle, place bottle, including nipple, with 4 oz. room temperature water in microwave; heat 15 seconds (high). 4 oz. of refrigerated milk requires 30-40 seconds (high).

• When heating bulky foods in a container, stir halfway through cooking time by rearranging the cool food in the center with hot foods around the circumference. If you have a **defrost or medium (50%) setting**, use it during the last half of reheating time to transfer heat more evenly.

• If you have a temperature **probe** place tip in center of the food and heat (using medium-high (70%) or high) to 155°F.

To **HEAT CASSEROLES**: Store foods in containers appropriate for reheating. Shallow reheats faster than deep. Stirring or rearranging is important. If this isn't possible, the outside of a large flat container may need shielding and rotating ¼ turn halfway through cooking. Cover with wax paper or lid to retain heat in the container. For a deep dish use Medium power.

Amount of Food	Power	Time	
1 cup	Medium-high (70%)	1-2	minutes
2 cups	Medium-high (70%)	2-3	minutes
3 cups	Medium-high (70%)	3-4	minutes
4 cups (1 qt)	Medium-high (70%)	4-5	minutes
8 cups (2 qts)	Medium-high (70%)	8-10	minutes

Guide to Quick Microwaving (High)•

Bacon.. 1-1½ minutes/slice
Beef, ground .... 5-6 minutes/lb.
Brownies....................................... 5-7 minutes/8x8-inch dish
Butter, melted .... 45 seconds/½ cup
Butter, softened............................. 15-30 seconds/½ cup
Cakes, bundt .... 8-12 minutes/cake
Cakes, layer .... 4-6 minutes/8-9-inch round
Cakes, sheet.............................. 9-11 minutes/12x8-inch dish
Cakes, upside-down .... 5-7 minutes/8-9-inch round
Casseroles (cooked ingredients) .... 1½-2 minutes/cup
.... 5-7 minutes/qt.
.... 10-14 minutes/2 qts.
Chicken, Turkey.................................... 7-9 minutes/lb.
Chocolate, melted.............................. 1½-2 minutes/1 oz. sq.
Chops .... 7-9 minutes/lb.
Coffee, Tea.. 1-2 minutes/cup
Cookies, drops .... 2-3 minutes/dozen
Crust, crumb .... 1-3 minutes/9-inch crust
Crust, pastry .... 4-5 minutes/9-inch crust
Cupcakes .... 2-2½ minutes/6 cupcakes
Defrosting .... 2-3 minutes/lb.
Eggs, Fried & Poached .... 30-40 seconds/egg
Eggs, Scrambled .... ¾-1 minute/egg
Fish & Seafood .... 4-5 minutes/lb.
Fruit .... 5-6 minutes/lb.
Ham, precooked whole .... 5-6 minutes/lb.
Hot Dogs .... 20-30 seconds/weiner
Meatloaf.. 8-10 minutes/lb.
Meatballs, Hamburger patties...................... 6-8 minutes/lb.
Milk, Cocoa .... 1-2 minutes/cup
Muffins .... 2-3 minutes/6 muffins
Onion, saute .... 1-2 minutes/½ cup
Pork.. 8-9 minutes/lb.
Potatoes.. 6-7 minutes/lb.
Pudding .... 5-7 minutes/3¼ oz. pkg.
Roast, beef....................................... 6-8 minutes/lb.
Roast, Lamb & Pork .... 8-9 minutes/lb.
Rolls, Doughnuts .... 5-15 seconds/one
Sandwiches................................. 20-30 seconds/sandwich
Sauce, Gravy................................... 1½-3 minutes/cup
Soup, Canned .... 1½-2½ minutes/cup
Vegetables, canned-drained .... 1-2 minutes/cup
Vegetables, fresh................................. 6-7 minutes/lb.
Vegetables, frozen .... 5-8 minutes/10-oz. pkg.
Water, boiling.................................. 2½-3 minutes/cup
Water, Hot.. 1-1½ minute/cup

- A scale will give you accurate weight to compute correct cooking time. Weigh empty dish first and turn back to 0 before adding ingredients.
- All times are high power. To reduce power, see chart (p. 14), or recipe category.
- Timing varies with starting temperature of the food, size and amount cooked.

Utensils

GENERALLY, glass, paper, plastic and some wood make good utensils because they allow microwaves to transmit into food without interference. Metal reflects microwaves so is not a good choice.

GLASS: Oven-proof and ceramic glass dishes are preferred for microwave cooking. They are available in numerous sizes and shapes, to accommodate many foods. A 4-cup and 2-cup glass measure are two of the most useful utensils. Dinnerware may be used; try dish test to see if o.k. Most Corning Ware and Pyrex work well — except Centura$^{(R)}$ dinnerware and covers with metal screws; Corelle$^{(R)}$ closed handle cups, and Pyrex$^{(R)}$ pitchers and flasks. Some glass dishes or painted bowls contain a metallic substance and are not suitable for use. They will absorb microwave energy. Dishes with decorative metal trim or seals cannot be used. **To test your dish for use:**

1. Place a cup of tap water and empty dish in oven.
2. Microwave (high) 1 minute.

If water gets hot and the dish doesn't, it CAN be used. If the dish gets hot, it cannot be used. Always test goblets, mugs, and several pieces of your dinnerware before using. If you have an infra-red browner in your oven, use only glass-ceramic dishes with it. Don't combine glass with freezer use unless glass can stand temperature extremes.

PLASTIC: Use only strong thermo-plastics that won't melt from heat in the food. Foam cups will heat liquids but may melt with fats and sugars. Boilable bags can be used for cooking. (Do not use twist ties! Secure with string or rubber band.) Plastic tubs can be used for **reheating** (not cooking) but eventually will melt and loose their shape. Plastic wrap is a good cover for cooking eggs and some vegetables to trap heat and steam. Melamines should be tested and generally can't be used.

PAPER: Paper plates and towels have several uses. Use paper cartons to cook vegetables and reheat foods. Avoid cooking foods for more than a few minutes (3-4) on paper unless it's polyester coated. Heat transfers to the paper; if food cooks too long, paper may ignite. Wax paper and paper towel make excellent covers for cooking containers with no lid. Paper towels and napkins let steam escape while absorbing splatters. Wax paper holds in steam as a lid does. Do not use **recycled** paper since it may contain substances that could ignite.

WOOD: Wooden spoons may be left in the dish for stirring. Rolls may be heated in a straw basket. Don't cook in wood more than 5 minutes.

METAL: Metal reflects microwaves (stopping cooking) and **is not suitable** as a cooking utensil. Do not use any metal unless recommended by your manufacturer (shielding is an exception). Some manufacturers allow the use of metal if at least 2 cups of food are present but it increases cooking time. The only advantage of using metal is for shielding. If metal isn't used correctly, it can pit walls of the oven or cause arcing (like welding) if not evenly shaped or gets too close to the walls.

Many glass utensils you have in your cupboards will probably eliminate the need for purchasing new. There are, however, microwave accessories entering the market (some are excellent and others are almost inconvenient to use). I feel they should have the following qualifications:

1. Do a good, easy job of cooking what they are designed to cook! The shape should give the best microwave pattern for a variety of uses.
2. Clean easily — including fit into a dishwasher.
3. Store easily.

You will want to purchase the following (which I feel are as necessary as measuring cups for baking!) for excellent cooking results:

1. The most essential utensil needed for microwaving is a slotted **roasting rack** which allows easy draining of juices but is supported to hold a heavy turkey or roast. It should withstand hot temperatures, be easy to clean, and fit into a 12x8-inch glass dish. (Those with wells around outer rim or in one corner allow drippings to collect in this area; drippings instead of food attract energy for inefficient cooking.) "Shield" corner wells if possible.

2. **Plastic (2 qt.) cake pans** do an excellent job of cooking. They don't absorb energy like glass and are lighter in weight. The sides are also higher for increased volume in cakes.

3. **Plastic (6 cup) ring mold** for bar cookies, cornbread, coffee cake, cakes, reheating quantities of food, etc. For meatloaf I prefer to place a glass in the center of a circular dish rather than having fat rest on my food. It's easier to baste off as it collects in the center. Scalloped shapes make the food more interesting when inverted.

4. **6-cup muffin pan** with holes for circulation of air in the bottom so condensation won't collect. Baking papers hold the batter.

5. **Bundt pan (12 cup)** for all 2-layer and specialty-type cakes. I prefer prettier scalloped shapes. Any 2-layer cake mix also fits in this dish which is designed for the best energy distribution.

Many of these dishes are available in **sets** which usually sell for a lower price than buying each individually. **Evaluate** pieces for good cooking design. One set has a lid that doubles as a pie plate which is nice for crumb crusts and other 1 qt. dishes. The **Udel**[R]-**Polysulfone label** assures you the dishes will withstand high temperatures which is important for foods high in fats and sugars. They are unbreakable. These are more expensive but last longer than those which you may have to replace. A toothbrush should never be necessary for cleaning. I am constantly searching and evaluating new utensils. To receive information on those I recommend as satisfactory, or a source, please send stamped, self-addressed envelope and 10 cents to address on cover.

A basic, practical set of cookware for a family of 4 for every day, every meal for a large variety of foods include the following:

1,2&4-cup glass measuring cups	4 qt. casserole (optl.)
10 oz. round glass dish	12x8-inch glass dish
1 qt. round glass dish	10-inch sq. glass-ceramic dish
1½ qt. round glass dish	9-inch glass pie dish
2 qt. round glass dish	Circular solid muffin pan (eggs)
3 qt. round glass dish	Wooden spoon set

Kitchen scale (metric and American standard measure)

I use the above constantly including the 5 microwave accessories. Duplicates may be added to suit your family needs. Extras which make your microwave more versatile are:

- Browning dish for grilling or searing
- Clay cooking pot for stews and roasts
- "Cook and serve" pieces to match or complement your dinnerware.
- Microwave Thermometer
- Plastic colander for browning ground beef for chili, spaghetti sauce, etc. (Place glass dish underneath to catch drippings.)
- Small containers for freezing and reheating leftovers
- Wicker baskets in which to cradle clear cooking dishes

I have covered the utensil topic more thoroughly in Bon Appetit magazine, Microwave Column, March 1979.

Converting Recipes

As you become familiar with microwave cooking, you will enjoy serving "family favorites" microwaved! Microwave "**basics**" need to be considered to make adjustments in recipe and cooking times. Some casseroles may need few changes if heated, steamed or baked. Major adjustments may need to be made for moisture, amount of cooking, amount of food, cooking container and whether or not all food is raw or some partially cooked.

Because **MOISTURE CONTENT** is important in determining cooking time, recipes that have a large amount of moisture may have to be adjusted because the microwave evaporates almost no liquid. Conventional cooking heat evaporates and dries food. The recipe formula contains a larger amount of liquid to prevent dried food as it heats. With microwave cooking, chemical properties of food heat more rapidly. A smaller amount of moisture is needed when preparing the recipe.

REDUCE LIQUID in the recipe by ¼ the conventional recipe, keeping in mind the desired texture of the cooked food. For example, in a conventional cake, a larger amount of water is needed to prevent the cake from drying out during cooking. Reduce the moisture content by ¼ for microwave cooking because it's faster. If the recipe calls for 1 cup of water, reduce it to ¾ cup. The base for a casserole may be 1 can of soup and 1 can of water. For microwave cooking add 1 can of soup and ½-¾ can of water. With a sauce such as spaghetti, you conventionally add a large amount of water which reduces during cooking. It doesn't reduce in the microwave so less liquid is added when preparing. Keep in mind the consistency of the food. With a little practice, you will learn to judge the consistency of foods that cook best in the microwave. Some breads, such as muffins, have a stiff batter. If already dry it will not be necessary to reduce the liquid. **For accuracy, compare the amount of liquid in the conventional recipe and a similar microwave recipe the first time.**

To **DETERMINE COOKING TIME,** remember that 1 cup of tap water boils in 2½-3 minutes (high) and 1 cup of food heats in 2-3 minutes (high). Cook refrigerated foods 2 minutes/cup (1½ minute/cup at room temperature). Sauces cook 2 minutes/cup. This is the standard used to cook liquids in most recipes. If your oven takes longer, you will need to add additional time to your recipe (and less if your time is less). If you are scalding milk, melting butter, bringing liquids to room temperature, all are liquid so 2½-3 minutes is the basis for determining cooking time. Foods cooked in a sauce generally adapt very well.

The average food requires ¼ conventional cooking time. A casserole that requires 1 hour conventionally will cook about 15 minutes in the microwave. The same is true with many other foods; however, the microwave will require even less time for some foods, such as custard. Conventional oven-cooked foods take about ¼ the time but foods cooked on the surface of the range will often require identical or more than ¼ time. You may prefer to continue cooking these foods conventionally. Rice and noodles are examples of foods requiring about the same time. **Consult a similar microwave recipe**

the first time you try converting and make a note with the recipe of your technique.

Other considerations are **shape, volume, weight, density, starting temperature, wattage of the oven, peak electric usage hours,** and the **container** selected for cooking.

When cooking an individual food such as Baked Potato, the recipe usually identifies the food by size — small, medium and large. There is a great deal of variation in each of our opinions about size. To be more accurate in determining cooking time, **weigh** food and cook it 6-7 minutes/lb. (high) depending on the wattage in your oven. If your oven is more than 650 watts it may require less cooking time and if less than 600 watts, it may be necessary to add more time. You will find a kitchen scale a good accessory to use with microwave cooking. It provides you with information for good, accurate results. For example, to cook an acorn squash conventionally, the cooking time would be 1-1¼ hours. By weighing and cooking in the microwave it will cook in 7-9 minutes. ¼ time would be too long and would overcook the squash. **WEIGHT is the most accurate method of determining cooking time.**

Increase cooking time as you **INCREASE THE AMOUNT OF FOOD.** Weigh and add 6-7 minutes/lb. (high) more cooking time. For example, when cooking a stuffed turkey, weigh the stuffing and add 6-7 minutes/lb. (high) for each pound of stuffing. As you increase the quantity of potatoes, corn on the cob, etc., weigh these and cook 6-7 minutes/lb. (high) for the total weight.

If you double the amount of food to be cooked, you don't necessarily double the cooking time. For this reason it is important to consult a cooking table, another similar microwave recipe, or weigh the food. For example, 1 egg cooks in 30-35 seconds; 2 eggs in 60-70 seconds; 3 eggs will require 1½ minute. Cooking times will be easy to remember as you use them often.

The **COOKING CONTAINER** makes a difference in cooking results. You will have better results when you make a sauce or scrambled eggs in a measuring cup or a deep glass dish than when using a dish with a flat surface, such as a cake or pie dish. In the deep dish microwaves surround the food more evenly; in the flat dish it cooks from outer edges leaving the center with very little cooking unless stirring often or energy is reduced. Select containers most practical for the results you are trying to achieve. Remember the importance of the ring or "donut" shape. When cooking foods that require longer cooking times with liquids at a boil, select a large container so food will not boil over. Scalloped potatoes, noodles and rice need large containers to allow liquid to boil.

Foods high in **FATS** and **SUGARS** tend to absorb energy faster than those without. Add ⅓ cup oil to a cake batter for more even cooking. Use less or powdered **SEASONINGS** so the flavors will penetrate more rapidly. **PRE-BROWNING** of meats is often not necessary. If you are preparing a **CONVENTIONAL MIX** (such as cake mix), allow batter to rest 5-10 minutes after mixed so leavening added for conventional cooking has time to "work." You will see air bubbles on top after 10 minutes.

Always remember to allow for **CARRY-OVER COOKING** as part of the total cooking time. Overcooked foods in the microwave dehydrate and toughen; there is no way of restoring the food when this occurs.

ALWAYS UNDERCOOK, ESPECIALLY WHEN YOU ARE EXPERIMENTING! You may have to try your favorite conventional recipe more than once before you achieve the best results. Make a note of your changes so you will remember the next time. And above all, try many of your favorites! You may find the food even better because of the many advantages of microwave cooking!!

Beverages

Heating and brewing beverages is a convenience at mealtime and for snacking with your microwave. Most beverages can be prepared and served in the same container. Coffee brewed in the morning can be reheated during the day. Instant coffee, tea and mixes can be prepared in almost a moment's notice.

Avoid overcooking milk because it has a tendency to boil over very quickly. Use a container large enough for the boiling action. For best results, heat or scald milk only. When heating more than 1 cup at a time, arrange on a plate for ease in rotating ¼ turn halfway through cooking. Beverages heated in quantity require about the same cooking time as on the range. Avoid using cups, mugs or containers with a metallic substance in the clay or those with "glued-on" handles. When reheating a beverage, remember to adjust time for the *beginning* temperature of the food (especially when warming coffee, etc.) Most mugs hold more than 1 cup of liquid and will require longer heating. Stir when warm to distribute heat more evenly. If you are using a probe, heat 150-170°F. Use high power. You may prefer to use medium-high (70%) for milk base.

BEVERAGE HEATING TIMES

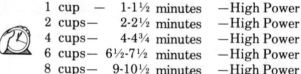

1 cup —	1-1½ minutes	—High Power
2 cups—	2-2½ minutes	—High Power
4 cups—	4-4¾ minutes	—High Power
6 cups—	6½-7½ minutes	—High Power
8 cups—	9-10½ minutes	—High Power

Notes: _____

HOT COCOA

Chocolate Milk: Fill cups or mugs with chocolate flavored milk or drink. Use heating times in above table.

Hot Cocoa Mix: Fill cups or mugs with milk. Use heating times in above table. Stir in cocoa mix as directed on package.

Unsweetened Cocoa: In a cup or mug, combine 1 Tbsp. cocoa, 2 Tbsp. sugar and a pinch of salt. Add enough milk to form a paste; mix until smooth. Add milk to fill cups. Stir. Use heating times in above table.

• *If you wish to add a marshmallow to each cup, add during the last 15 seconds of cooking.*

Notes: _____

COFFEE: Add instant coffee in quantity desired. Fill with water. Use heating time in table (p. 28). Heat until steaming.

● *Do not boil coffee because it becomes bitter.*

● *My husband likes to mix 1 tsp. instant coffee and 2 tsp. cocoa mix for a special treat on a cold morning.*

TEA: Add tea bags in quantity desired. Fill with water. Use heating time in table (p. 28). Heat until steaming.

● *Do not boil tea because it becomes bitter.*

HOT BUTTERED RUM: Place 1 Tbsp. brown sugar in mug and fill to ¾ full water. Heat, using beverage time table (p. 28). Add 1 jigger (1½ Tbsp.) rum and top with 1 tsp. butter. Serve hot.

SPICED TEA MIX

1 cup instant Tang	½ cup instant tea
½ envelope (1.7 oz) presweetened lemon drink mix	1 tsp. ground cloves
	½ tsp. ground allspice
1 cup sugar	1 tsp. cinnamon

Mix and store in air-tight container. Use 1½-2 tsp. per cup; fill with water. Heat, using time in table (p. 28).

● *This tea mix is a pleasant change for a snack or after dessert. Add seasonings of your own choosing for substitution in the recipe. It also makes a nice gift.*

HOT LEMONADE OR TANG is a delightful change and can easily be heated using beverage time table (p. 28).

Notes: _____

_____

MULLED CIDER — *An autumn favorite!*

1 qt. apple cider	1-2 cinnamon sticks
2 whole allspice	5 Tbsp. brown sugar
2 whole cloves	½ orange, thinly sliced with peel

In a 2 qt. glass container, combine all ingredients. Microwave (high), covered with wax paper 8-10 minutes, stirring halfway through cooking time. Serve when cider is steaming. Serves 4-5.

● *Tea may be substituted for cider in above recipe.*

WASSAIL PUNCH — *Delicious on any cold evening.*

2 qts. water	1 (46 oz) can pineapple-
1 (1 lb) pkg. fresh cranberries	grapefruit juice
5 whole cloves	2-3 cinnamon sticks
	Sugar, to taste

Boil water. Add cranberries; soak overnight until soft. Mash and strain pulp, saving juice. Add remaining ingredients. Microwave (high) 12-15 minutes, stirring once or twice. Makes 8,1-cup servings.

● *Add alcoholic beverage (rum, bourbon, etc.) if desired.*

Hors d'Oeuvres

Many social occasions center around food. Whether a party, an office function, a midnight snack, cocktails, drop-in guests, or an impromptu get-together, hors d'oeuvres are usually part of the occasion. It is good planning to keep several on hand for emergencies. Many can be prepared ahead, frozen and reheated as needed. Others can easily be combined as the occasion arises. Buy ingredients for last minute notice. Heat, using high or medium-high (70%) power.

HOT CHEESE DIP — *Always a favorite at cooking schools.*

1 (5 oz) jar sharp cheese spread	2 finely sliced green onions (& tops)
1 (7 oz) can drained minced clams	
¼ medium finely minced green pepper	3 dashes hot sauce
	Garlic salt to taste

In 1 qt. casserole, combine ingredients. Microwave (high) 2½-3 minutes, stirring every minute. Serve hot with crisp corn chips. Makes about 1½ cups.

- *Substitute 1 (7 oz) can shrimp to make a* **SHRIMP DIP**.
- *Dip also makes a wonderful* **CHEESE SPREAD** *when served cold.*

Notes: _____

RUMAKI — *A conventional favorite that microwaves well!*

¼ lb. bacon strips, cut in thirds	½ lb. chicken livers
1 (6 oz) can water chestnuts	Soy sauce

Heat bacon 30 seconds (high) to separate. Drain and slice each chestnut into thirds. Cut chicken livers in 1-inch pieces. Dip livers in soy sauce. Layer chestnut with liver on bacon slice, roll bacon and secure with a toothpick. Arrange 10 Rumaki on a double layer of crumpled paper towels or roasting rack in 12x8-inch dish. Microwave (high), covered with paper towel, 5-7 minutes, rotating ¼ turn halfway through cooking. Serve hot.

Maxi-Time: Medium-high (70%) 7-9 minutes.

- *If desired, brown Rumaki under broiler a few minutes.*

Notes: _____

BARBECUED HOT DOGS — *An easy favorite of adults and kids.*

1 (12 oz) pkg. wieners	2 Tbsp. honey
1 cup barbecue sauce	½ tsp. prepared mustard

Slice each wiener into 4 pieces. Cut a ¾-inch deep cross in end of each. In a 2 cup glass measure, blend barbecue sauce, honey and mustard. Microwave (high) 1 minute. Arrange 10 wieners in a circle on a glass pie plate. Pour a little sauce over each piece. Microwave (high) 2-2½ minutes, rotating dish ¼ turn halfway through cooking. Serve hot with toothpicks.

- *Quick to prepare and easy to eat. Keep ingredients on hand for unexpected occasions or children's snacks.*

Notes: _____

_____

CRAB PUFFS — *An elegant, easy favorite.*

1 (6½ oz) can crab (or ½ lb. fresh)	2 Tbsp. finely minced celery
¼ cup chopped olives	3 drops tabasco sauce
2 Tbsp. finely minced onion	½ to ¾ cup mayonnaise
2 Tbsp. finely minced green pepper	24 baked miniature cream puff shells, halved

In 1 qt. bowl, combine crab, olives, onion, green pepper, celery, tabasco sauce and enough mayonnaise to make a smooth filling. Fill shells; microwave (high), uncovered, on paper plate allowing 1½-2 minutes for 12 shells. Serve immediately. Makes 24 puffs.

- *May be made ahead and frozen. To serve, defrost a few minutes and heat as needed for serving.*
- *Substitute Shrimp or Tuna for* **SHRIMP PUFFS** *or* **TUNA PUFFS.**

Notes: _____

STUFFED MUSHROOMS — *A cooking school favorite for 9 years!*

2 Tbsp. butter	2 Tbsp. chili sauce
¾ cup soft bread crumbs	1 tsp. salt
½ cup finely chopped walnuts	2 Tbsp. lemon juice
⅓ cup finely grated onion	Dash pepper
	50 medium mushroom caps

In 1 qt. glass casserole microwave (high) butter 30 seconds. Combine with bread crumbs and walnuts. Microwave (high) 2½-3½ minutes, stirring halfway through cooking. Blend with onion, chili sauce, salt, lemon juice and pepper. Stuff mushrooms using about 1 Tbsp. stuffing per cap. Arrange 10-12 mushrooms on paper plate. Microwave (high), covered with wax paper, 5-6 minutes, rotating dish ¼ turn halfway through cooking. Serve hot. Makes 50.

- *Small, moist appetizers may be cooked on paper towel, plate or roasting rack to absorb excess moisture. Transfer to dish or tray for serving.*
- *To make these easy to eat — after filling, top with stem from mushroom; place toothpick through stem, filling and cap before heating.*

Notes: _____

MARINATED MUSHROOM CAPS

These used to be in the "Salads." After being a hit at a large party, it was suggested they be moved to "Appetizers" for ease of finding!

1 lb. small fresh mushrooms
6 Tbsp. olive oil
¾ cup dry white wine
1¼ tsp. salt
¼ tsp. dried oregano
¼ cup chopped parsley
2 Tbsp. chopped onion
3 Tbsp. lemon juice

Clean mushrooms. Remove stems if desired. In 4 cup glass measure combine all ingredients except mushrooms. Microwave (high) 3-4 minutes until mixture boils. Pour over mushrooms. Chill, covered, several hours, stirring occasionally. Makes about 4 cups.

● *Delicious in salads or served alone as an hors d'oeuvre.*

NIBBLES — *A favorite to have year round or to give as a gift.*

1 (10 oz) box round cereal (Cheerios)
2 cups wheat cereal squares (Wheat Chex)
1 small box pretzel sticks
1 (1 lb) can mixed nuts
½ cup butter
¼ cup Worcestershire sauce
1 Tbsp. garlic salt
1 Tbsp. celery salt
1 Tbsp. onion salt

In large glass bowl, combine cereals, nuts, and pretzels in bite size pieces. In a 2 cup glass measure, combine remaining ingredients. Microwave (high) 1-1½ minutes until butter melts. Mix well; pour over dry ingredients. Microwave (high) 6-8 minutes, stirring to mix ingredients every 2 minutes. Cool and serve as needed.

● *Store in air-tight container. May be frozen.*

NACHOS — *A southwest favorite which makes a hit anywhere.*

1 lg. pkg. Dorito corn chips
1 (7 oz) jar taco sauce, hot or mild
1 (4 oz) can sliced ripe olives
1 cup grated sharp cheddar cheese

Arrange Doritos on large paper plate. Pour taco sauce evenly over chips. Sprinkle olives and grated cheese over sauce and chips. Microwave (high) 2-2½ minutes, rotating dish ¼ turn halfway through cooking. (Cheese should be bubbling.) Serve hot to a crowd.

● *These are easy to serve for a crowd. Heat more as needed.*
● *For variety heat 1 tsp. Refried Beans on each corn chip; top with grated cheese. Microwave (high) 2-2½ minutes per plate following directions above.*

Notes: _____

CHEESY SNACKS — *Make ahead and serve when needed.*

1 cup grated sharp cheddar cheese	1 tsp. garlic salt
1 Tbsp. flour	1 Tbsp. dry white wine
1 tsp. curry powder	2 egg whites

In small bowl combine cheese, flour, curry, garlic salt and wine. Beat egg whites until stiff; fold into first mixture. Drop by teaspoons on wax paper. Place each cheese puff on cracker on roasting rack. Microwave (high) 1-1½ minutes for 12 crackers, rotating dish ¼ turn halfway through cooking, until cheese begins to bubble. Serve while hot. Serves 10-12.

● *Cheese mixture can be shaped around a green olive for an interesting variation.*

● *To freeze, place in freezer on cookie sheet. When frozen, transfer to plastic bag. Microwave (high) 1½-2½ minutes, rotating dish ¼ turn halfway through cooking to serve.*

Notes: _____

TERIYAKI CHICKEN WINGS — *Always a party favorite!*

2½-3 lbs. chicken wings	2 Tbsp. catsup
½ cup Teriyaki sauce	¼ cup water
	2 tsp. cornstarch

Cut wings at joints (save tips for chicken soup). Blend Teriyaki and catsup; marinate wings, chilled, 3-4 hours, stirring once or twice. In glass measuring cup pour off marinade; combine with water and cornstarch. Microwave (high) 2-3 minutes stirring every minute until boiling. On glass plate arrange chicken "spoke fashion." Baste with sauce. Microwave (high), covered, 4-5 minutes. Rotate dish ¼ turn and baste. Microwave (high), uncovered, 4-5 minutes. Broil if desired. Serve immediately. Serves 10-12.

● *For a large party we find it easier to cook a large pan of these in the conventional oven. Reheat 2-3 minutes in microwave at serving. Can also prepare early in the day and reheat.*

Notes: _____

Magic: *Stale crackers, potato chips, corn chips, pretzels, popcorn and other snack foods can be refreshed in the microwave by heating ½-1 minute (high), depending on quantity. Rest outside oven 1-3 minutes until crisp.*

CHOPPED CHICKEN LIVER
A delicious appetizer for a crowd. Very hearty to serve before late dinner.

1 lb. chicken livers	1 tsp. Worcestershire sauce
⅓ cup finely chopped onion	1 Tbsp. lemon juice
⅓ cup rendered chicken fat	1 tsp. salt
3 hard-cooked eggs (p. 92)	¼ tsp. pepper

Chop liver so it won't pop during cooking. In 1½ qt. glass casserole combine liver, onion and rendered fat. Microwave medium (50%) 8-10 minutes, stirring every 3 minutes until liver is no longer pink but not hard. Chop into tiny pieces. (Use food processor if you have one.) Mince eggs, saving ½ yolk for garnish. Blend with liver, sauce, lemon juice, salt and pepper. Chill before serving. Makes 2 cups.

- *At serving time place mixture on lettuce leaf. Garnish with remaining sieved egg yolk. Serve on crackers.*
- *Prepare the day before to blend flavors and chill well.*

Notes: _____

BEEF JERKY — *Homemade nourishment for snacking or hiking.*

1½ lb. round or flank steak	¼ tsp. garlic powder (optl.)
2 tsp. seasoned salt	¼ tsp. pepper

Trim meat and slice* 1/8-inch thick. Shake meat in seasonings in paper sack. On rack in 12x8-inch glass dish lay 6 pieces over rack ribs. Microwave (high), covered with paper towel, 3-4 minutes, rearranging once. Finish drying at room temperature on paper towel if necessary. Store in covered container. Makes 40.

*Freeze 30 minutes for easier slicing.
- *Venison may be substituted for beef.*

Notes: _____

TERIYAKI ROLL-UPS — *An easy Rumaki variation.*

1 Tbsp. finely chopped onion	¼ tsp. salt
1 clove finely minced garlic	½ lb. round or sirloin steak,
1 tsp. Worcestershire sauce	cut diagonally in very thin
¼ cup soy sauce	strips
1 Tbsp. sugar	1 (6 oz) can halved water
¼ tsp. ground ginger	chestnuts

In mixing bowl, combine onion, garlic, Worcestershire sauce, soy sauce, sugar, ginger and salt. Add meat strips; coat evenly. Marinate 30 minutes, stirring occasionally. Drain strips on paper towel. Wrap 1 around water chestnut and secure with toothpick. Arrange on glass plate. Microwave (high) 3-4 minutes, rotating dish ¼ turn

halfway through cooking. Rest 5 minutes. Serve hot. Makes 50.
- *⅓ cup prepared teriyaki sauce may be substituted for the Worcestershire sauce, soy sauce, sugar, ginger and salt.*

Notes: _____

COCKTAIL MEATBALLS
An excellent recipe to prepare, shape, and freeze.

1 lb. lean ground beef	1 egg
½ cup soft bread crumbs	½ tsp. salt
½ cup dry white wine	½ tsp. pepper
½ cup minced onion	½ tsp. oregano
1 clove minced garlic	¼ tsp. dried mint
1 Tbsp. dried parsley flakes	¼ tsp. ground thyme

Combine all ingredients, mixing lightly but thoroughly. Chill 2 hours for easy shaping and to blend seasonings. Shape in 1-inch meatballs; place 10 in a circle on paper plate or roasting rack in 12x8-inch glass dish. Microwave (high), covered, 1½-2½ minutes, rotating ¼ turn halfway through cooking. Serve hot. Makes 40.
- *Use to fill stuffed mushrooms or for hamburgers.*
- *For easy mixing, combine ingredients in plastic bag and squeeze.*

Notes: _____

SNACKIN NUTS — *Good nibbles to have on hand!*

2 Tbsp. butter	¼ cup sugar
2 cups pecan or walnut halves	½ tsp. cinnamon
	1 Tbsp. brown sugar

In 2 qt. glass measure melt (high) butter 30 seconds; add nuts. Microwave (high) 4-5 minutes, stirring every minute. Combine sugar, cinnamon and brown sugar; add to nuts coating evenly. Cool spreading evenly on bread board. Serve warm or cold. Makes 2 cups.
- *Store in freezer for use later if desired.*

SWEET AND SOUR WEINER FONDUE — *For quick snacking!*

1 (5 oz) jar currant jelly	1 (1 lb) pkg. weiners, in bite-
⅓ cup prepared mustard	size pieces

In 4 cup glass measure blend jelly and mustard. Microwave (high) 2 minutes, stirring once. Add weiners; microwave (high) 3-4 minutes stirring once. Serve hot. Makes 60-70.

Notes: _____

Breads

Breads are porous and cook very fast. It may be difficult to believe a roll can be heated in 10-15 seconds. If heated 20-25 seconds, it could be hard and tough after cooling (overcooking). Small amounts heat in about the same time as cooking. (15 seconds are needed to cook a small muffin or heat a dinner roll.) "Carry-over cooking" is important since foods are continuing to cook. Breads may feel soft or cool when touched. Always carry-over cook before adding more time.

Questions about browning in the microwave have been asked for years. Breads are one of the few foods that do not brown. Because they cook and heat so quickly, there is no time to dry to form a brown crust. "Cosmetically decorate" by coating with cinnamon, cinnamon and sugar, cornmeal, cocoa, etc. Select foods with a naturally colored dough for less coloring concern. "Decorate" with a contrast (frosting on zucchini bread) to improve the appearance. Browning shouldn't discourage you from preparing foods your family can enjoy in less than ¼ conventional time. If you are converting a recipe use less baking powder and liquid. Reduce the leavening by ⅓ so you won't get a bitter aftertaste. Liquid can be reduced up to ¼ less. You can also use a medium-high (70%) to medium (50%) power.

Cook most breads uncovered to prevent becoming moist and soggy. Heating on a paper towel, napkin or roasting rack will help prevent a soggy bottom. They may be heated in a wicker basket surrounded by a cloth (if the basket has no metallic paint or staples). Refresh day-old breads by heating a very short time.

 TO REHEAT DINNER ROLLS: Arrange on a paper napkin, paper towel, cloth or roasting rack; heat until rolls feel warm to the touch. Serve immediately.

1	10-15	seconds	High Power
2	20-30	seconds	High Power
3	25-35	seconds	High Power
4	40-60	seconds	High Power
6	60-75	seconds	High Power
8	1¼-1½	minutes	High Power

- *When roll is combined with a moist filling or topping, these are more dense and heat faster. Raisins and icing become extremely hot! They can be heated on medium (50%) to medium-high (70%) power.*
- *Heating a loaf or ring will require 1-1½ minutes.*
- *Heat large rolls longer and small rolls the shorter time.*

Notes: _____

FRENCH BREAD WITH GARLIC SPREAD — *Always a winner!*

1 loaf French bread	½ tsp. garlic salt or garlic
⅓ cup soft butter	powder

Cut bread in half lengthwise and crosswise. Slice into ½-inch slices (do not slice through bottom of loaf). In glass cup, melt butter with garlic (high) 30-40 seconds. Brush butter on each slice. Place halves together to reform loaf. Move center slices toward outside edges. Microwave medium-high (70%) wrapped in paper towel or cloth 45-60 seconds, rotating ¼ turn halfway through cooking.

- *Seasonings such as dill weed, parsley, etc. may be added with butter.*
- *Heat only the portion needed for immediate serving. Reheat remaining bread later, as desired.*

Notes: _____

_____

CORNBREAD — *An easy microwave bread!*

1 cup cornmeal	⅓ cup oil, soft butter or
1 cup flour	shortening
1 Tbsp. baking powder	1 cup milk
1 tsp. salt	1 egg

Combine cornmeal, flour, baking powder and salt in mixing bowl. Add oil. Beat milk and egg together; mix with dry ingredients. Pour into 6 cup plastic ring mold. Microwave (high) 4-5 minutes, rotating ¼ turn halfway through cooking. Rest 5 minutes. Serves 6-8.

Maxi-Time: Medium (50%) 4 minutes. Rotate ¼ turn; microwave (high) 2-3 minutes.

- *I prefer to cook in a ring mold. You can also use a 9-inch round glass cake dish. Place a small glass in the center of the dish, pour cornbread around glass. Follow directions above.*
- *Add ½ cup grated cheddar cheese or chopped crisp bacon (optl.)*
- *For richer bread add another egg.*
- *To make* **MUFFINS**, *pour batter in baking papers in 6 cup muffin pan. Fill each with ¼ cup batter (half full). Microwave following muffin chart (p. 38).*
- *The muffin pan cooks better and is handier than custard cups.*

Notes: _____

_____

BRAN DATE MUFFINS — *An easy breakfast or snack muffin!*

¼	cup water	⅔	cup flour
2	Tbsp. butter	½	tsp. baking powder
¾	cup All-Bran cereal	¼	tsp. salt
⅓	cup sugar	¼	cup milk
1	egg	6	dates, chopped (optl.)

In 1 qt. glass bowl microwave (high) water and butter 1 minute. Stir in cereal. Add sugar and egg. Blend in remaining ingredients. Place baking papers in plastic muffin pan. Fill half full with muffin mixture. Microwave as follows:

1 muffin	30-40	seconds	High Power
2 muffins	45-55	seconds	High Power
4 muffins	1¼-1¾	minutes	High Power
6 muffins	1¾-2¼	minutes	High Power

Rotate muffins ¼ turn halfway through cooking.
- *Chilled batter will require additional 12-15 seconds.*
- *Vary basic mixture by substituting raisins, nuts, grated apples or jelly in center of muffins. Finished muffins may be dipped in mixture of brown sugar, cinnamon and nuts.*

Notes: _____

BRAN MUFFINS (Basic Mix) — *Make your own mix!*

5½	cups All-Bran cereal nuggets	1	cup shortening
2	cups boiling water	4	eggs
1½	cups sugar (¾ cup white	3	cups buttermilk
	& ¾ cup brown)	5	tsp. baking soda
1	tsp. salt	5	cups flour
		1	cup chopped walnuts

Place All-Bran cereal in large bowl and cover with 2 cups boiling water. Soak 15-20 minutes. In another bowl blend sugars, salt, shortening, eggs, buttermilk, soda and flour. Combine with bran mix and nuts. Store in airtight container in refrigerator up to 6 weeks. Microwave as follows:

Spoon ¼ cup batter in baking papers in 6 cup plastic muffin pan. Microwave (high) rotating ¼ turn halfway through cooking using Muffin times (above). Makes about 50 muffins.
- *A good snack food to make as needed. Children can make these for breakfast and snacks after school and will never burn themselves!*

Notes: _____

_____

GINGERBREAD — *Serve with meals or dessert.*

½ cup water	½ tsp. salt
1 cup molasses	2 tsp. ginger
¼ cup butter or oil	1 tsp. baking soda
1 Tbsp. sugar	2 cups flour

In 2 cup glass measure microwave (high) water, molasses and butter 1-2 minutes until boiling. Add sugar, salt, ginger and baking soda. Blend in flour. Pour into 6 cup plastic ring mold. Microwave (high) 6-8 minutes rotating ¼ turn halfway through cooking. Rest 5 minutes. Invert from pan. Serves 6-8.
Maxi-Time: Medium-high (70%) 8-10 minutes.
- *Bread may be reheated. Serve warm with Lemon Sauce.*

Notes: _____

NUT BREADS (convenience mixes): Prepare as directed on package, reducing liquid by 2 Tbsp. Line bottom of 9x5x3-inch glass loaf pan with wax paper. Pour batter into pan. Rest 5 minutes. Sprinkle top with Streusel mixture of brown sugar, cinnamon and chopped nuts. Microwave medium-high (70%) 8-10 minutes, rotating dish ¼ turn halfway through cooking. Test with toothpick. Makes 1 loaf.

Notes: _____

DUMPLINGS — *No worry about these browning!*

2 cups flour	¾ cup milk
2 tsp. baking powder	2 eggs
¾ tsp. salt	1 Tbsp. vegetable oil
1½ tsp. parsley flakes	2½ cups boiling stock

Combine flour, baking powder, salt and parsley flakes. Blend milk, eggs and oil and mix with dry ingredients just until moistened. Drop by rounded spoonfuls into boiling stock. Sprinkle with parsley flakes. Microwave (high), covered, 7-10 minutes rotating ¼ turn halfway through cooking. Rest 5 minutes. Serves 5-6.
- *Dumplings are ideal because they look best when "snowy" white!*
- *Parsley adds a little extra, as would paprika, chives, etc. Cook over soups, stews, short ribs, etc.*

Notes: _____

_____

- **Thaw and heat frozen French toast, pancakes & waffles** medium-high (70%) 1-2½ minutes for 1-2 pieces; 3-4 minutes for 3-4. If refrigerated, allow 15-45 seconds less time.

Magic: To make **BREAD CRUMBS**, tear 4 slices fresh bread into tiny pieces, or crumb in blender. Add to ¼ cup butter. Season as desired. Cook 1-2 minutes (high) stirring every 30 seconds. Use in favorite recipes as a topping. Store in covered container in the refrigerator. For **BREAD CROUTONS**, substitute ¼-inch bread cubes for the crumbs. Makes about 2 cups crumbs or croutons.

DANISH COFFEE CAKE

Combine microwave and conventional oven for this delicious pastry. It is gorgeous and yummy for a formal or informal occasion.

1 cup flour	1 cup flour
½ cup butter	3 eggs
2 Tbsp. water	1½ cups powdered sugar
½ cup butter	2 Tbsp. warm water
¾ cup water	1 tsp. almond or orange
1 tsp. almond flavoring	flavoring
	Sliced almonds

With pastry blender cut flour into butter. Sprinkle with water; blend with fork. (A food processor does this in 30 seconds.) Form a ball; divide in half. Pat dough into two 12x3-inch strips on cookie sheet. Form a little rim around edge with heel of hand.

In 2 cup glass measure combine water and butter. Microwave (high) 2½-3 minutes until boiling. Add almond. In medium mixing bowl quickly beat in flour with whip. Add eggs, beating well after each. Divide evenly to cover dough mixture spreading out to sides and ends. Bake at 350°F. for 40-50 minutes until top is crisp.

In 2 cup glass measure combine powdered sugar, water and almond or orange flavoring. Frost pastry while warm. Sprinkle with sliced almonds. Serve in small strips. Serves 8-10.

● *An excellent hostess gift for special occasions. It's very rich. Our family appreciates this on a holiday or birthday breakfast.*

ZUCCHINI BREAD — *Only 8-10 minutes — not 1 hour at 350°F.*

3 eggs	¼ tsp. baking powder
2 cups sugar	1½ tsp. baking soda
1 cup oil	1 Tbsp. cinnamon
2 cups raw grated zucchini	½ tsp. ground cloves
2 cups flour	1 cup chopped nuts
1 tsp. salt	2 tsp. vanilla

In large mixing bowl blend eggs and sugar. Combine with oil and zucchini. Stir in remaining ingredients. Pour into 12-cup microwave bundt pan or 2-6 cup baking rings. (A 2 qt. casserole with glass in the center may also be used.) Microwave (high) 8-10 minutes, rotating ¼ turn halfway through cooking. Bread looks dry and begins to pull away from side when cooked. Cool 10 minutes in pan.

Invert onto serving platter. Frost with cream cheese frosting when cool. Makes 1 large or 2 small loaves.

● *This bread won't brown but when it's frosted no one will ever know. I prepare in quantity and freeze. At Christmas, they are a great substitute for fruitcake.*

● *If cooking in 6-cup ring — microwave 4-6 minutes each, rotating halfway through cooking.*

Notes: _____

WHOLE WHEAT BREAD

The best way to bake yeast bread is conventionally. The quality of microwaved bread is very different. The top crust does not brown. After baking many loaves of bread with so many differences in quality, I couldn't begin to tell you (!!!!), this whole wheat with a good natural color was the most acceptable (but better cooked conventionally!) My husband did buy me a mixer with a dough hook after the first 25 loaves — so maybe that will be an incentive. And I hope you have better luck!!

1 cup lukewarm water	2 Tbsp. shortening
1 pkg. active dry yeast	2 Tbsp. molasses
2 cups all-purpose flour	2 Tbsp. granulated sugar
1 cup milk	2½ tsp. salt
	4 cups whole wheat flour

In 2 cup glass measure microwave (high) water 30-45 seconds until lukewarm. Add yeast to soften. Stir into flour making a thick, smooth batter. (Cover; rest overnight in warm place.)

In a 4 cup glass measure, scald milk with shortening, molasses, sugar and salt about 2-3 minutes (high). Cool until lukewarm. Stir the yeast sponge and combine with milk mixture. Add whole wheat flour, 1 cup at a time, making a stiff dough. Turn dough onto lightly floured board and knead until smooth. Divide into 2 equal portions. Cover with a towel; rest 10 minutes. Shape into loaves; place in 9x5x3-inch loaf pans. Cover; rise for about 1½ hours, or until double in bulk. (Hurry by placing a 4 cup glass measure boiling water in microwave with bread dough until water cools. Reheat water and repeat until dough doubles in size.) Microwave (high) 1 loaf, 3-4 minutes, rotating ¼ turn once or twice as needed for even shaping. Test for doneness with a toothpick. Brush with melted butter (optl.) and place under a hot broiler element 1-2 minutes to brown. Cool 10 minutes. Remove from pan, cool on rack.

● *If preferred, bread may be cooked in microwave 3 minutes and finished in conventional oven as you would for Brown 'n Serve rolls or bread.*

● *Toast slices for brown color.*

Magic: To **THAW FROZEN BREAD DOUGH**, boil 4 cups water. Place in microwave with frozen bread in glass loaf pan. Microwave (high) ½ minute; rest 20 minutes. Repeat 3 times, rotating dish ¼ turn with each heating. Rest in microwave until double in size (15-20) minutes. (Reheat water if it cools.) Cook in conventional oven following package directions. Or use method p. 197.
• When **thawing frozen bread,** be certain to remove metal twist or it will arc!

STEAMED BOSTON BROWN BREAD — *A New England favorite.*

½ cup whole wheat flour	½ tsp. salt
½ cup flour	½ cup dark raisins
½ cup cornmeal	1 cup buttermilk
1 Tbsp. sugar	¼ cup oil
1 tsp. baking soda	⅓ cup molasses

In mixing bowl combine all ingredients, blending well. Pour half the mixture (1½ cups) into 2 cup measure with wax paper in bottom. Cover with plastic wrap to steam. Microwave medium (50%) 6-8 minutes, rotating dish ¼ turn halfway through cooking. Rest 5-10 minutes. Invert; cool to slice easier. Microwave remaining batter. Makes 2 small loaves.
● *Reheat to serve if desired.*

Notes: _____

CARAMEL BREAKFAST RING — *A cooking school favorite.*

⅓ cup brown sugar	¼-½ cup chopped walnuts
3 Tbsp. butter	1 (8 oz) can refrigerated
1 Tbsp. water	biscuits

In 6 cup plastic ring mold or 1 qt. glass dish, add brown sugar, butter, water; heat 1 minute. Blend ingredients and stir in nuts. Separate biscuits; arrange in overlapping ring (or for a crowd, cut each biscuit in quarters). Spoon caramel mixture over biscuits (or stir to coat and push to sides, placing a small glass in the center). Microwave (high) 2-3 minutes, rotating ¼ turn halfway through cooking. Rest 2-3 minutes. Biscuits should be firm and no longer doughy — but not tough! Remove center dish; invert on serving plate. Serve warm by pulling sections apart. Serves 4-6.
Maxi-Time: Medium (50%) 4-6 minutes.
● *I prefer medium (50%) if you have it.*
● *One of the easiest, most beautiful dishes you can make in the microwave. Let your children make it and serve you "breakfast in bed!" Keep ingredients on hand for late night snacks!*
● *Add chopped maraschino cherries with pecans for variety.*

- *For* **HERBED RING,** *blend 1 Tbsp. Parmesan cheese, ½ tsp. minced parsley, ¼ tsp. paprika and pinch garlic powder. Break 1 (8 oz) can refrigerator biscuits apart. Dip one side in 1 Tbsp. melted butter, then in herbs. Arrange overlapping, butter side down in 6 cup plastic ring mold. Microwave as above.*

COFFEE CAKE — *Good for variety at breakfast.*

2 cups biscuit mix	½ cup milk
2 Tbsp. sugar	½ Tbsp. brown sugar
1 egg	1 tsp. cinnamon
	2 Tbsp. chopped walnuts

In medium mixing bowl combine biscuit mix, sugar, egg and milk. Pour into 9" cake pan. In small bowl combine brown sugar, cinnamon and walnuts; sprinkle evenly over top. Microwave (high) 6-7 minutes rotating dish ¼ turn halfway through cooking. Rest 5 minutes before serving. Serves 6-8.

Maxi-Time: Medium-high (70%) 4 minutes. Rotate ¼ turn. High, 3-4 minutes. Rest 5 minutes.

- *Make 2 layers and stack to serve for brunch. For ease in removing from dish, line with wax paper; remove after cooling 5 minutes.*

- *A 9 ounce yellow or white cake mix may be substituted for biscuit mixture. Cook as directed above, using mini or maxi time.*

- *For* **EASY COFFEE CAKE,** *blend 1 (7 oz) muffin mix, any flavor, following package directions. Pour into 6 cup plastic ring mold. Combine 1 Tbsp. brown sugar, ½ tsp. cinnamon and ¼ cup chopped walnuts; sprinkle on top. Microwave (high) 3-5 minutes, rotating ¼ turn halfway through cooking. Serves 5-6.*

- **PIZZA** can be successfully prepared in the microwave by using the *Microwave Browning Grill.* Thaw or select fresh small or medium pizza. Preheat grill (high) 5-6 minutes. Place pizza on hot grill. Microwave (high) 3-5 minutes until hot and bubbling. Serve immediately.

    Wipe with paper towel and reheat 2-3 minutes before cooking another. Clean with a baking soda paste and paper towel.

    * The size of pizza and ingredients alters time.
    * Remove cardboard from bottom of purchased pizza.
    * Reheat cooked pizza (high) 1-1½ minutes/slice. Rest 1 minute before biting because the sauce will be hotter than the crust and could burn your mouth!

Magic: To **HEAT TORTILLAS a la NO EXTRA CALORIES!** pierce paper wrapper with fork or remove and wrap in a cloth. Microwave (high) 4 minutes, rotating ¼ turn halfway through cooking. (Saves extra oil normally used for frying.) Shells are more versatile as a bread to serve with meals.

Sandwiches

Day old bread which has lost some of its moisture heats with better results than fresh. Moisture in the sandwich filling is sufficient. A common complaint about heating sandwiches — they become "soggy" on the bottom as moisture in the filling transfers to porous bread. Moisture also presents a steaming problem. For this reason, toasted bread is preferred, reducing moisture. For heating sandwiches place on a napkin which will absorb moisture, or a roasting rack.

Catsup, mustard, pickles, etc. should be added after the sandwich is heated. For more uniform heating, edges of the filling or patty should be higher or bulkier than the center. Slice the sandwich and place outside edges together when heating.

Bread is porous, and meats and fillings are dense; therefore, the filling determines cooking time. Because fillings absorb more energy, they become hotter than the bread. **A word of caution:** allow rolls, sandwiches and breads to rest a few minutes before biting or the filling may burn your mouth!! (For example, jelly filling or icing on breakfast rolls will be hotter than the bread.)

Roasting racks for microwave oven use make good utensils for heating sandwiches because they allow more even air circulation. To reheat pizza, place it on a roasting rack.

HOT DOGS: Place a hot dog in bun and wrap in paper napkin or place on rack. Arrange in a circle and cook until warm as follows:

1 hot dog	20-25 seconds	High Power
2 hot dogs	45-50 seconds	High Power
3 hot dogs	1 minute	High Power
4 hot dogs	1 min., 10 seconds	High Power
6 hot dogs	1 min., 45 sec.	High Power

TOASTED CHEESE SANDWICHES: Toast bread conventionally and slice cheese for each sandwich. Butter is optional but if watching calories, leave it off; there is no difference in cooking. Place sandwich on a napkin or glass dish. (See table above.) Cheese will be very hot so cool a few minutes before biting!

- *For browning dish, preheat 4-5 minutes (high) Place buttered sandwich on hot dish. Flatten sandwich. Turn over after 15-20 seconds. Second side may take 20-30 seconds. (We feel it's easier to follow directions above.)*
- *If your bread is tough, it is overcooked! Toughness is usually an indication of overcooking for all foods.* **It doesn't take long!!**
- **Magic:** *We toast a loaf of bread in the broiler and keep frozen for snacking or quick sandwich making! This is great for kids!*

HAMBURGERS — *An even faster favorite with a microwave.*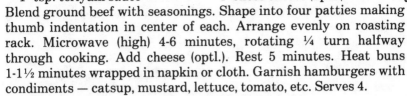
1 lb. ground beef	½ tsp. salt
¼ cup finely chopped onion	Dash pepper
2 Tbsp. chili sauce	8 split hamburger buns
1 tsp. teriyaki sauce	4 slices cheese (optl.)

Blend ground beef with seasonings. Shape into four patties making thumb indentation in center of each. Arrange evenly on roasting rack. Microwave (high) 4-6 minutes, rotating ¼ turn halfway through cooking. Add cheese (optl.). Rest 5 minutes. Heat buns 1-1½ minutes wrapped in napkin or cloth. Garnish hamburgers with condiments — catsup, mustard, lettuce, tomato, etc. Serves 4.

● *You may substitute your favorite hamburger mix.*

● *A natural browning agent is available to sprinkle on burgers before cooking if more browning is desired. Soy or teriyaki sauce may also be brushed on outside or make your own p. 190.*

● *For* **BROWNING DISH**, *preheat 5 minutes. Place patties on hot dish. Cook (high) 1-1½ minutes. Turn over and cook 1-1½ minutes.*

Notes: _____

_____

CRAB SANDWICH SUPREME — *Use fresh crab in season.*
8 oz. fresh crab	½ cup mayonnaise
½ cup finely chopped celery	6 slices toasted bread (or bun)
½ tsp. Worcestershire sauce	1 cup grated sharp cheddar
¼ tsp. salt	cheese

Blend crab, celery, Worcestershire sauce, salt and mayonnaise to moisten. Spread on toast or buns; sprinkle with grated cheese. Heat on napkin or rack until cheese melts or use timetable below. Rest a few minutes before serving. Serves 6.

● *1 (6½ oz) can crab may be used. Shrimp is also excellent.*

Notes: _____

MEAT, POULTRY OR FISH SANDWICHES: Arrange 3-4 thin slices of cooked meats, poultry or fish on bread or bun. Cover with gravy, barbecue sauce, etc. Heat open-face or closed (timing varies little since sauce and meat will absorb most of the energy). Place on napkin, or plate and heat as follows:

1 sandwich	½ to 1 minute	High Power
2 sandwiches	1 to 1½ minute	High Power
4 sandwiches	2 to 3 minutes	High Power

I prefer to thinly slice meat and fold before layering on bread for more even heating.

MICROWAVE PIZZA — *Delicious treat for teenagers!*

English Muffins   Sliced pepperoni
Butter   Grated mozzarella cheese
Taco sauce   Italian seasoning
     Parmesan cheese

Split muffins. Spread with butter. Top with spoonful of taco sauce, sliced pepperoni and mozzarella cheese. Sprinkle with Italian seasoning and Parmesan cheese. Arrange muffins on roasting rack in 12x8-inch glass dish. Microwave (high) 1-1½ minutes per muffin (2 halves). Rotate dish ¼ turn; microwave (high) ¾-1½ minutes.

- *Great food for slumber parties. Let everyone fix their own.*
- *Muffins may be toasted if desired.*

Notes: _____

_____

FRANKFURTER REUBEN — *A quick, tasty sandwich!*

12 slices rye bread   ⅓-½ cup Thousand Island
     butter   dressing
6 large frankfurters   1 cup sauerkraut, well drained
     6 slices Swiss cheese

Toast and butter bread. Split frankfurters in half lengthwise; place on 6 bread slices. Divide dressing on frankfurters; add 2 Tbsp. sauerkraut per sandwich. Top each with cheese slice. Cover with remaining bread. Microwave (high) as follows, rotating ¼ turn half-way through cooking:

     45-60 - 1 sandwich
     2-2½ minutes - 3 sandwiches
     3-4 minutes - 6 sandwiches

Serve warm. Makes 6 sandwiches.

- *Sliced corn beef or pastrami may be substituted for frankfurters.*

Notes: _____

Pasta

Microwave and conventional cooking times are about the same for pasta products. Many people have said they prefer the texture of microwave cooked pastas. Others say it is their favorite micro-waved food. The microwave gives perfect "al dente" texture a true Italian would love! Which way you cook it will often be determined by other foods in your menu. For example, when cooking spaghetti you may prefer making sauce in the microwave while cooking spaghetti on the range. Pasta can easily be reheated in the micro-wave. Allow 1-2 minutes for each cup. You may prefer cooking large quantities conventionally to reheat as needed. Undercook 2-4 minutes for use in a casserole with further cooking.

Use a large container so water won't boil over. Greasing rim of the dish with oil helps prevent boiling over. If you have a large family, microwaving pasta will not be practical. Remember, use the micro-wave for what it does best!

LASAGNA NOODLES

8 oz. (4 cups) Lasagna noodles	1 tsp. salt
1 qt. (4 cups) water	1 tsp. vegetable oil

In 12x8-inch glass dish arrange noodles. In 4 cup glass measure, microwave (high) water, salt and oil 6-8 minutes until boiling; pour over noodles. Microwave (high), covered, 7-9 minutes, stirring half-way through cooking. Rest, covered, 10 minutes. Drain extra liquid before serving. Serves 4-6.

MACARONI

1 qt. (4 cups) water	1 tsp. salt
1 tsp. vegetable oil	2 cups (7 oz) macaroni

In 4 cup glass measure, microwave (high) water, oil, and salt 6-8 minutes until boiling. Place macaroni in 3 qt. glass dish, pour boil-ing water over macaroni. Microwave (high), covered, 6-8 minutes, stirring halfway through cooking. Rest, covered, 10 minutes. Drain extra liquid before serving. Serves 4-6.

MANICOTTI

1 qt. (4 cups) water	1 tsp. salt
1 tsp. vegetable oil	16 manicotti shells

In 4 cup glass measure microwave (high) water, salt and oil 6-8 minutes until boiling. In 12x8-inch glass dish arrange noodles, pour boiling water over manicotti. Microwave (high) 6-8 minutes rotating dish ¼ turn halfway through cooking. Rest, covered, 10 minutes. Drain extra liquid. Fill shells with cheese or meat filling. Microwave (high) additional 10-12 minutes. Serves 5-6.

NOODLES

1 qt. (4 cups) water	1 tsp. salt
1 tsp. vegetable oil	8 oz. (4 cups) noodles

In 4 cup glass measure microwave (high) water, oil and salt 6-8 minutes until boiling. Place noodles in 3 qt. glass casserole, pour boiling water over noodles. Microwave (high), covered, 6-8 minutes, stirring halfway through cooking. Rest, covered, 10 minutes. Drain extra liquid before serving. Serves 4-6.

SPAGHETTI (Long)

1 qt. (4 cups) water	1 tsp. salt
1 tsp. vegetable oil	7 oz. long spaghetti

In 4 cup glass measure microwave (high) water, oil and salt 6-8 minutes until boiling. In 12x8-inch glass dish spread spaghetti, pour boiling water over spaghetti. Microwave (high), covered, 6-8 minutes, stirring halfway through cooking. Rest, covered, 10 minutes. Drain extra liquid before serving. Serves 4-6.

Notes: _____

- *For other pastas not mentioned, use cooking directions for a similar product. For example, shell macaroni would be cooked like macaroni and fettucine like noodles.*
- *When cooking dishes such as Macaroni and Cheese, cooking time is reduced if pasta is precooked before combining with sauce. Precooked pasta in the freezer is one of the best convenience foods to keep on hand. Substitute for potatoes at mealtime. Reheat quickly for meals in shifts. (I always cook extra for freezing.)*
- *When converting recipes precook pasta first.*

ALMOND NOODLES — *A very rich side dish.*

8 oz. Fettucine noodles	½ cup finely chopped parsley
6 Tbsp. butter	Pepper
2 tsp. olive oil	¼ cup toasted sesame seeds
1 clove minced garlic	¼ cup toasted slivered almonds
	½ cup Romano cheese

Cook noodles (above). Microwave (high) butter, oil, garlic, and parsley. Blend with noodles. Pepper to taste. Add sesame seeds, almonds, and cheese. Toss well to blend. Serves 4.

- *½ cup cream cheese or cream may be added with butter and oil.*

Notes: _____

_____

NOODLES AND CHEESE SUPREME — *Use as a main dish.*

8 oz. noodles	1 tsp. Worcestershire sauce
2 cups sour cream	Dash of tabasco
2 cups cottage cheese	¼ cup chopped onions
1 clove minced garlic	¼ cup butter
	Salt and pepper to taste

Cook noodles (p. 48). In 3 qt. glass casserole, combine noodles, sour cream, cottage cheese, garlic, and Worcestershire sauce. In 2 cup glass measure, microwave (high) tabasco, onions and butter 2-3 minutes, stirring every minute. Stir into noodles. Salt and pepper to taste. Microwave (high) 10-12 minutes, or until set, rotating ¼ turn once. Rest 10 minutes. Serves 4-6.
● *Serve with grated Parmesan cheese.*

Notes: _____

EASY MACARONI AND CHEESE — *Easier dishes are hard to find.*

8 oz. (2 cups) macaroni	½ cup grated sharp cheddar
½ cup evaporated milk	cheese

Cook macaroni (p. 47). In 2 qt. glass casserole, blend macaroni and milk, sprinkle with grated cheese. Microwave (high) 3-5 minutes rotating ¼ turn halfway through cooking. Rest, covered, 10 minutes. Serves 4-6.
● *Blend seasonings such as thyme, saffron, oregano, etc. with macaroni and milk. Garnish with chives, bacon bits, etc.*
● *Prepare Cheese Sauce (p. 100) and combine with cooked macaroni for an alternate method.*

Notes: _____

Cereals

Cereals may be cooked individually in serving dishes or in quantity for the entire family. If you have food likes and dislikes, let teenagers and Dad fix their own to suit their taste. They have a tendency to boil over so select a dish large enough for boiling water. Stir several times during cooking to distribute heat evenly. Carry-over cooking, covered, is important.

QUICK OATMEAL - Individual Servings
¼ cup quick-cooking oatmeal   Pinch salt
½ cup water

In glass serving bowl, blend oatmeal, water and salt. Microwave (high) 1-1½ minutes. Stir, cover and rest 2-3 minutes before serving. Serves 1.

● *Top with brown sugar or maple syrup to enhance flavor!*
● *Add one minute more for each additional serving.*

Notes: _____

QUICK OATMEAL - Quantity Servings
1½ cups quick-cooking oatmeal   ¾ tsp. salt
3 cups water

In 2 qt. glass casserole, blend oatmeal, water and salt. Microwave (high) 4 minutes. Stir; microwave (high) 2-3 minutes longer. Stir. Cover and rest 5 minutes before serving. Serves 4-6.

● *If cereal is left over from breakfast, store in refrigerator in covered container. Reheat 1-1½ minutes per cup as needed.*

Notes: _____

OATMEAL - Regular or Old Fashioned
Follow directions for Quick Oatmeal, stirring several times after mixture boils. Stir; cover; rest 5 minutes before serving. Serves 4-6.

● *Watch mixture closely so it does not boil over. The secret is to stir frequently. Grease rim with a little oil.*

Notes: _____

● *Prepare other cooked cereals using methods above for cereals of the same type. To prepare* **CREAM OF WHEAT***, allow 3 Tbsp./serving; follow package directions, stirring to prevent lumping.*

Notes: _____

GRANOLA — *Make your own speedy cereal.*

4 cups oats	½ cup honey
1 cup coconut	½ cup melted butter
¾ cup wheat germ	½ tsp. salt
1 cup chopped nuts or seeds	1 tsp. vanilla
½ cup brown sugar	½ cup raisins

In 3 qt. glass bowl blend ingredients except raisins. Microwave (high) 10-12 minutes or until ingredients are toasted, stirring every 4 minutes. (Add raisins last 4 minutes.) Cool, sprinkled on cookie sheet. Store in covered container. Makes 6 cups.

● *A good topping for cakes, pudding and ice cream.*

Rice

Rice appears many places in our menu served alone, seasoned with butter, parsley flakes, seasonings, etc. or in combination with foods at almost every course. It can be microwaved, but many people prefer cooking it conventionally because the same cooking time is required. Because of the long cooking time for brown and wild rice, I recommend you cook these on the range. All rice reheats easily without drying or changing texture (unless you overcook!). Allow 1-2 minutes/cup to reheat.

Rice is a dry food rehydrated by absorbing water. Select a large container for boiling action. I recommend quick-cooking rice for most recipes since it takes about the same time as other ingredients or precook before adding to a recipe. Three methods are recommended for cooking rice.

LONG-GRAIN RICE

1 cup long-grain rice	1 tsp. butter
1 tsp. salt	2 cups water

In 3 qt. glass casserole, combine rice, salt, butter and water. Microwave (high), covered, 12-14 minutes, stirring halfway through cooking. Rest, covered, 10 minutes. Serves 4.

AN ALTERNATE method requiring less time in the microwave:
Combine amounts above. Microwave (high), covered, 6-8 minutes until mixture boils. Rest, covered, 10-12 minutes. Microwave (high), covered, 2-4 minutes. Rest 5-10 minutes.

●*With this method you utilize the microwave for other foods during resting times.*

ANOTHER ALTERNATE cooks a large quantity conventionally and utilizes the microwave for reheating.

2 cups long-grain rice	1 Tbsp. butter
2 tsp. salt	4 cups water

In 4 qt. saucepan, combine rice, salt, butter and water. Bring to a vigorous boil, covered with tight-fitting lid on range. Reduce heat as low as possible. Cook 20-25 minutes. **Do not** stir or lift cover. Remove from heat. Rest, covered, 10-15 minutes. Makes about 6 cups.

- *To serve, reheat, covered, 8-10 minutes* **or** *1-2 minutes/cup,* **or** *freeze in serving size containers and reheat 2-3 minutes/cup.*
- *Cook rice in meat stocks, instead of water, for more flavor.*

Notes: _____

QUICK-COOKING RICE

1½ cups water	2 tsp. butter
1 tsp. salt	1½ cups quick-cooking rice

In 1 qt. glass casserole, combine water, salt and butter. Microwave (high), covered, 3-4 minutes until water boils. Stir in rice. Rest, covered, 5-7 minutes. Serves 4.

- *If desired, blend other seasonings with rice before resting.*

Notes: _____

WHITE AND WILD RICE MIXES

6 oz. pkg. rice	2 tsp. butter
1 tsp. salt	1¾ cups water

In 3 qt. glass casserole, combine rice, salt, butter and water. Microwave (high), covered, 15-18 minutes, stirring halfway through cooking. Rest, covered, 10 minutes before serving. Serves 3-4.

Notes: _____

- *These Rice Blends complement main dishes for variety in meals.*

HERB RICE BLEND

2 beef bouillon cubes	½ tsp. crushed marjoram
¼ tsp. crushed rosemary	1 tsp. dry onion flakes
½ tsp. crushed thyme	

Add to rice during cooking to blend flavor.

CURRIED RICE BLEND

2 chicken bouillon cubes	1 Tbsp. dried mushroom flakes
1½ tsp. curry powder	½ tsp. parsley flakes
1 tsp. dry minced onion	¼ tsp. paprika

Add to rice during cooking to blend flavor.

ORANGE-RAISIN RICE BLEND

2 chicken bouillon cubes	½ cup golden raisins
2 tsp. dried orange rind	⅓ cup slivered, toasted almonds

Add to rice during cooking to blend flavor.

Notes: _____

RICE-A-RONI MIX

1 (8 oz) Rice-A-Roni mix   2½ cups boiling water
2 Tbsp. butter

In 2 qt. glass casserole, combine rice-vermicelli mixture and butter. Microwave (high) 3-4 minutes, stirring every minute until vermicelli browns. Add boiling water and envelope contents. Microwave (high), covered, 12-14 minutes, stirring halfway through cooking. Rest, covered, 10 minutes. Serves 4-6.

CHEESE RICE RING — *A custard-type side dish.*

½ cup quick-cooking rice   ¾ cup milk
1 cup water   2 eggs
½ tsp. vegetable oil   1 tsp. salt
1 cup grated cheddar cheese   1 tsp. dry mustard

In 2 qt. glass casserole combine rice, water and oil. Microwave (high), covered, 4-5 minutes. Rest, covered, 5 minutes. Combine with cheese, milk, eggs, salt and mustard. Pour into 6-cup baking ring. Microwave (high), covered, 5-7 minutes, rotating ¼ turn halfway through cooking. Rest, covered, 5 minutes. Serve with ham, fish or poultry. Serves 4-5.

RICE PILAF — *Delicious with fish or poultry.*

2 Tbsp. butter   ½ tsp. salt
½ cup finely diced onions   1 (14 oz) can chicken broth (or
¼ cup minced parsley   bouillon crystals and water)
¾ cup diced celery   ¾ cup water
1 cup long-grain rice   1 (4 oz) can sliced mushrooms

In 2 qt. glass casserole blend butter, onion, parsley and celery. Microwave (high) 3-4 minutes stirring once. Combine with rice, salt, chicken broth, water and undrained mushrooms. Microwave (high), covered, 10-12 minutes, rotating dish ¼ turn halfway through cooking. Rest, covered, 5-10 minutes before lifting lid. If rice isn't tender, recover and cook 1-3 minutes longer. Serves 3-4.

Notes: _____

_____

Think Time — Not Heat!!

Salads

Most salads do not require cooking but your salad menu can be varied with your microwave. Cooking or heating salad dressing, cooking bacon, and heating water for gelatin salads is accomplished with ease. Some salads may be served warm.

HOT GERMAN POTATO SALAD — *An easy hot salad.*

4 medium potatoes	1 tsp. salt
6 slices bacon	½ tsp. celery seed
⅔ cup chopped onion	¼ tsp. pepper
3 Tbsp. flour	⅔ cup water
2 Tbsp. sugar	⅓ cup vinegar

Microwave potatoes (p. 64). Peel and slice thinly. Microwave (high) bacon (p. 138). Microwave (high) onion in bacon fat 3 minutes, stirring every minute. Blend flour, sugar, salt, celery seed, and pepper with onions. Microwave (high) 2-3 minutes, stirring every minute until smooth and bubbly. Stir in water and vinegar; bring to boil. Add potatoes and crumbled bacon. Microwave (high), covered, 3 minutes. Rest 5 minutes before serving. Serve hot or chilled. Serves 4-6.

● *2 (12 oz) pkgs. frozen hash browns may be substituted for whole potatoes. Microwave (high), covered, 12-14 minutes, stirring halfway through cooking until done. Combine with remaining ingredients.*

Notes: _____

_____

WILTED LETTUCE SALAD — *This luscious salad is a treat!*

5 slices bacon	½ cup vinegar
1 medium head lettuce	½ tsp. seasoned salt
2 thinly sliced green onions (tops too!)	Dash lemon pepper
	½ tsp. garlic powder
¼ cup bacon drippings	¼ tsp. dry mustard
½ cup sugar	2 sliced hard-cooked eggs

Cook bacon (p. 138); crumble, reserving ¼ cup drippings for dressing. Tear lettuce and combine with onions in salad bowl. Heat bacon drippings and pour over salad. In 2 cup glass measure mix sugar, vinegar, salt, pepper, garlic powder and mustard. Microwave (high) until mixture boils (1 minute). Stir to dissolve sugar and immediately pour over salad greens, mixing well until evenly coated with dressing. Garnish with bacon and eggs. Serves 6-8.

● **Fresh spinach,** *when available, is an excellent substitute for lettuce.*
● *Hard cook eggs in microwave (p. 92).*

VINAIGRETTE DRESSING

Serve on chilled, fresh-cooked asparagus for a spring treat. (The rest of the year frozen or canned asparagus is a good substitute.)

½ cup vegetable oil	½ tsp. seasoned salt
2 Tbsp. vinegar	1 tsp. sugar
2 Tbsp. lemon juice	½ tsp. paprika
	½ tsp. dry mustard

In 2 cup glass measure combine all ingredients. Microwave (high) 2-3 minutes until mixture boils. Chill. Serve on greens. Makes 1 cup.
- *Bottled salad dressings may be heated to pour over tossed salads with excellent results.*

CRANBERRY MOLDED SALAD

A Christmas salad that's good throughout the year.

1 envelope unflavored gelatin	2 oranges; peel 1
½ cup cold water	1 apple, peeled, cored
1 cup mayonnaise	½ cup sugar
1 (3 oz) pkg. cream cheese	2 cups boiling water
1½ tsp. grated orange rind	1 (3 oz) pkg. cherry gelatin
2 cups fresh cranberries	1 (3 oz) pkg. lemon gelatin

In 4 cup glass measure soften gelatin in cold water. Microwave (high) 1 minute until dissolved. Gradually add mayonnaise to cream cheese (softened in microwave 30 seconds). Mix until well blended. Stir in gelatin and orange rind; pour into tall 2 qt. mold. Chill until firm. Grind together cranberries, oranges and apple. Stir in sugar. Heat water (high) to boiling (4-5 minutes). Dissolve cherry and lemon gelatins in boiling water. Chill until slightly thickened. Fold in cranberry mixture; pour over molded gelatin layer. Chill until firm. Unmold. Serves 8-10.

Notes: _____

MOLDED MUSTARD SALAD

An excellent accompaniment and a little out of the ordinary, especially for a company ham or roast beef dinner.

1 envelope unflavored gelatin	¼ tsp. salt
½ cup cold water	¼ tsp. paprika
1 cup mayonnaise	½ cup whipped cream
⅓ cup prepared mustard	1 (8 oz) can mandarin oranges

In 4 cup glass measure soften gelatin in cold water. Microwave (high) 1 minute until dissolved. Cool. Blend mayonnaise, mustard, salt, and paprika. Stir in gelatin. Chill until slightly thickened; fold in whipped cream. Pour into 1 qt. tall mold. Chill until firm. Unmold and decorate with oranges. Serves 4-6.

THREE BEAN SALAD
I've been taking this to potlucks for years and it's still requested.

4 slices diced bacon
½ cup sugar
1 Tbsp. cornstarch
1 tsp. salt
¾ tsp. pepper
⅔ cup cider vinegar

1 (1 lb) can French-style
 green beans
1 (1 lb) can cut wax beans
1 (1 lb) can kidney beans
1 medium sliced onion

In 2½ qt. glass casserole microwave (high) bacon 3-4 minutes, stirring halfway through cooking. Remove cooked bacon to drain on paper towel. Add to drippings sugar, cornstarch, salt, pepper, and vinegar. Microwave (high) 3-4 minutes, stirring every minute until thick. Stir in drained beans and onion. Microwave (high), covered, 6-8 minutes, stirring once. Rest, covered, 10 minutes. Sprinkle with bacon. Serve either warm or cold. Serves 6-8.

PRETTY AS A PICTURE VEGETABLE MEDLEY
This salad serves a crowd and utilizes vegetables in season. Fall is one of the best times for an assortment! We could call this Autumn Harvest Salad since it looks like harvest bounty.

2 bunches broccoli, cut in
 thin stalks
1 small cauliflower, cut in
 flowerets
1 large zucchini,
 sliced ¼-inch thick
1 large crookneck squash,
 sliced ¼-inch thick
1 large pattypan squash,
 sliced ¼-inch thick

6 large fresh mushrooms,
 sliced
1 red pepper, cut into strips
1 medium green pepper, cut
 into strips
¼ cup butter
½ tsp. garlic salt
¼ tsp. pepper
¼ tsp. dry mustard

On large flat glass serving platter, arrange broccoli around outside edge of dish; cauliflower inside broccoli; squash, mushrooms and peppers should be arranged alternately near the inside of the dish to distribute color.

In 1 cup glass measure combine butter, garlic salt, pepper and mustard. Microwave (high) 30-45 seconds to melt butter. Drizzle over vegetables. Microwave (high) covered with wax paper or plastic wrap 10-15 minutes or until vegetables are done as desired, rotating dish ¼ turn every 5 minutes. Rest, covered, 5 minutes before serving. Serves 10-12.

● *This salad has such an assortment of vegetables, it should please the tastes of everyone. I prefer not to peel squash for added color.*
● *For a smaller amount of salad omit vegetables as desired. Microwave (high) 6-7 minutes/lb.*

PARTY FRUIT SALAD

At party time, this recipe eliminates last minute rushing because it is made the day ahead. And it will be a hit!

1 (20 oz) can pineapple chunks, save 2 Tbsp. juice	2 egg yolks
	2 Tbsp. sugar
1 (11 oz) can mandarin oranges, drained	2 Tbsp. pineapple juice
	2 Tbsp. brandy or rose wine
2 cups seeded grapes	½ tsp. dry mustard
2 cups miniature marsh-mallows	½ cup almonds, blanched and diced
1 (1 lb) can Royal Anne cherries, drained and pitted	½ cup heavy cream whipped, or sour cream

In large salad bowl, combine pineapple chunks, oranges, grapes, marshmallows, and cherries. Chill. In 2 cup glass measure combine egg yolks, sugar, pineapple juice, brandy or wine, and dry mustard. Microwave (high) 2-3 minutes, stirring every 30 seconds until thick and light. Chill. Just before serving, drain liquid from fruit. Fold cooled salad dressing, almonds, and cream into fruit until evenly blended. Chill until serving time. Serves 8-10.

CRAZY ORANGE SALAD

We all have favorite recipes. My mother gave me this. Since I have so many recipes going through my kitchen, I have included it so it will be easy to find even though it is not a microwave recipe. It does, however, enhance any microwave meal! Yum!

1 (3 oz) pkg. **dry** orange jello
1 (8 oz) tub cottage cheese, well drained
1 (11 oz) can mandarin oranges, drained
1 (8 oz) can crushed pineapple, drained
1 (4½ oz) tub Cool Whip

In medium mixing bowl combine dry jello and cottage cheese. Stir in oranges and pineapple. Blend with Cool Whip until mixture starts to congeal. Chill until serving time. Serves 5-6.

• *Make* **FRESH FRUIT AMBROSIA** *by combining fresh pineapple cubes, mandarin oranges, canned bing or maraschino cherries and other fruits as desired with ½-¾ cup coconut. Arrange in fruit shell (pineapple or melon) for serving. Microwave (high), covered, 8-10 minutes (120°F.) rotating ¼ turn halfway through cooking. If desired, 3-4 oz. rum or vermouth may be heated (high) 20 seconds; pour over ambrosia to flame and toast coconut. This will be a highlight with any meal.*

CHEESY FRUIT SALAD
A delicious combination for a frosted salad.

1 cup water	12 marshmallows (or cover with miniatures)
1 (3 oz) pkg. orange jello	
½ cup apricot or pineapple juice	½ cup sugar
	2 Tbsp. flour
1 (8 oz) can crushed, drained pineapple	1 cup fruit juice
	1 egg
1 (1 lb) can apricots, drained	1 cup whipped cream
	½ cup grated cheddar cheese

In 1 cup glass measure microwave (high) water 1½ minutes. In 12x8-inch glass dish combine with jello, juice, pineapple, and apricots. Cover with marshmallows. Chill until congealed.

In 2 cup glass measure combine sugar, flour, fruit juice, and egg. Microwave (high) 2-3 minutes, stirring every minute until thick. Cool. Combine with whipped cream and spread on jello. Sprinkle with grated cheese. Chill until serving. Serves 8-10.

MEXI-SALAD
A colorful vegetable salad. It also stretches protein in your meal.

1 lb. ground beef	1 Tbsp. chili powder
¼ cup chopped onion	4 cups shredded lettuce
1 (1 lb) can kidney beans, drained	½ cup sliced green onions
	2 cups grated sharp cheddar cheese
½ French dressing	
¼ cup water	

In 2 qt. glass casserole, microwave (high) ground beef and onion 4-6 minutes, stirring every 2 minutes. Pour off drippings. Stir in kidney beans, French dressing, water, and chili powder. Microwave (high) 4-6 minutes, stirring halfway through cooking.

In large mixing bowl, combine lettuce and green onions. Add cooked sauce and 1½ cups cheese; toss lightly. Arrange in lettuce-lined serving bowl. Sprinkle with additional ½ cup cheese. Serve hot or cold with crisp tortillas or corn chips. Serves 4-6.

●*Serve this salad for a main dish or a luncheon.*

FROSTED LIME SALAD
A delightful combination pretty enough to serve any time.

1 cup water	¾ cup finely diced celery
1 (3 oz) pkg. lime jello	½ cup chopped walnuts
1 (8 oz) can crushed, drained pineapple	1 (3 oz) pkg. cream cheese
	1 Tbsp. mayonnaise
1 cup small curd cottage cheese	1 tsp. lemon juice

In 1 cup glass measure microwave (high) water 2½-3 minutes to boil. In medium mixing bowl, dissolve gelatin in water. Chill until thick but not set, about 20 minutes. Fold in pineapple, cottage cheese, celery and walnuts. Pour into mold and chill until firm.

In 2 cup glass measure microwave (high) cream cheese 30 seconds. Whip with mayonnaise and lemon juice. Unmold firm gelatin and frost with cream cheese mixture. Serves 6-8.

COOKED SALAD DRESSING — *Good on fruit salads.*

1 Tbsp. butter	½ cup sugar
1 Tbsp. flour	½ cup vinegar
1 Tbsp. prepared mustard	1 egg, beaten
¼ tsp. salt	2 Tbsp. poppy seeds (optl.)

In 2 cup glass measure microwave (high) butter 15 seconds. Stir in flour, mustard, and salt. Add sugar. Slowly blend in vinegar and egg. Microwave (high) 2-3 minutes, stirring every minute until mixture is very thick. Fold in poppy seeds. Chill before using.
● *Thin with fruit juice for fruit salad.*

Notes: _____

_____

OVERNIGHT LETTUCE SALAD — *Great for Entertaining!*

1 med. head shredded lettuce	½ cup shredded cheddar cheese
1 bunch diced green onions	2 Tbsp. sugar
1 cup diced celery	1 tsp. seasoned salt
1 (10 oz) pkg. **frozen** peas	¼ tsp. garlic powder
½ lb. sliced fresh mushrooms	4 eggs
1 cup mayonnaise	8 slices diced bacon

In large glass salad bowl layer lettuce, green onions, celery, **frozen** peas, and mushrooms. Spread mayonnaise over top, sealing edges. Sprinkle with cheese, sugar, salt, and garlic powder. Refrigerate covered overnight. Hardcook eggs (p. 92). Chill.

In 1 qt. glass dish, microwave (high) bacon 5-6 minutes, stirring and removing drippings halfway through cooking. When crisp, drain on paper towel. Sprinkle with bacon and minced eggs before serving. Serves 8-10.
● *Joanne Magee, Portland, Ore., serves this delicious salad often and shared the recipe. Water chestnuts may be substituted for celery and Parmesan cheese for cheddar.*

Notes: _____

_____

Vegetables

Exciting things happen to vegetables cooked in the microwave! They are picture pretty. I have heard many mothers say their children would not eat conventionally cooked vegetables but love the same microwaved vegetable. This tells us something about quality and flavor. They can be *al dente* or soft to suit tastes. **Very little water** is added to most vegetables, retaining fresh vegetable flavor and color. Water clinging to vegetables after washing will often be enough for cooking. Some vegetables can be cooked in their own container, such as potatoes, acorn squash, corn on the cob, etc. This gives an added advantage — no dishwashing! When cooked in the skin, pierce to allow steam to escape. Since vegetables are exposed to less air, water and heat, they have about a 12% higher nutritive value. Substitute for good seasonal buys. When green peppers are $1.49/lb., use an alternate (stuff eggplant, etc.).

To determine **cooking times** for vegetables:

1. **Weigh** the total amount of food to be cooked.
2. Multiply the total weight times 6-7 minutes/lb.

   (6 minutes — 650 watt oven; 7 minutes — 600 watt oven.)
3. Set timer for total cooking time, **or** one-half total time to help you remember foods must be rotated ¼ turn or stirred halfway through cooking. Foods such as baked potatoes and baked squash may be placed on a roasting rack or turned over to prevent becoming soggy on the bottom.
4. Rest about 5 minutes, covered, to allow for "carry-over cooking."

When possible cook vegetables in a **covered** container to provide more even heating. Wax paper makes an ideal cover for many vegetables. To use, simply wrap the vegetable in the paper, place on any flat or round glass dish, or lay over the top as you would for a lid. Skins and husks are containers and won't need another covering.

Pierce skins if you are using a natural container to allow internal heat to escape (or they may burst). You can cook in a heat-proof plastic pouch but this must be pierced or slashed. If cooking frozen vegetables in the carton, remove paper from one end for ease of pouring at end of cooking.

If **salting** the vegetable is desired, dissolve salt in cooking liquid before adding vegetable. Salt sprinkled directly on vegetables will cause brown "freckles." It distorts the natural microwave cooking pattern. Other seasonings may be used as desired. A pinch of sugar brings out the flavor in many vegetables.

Arrange vegetables as evenly as possible. Place one near center of the cavity; two separated by one inch; three in a triangle with a 1-inch space between each; four in a square with a

1-inch space; etc. Do not place a single item in the center of circular arrangement because this area attracts fewer microwaves than outside surfaces. For your convenience you may wish to place multiple foods on a dish (or rack) for rotating. If you are slicing vegetables, slice so all pieces are about the same size. Small pieces cook faster than large. Arrange small or flower ends near center of the dish. Stir small vegetables to redistribute energy.

Be careful not to **overcook** vegetables! Overcooking makes them dry and tough. Always use the shortest cooking time in any recipe. Add more after "carry-over cooking." Butter, cheese, sauces, and accompaniments may be added to vegetables during or after cooking, depending on the results you want. You will have far more variety in texture, method, serving, and number of vegetables in your menu when you microwave.

If you are **DIETING** use your microwave for quick-cooking foods on your diet as well as snack foods for more variety. Foods selected from the following list contain 25 calories or less per ½ cup serving:

Asparagus	Celery	dandelion, kale,	Lettuce
Broccoli	Cucumbers	mustard,	Mushrooms
Cabbage	Green Beans	spinach, turnip	Summer squash
Carrots	Greens: beet,		Tomatoes
Cauliflower	chard, collard,		Turnips

The following vegetables contain about 40 calories per ½ cup serving when cooked:

Beets	Peas, green	Tomato Juice
Brussels Sprouts	Pumpkin	Winter Squash
Onions	Rutabagas	

All of these are easy to microwave without the addition of fats, oils, and sugar. For effective results with any diet, quantities of food you eat are very important and in most cases, should be measured!

MAGIC: Parsley, celery leaves and other **herbs can be dried** in your microwave. Clean, pat semi-dry between paper towels; microwave (high) 2-4 minutes/cup, mixing after every 30 seconds. Remove from oven; cool. Rub between towel to crumble. Repeat if necessary.

FRESH VEGETABLE COOKING CHART

ARTICHOKE — 1 medium (4-inches diameter).
Wash thoroughly, allowing a small amount of water to cling to leaves. Add 1 Tbsp. butter if desired. Wrap in wax paper. Place on glass plate or dish. Microwave (high) 6-7 minutes/lb., rotating ¼ turn halfway through cooking. Rest, covered, 5 minutes before serving. (Use desired seasonings — see p. 71 .)

ASPARAGUS — Fresh cut or spears-15 medium stalks=¾ pound. Pop white portion off bottom of each spear. Wash thoroughly, allowing a small amount of water to cling to spears. Arrange in a oblong glass dish (loaf pan) with approximately one-half the stalks pointing each way. Microwave (high), covered, 6-7 minutes/lb., rotating ¼ turn half-way through cooking. Rest, covered, 5 minutes before serving. Season as desired.

● *Asparagus may be peeled if desired.*

BEANS — GREEN OR WAX — 3 cups = 1 lb.
Wash thoroughly. Add ¼ cup water to 1½ qt. glass dish. Salt (optl.). Add beans to dish. Microwave (high), covered, 6-7 minutes/lb., stirring halfway through cooking. Rest, covered, 5 minutes before serving. Season. (For a more tender bean, add 2-3 Tbsp. more water; cook 2-4 minutes more.)

BEETS — 4 medium whole beets = 1 lb.
Clean beets. Place in 2 qt. glass dish. Cover with water. Microwave (high), covered, 15-17 minutes, stirring halfway through cooking. Rest, covered, 5 minutes before serving. (Reduce cooking time by boiling water first.) Peel, slice and season.

BROCCOLI — 1 small bunch = 1 lb.
Wash stalks and split to uniform size. Peel if desired. Add ¼ cup water and ½ tsp. salt (optl.), to 12x8-inch glass dish. Arrange broccoli with stems along outside and flowers in center. Microwave (high), covered, 6-7 minutes/lb., rotating dish ¼ turn halfway through cooking. Rest, covered, 5 minutes before serving. Season.

BRUSSELS SPROUTS — 1 tub = 10 ounces.
Wash and remove dried leaves. Add 2 Tbsp. water and ½ tsp. salt (optl.), to 1 qt. glass dish. Add sprouts. Microwave (high), covered, 6-7 minutes/lb., rotating dish ¼ turn halfway through cooking. Rest, covered, 5 minutes. Season.

CABBAGE — 1 small head = 1 lb.
Wash and shred, cut in wedges, or cook whole. Add 2 Tbsp. water and ½ tsp. salt (optl.), to 1½ qt. glass dish. Add cabbage. Microwave (high), covered, 6-7 minutes/lb. Rotate dish ¼ turn halfway through cooking. Rest, covered, 5 minutes. Season.

CARROTS — 6 whole medium = 1 lb.
Peel and wash carrots. Slice in equal rounds, dice in even strips, or cut lengthwise in even shape. Add ¼ cup water and ½ tsp. salt (optl.), to 1½ qt. glass dish. Add carrots. Microwave (high), covered, 7-8 minutes/lb., stirring halfway through cooking. Rest, covered, 5 minutes. Season. (Diagonally sliced carrots are pretty when serving.)

CAULIFLOWER — 1 small head = 1 lb.
Wash and trim. Leave whole and remove woody stalk with apple corer, or trim flowers from stem. Add 2 Tbsp. water and ½ tsp. salt

(optl.), to 1½ qt. glass dish. Add cauliflower. Microwave (high), covered, 6-7 minutes/lb. If left whole, rotate dish ¼ turn halfway through cooking. If cut in flowers, stir halfway through cooking. Rest, covered, 5 minutes. Season. (If left whole, the head may be wrapped in wax paper and placed on glass dish for cooking.)

CELERY — 3 cups sliced = 1 lb.

Wash and slice. Add 2 Tbsp. water and ½ tsp. salt (optl.), to 1½ qt. glass dish. Add celery. Microwave (high), covered, 6-7 minutes/lb., stirring halfway through cooking. Rest, covered, 5 minutes. Season.

CORN — 2 cups = ¾ lb.

Shuck ears and cut corn off cob. Add 2 Tbsp. water or cream and ½ tsp. salt (optl.), to 1 qt. glass dish. Add corn. Microwave (high), covered, 6-7 minutes/lb., stirring halfway through cooking. Rest, covered, 5 minutes. Season.

CORN ON THE COB — 1 medium ear = approximately ½ lb.

Pull back husks to check condition of corn. Remove husks except for about 2 layers, leaving silk in place. (Husks are the container to trap steam when cooking.) Arrange corn evenly on oven shelf. Microwave (high) for the following times, rotating ¼ turn halfway through cooking:

1 ear	2 - 3 minutes	High power
2 ears	4 - 5 minutes	High power
4 ears	6 - 7 minutes	High power
6 ears	8 - 9 minutes	High power
8 ears	10-12 minutes	High power

Rest, with husks on, 5 minutes. Remove husks and silks with clean hot pads. Dip in butter, if desired.

● *Corn may be husked and silked before cooking. Wrap in wax paper or place in a covered glass dish. Cook, following above times, rotating halfway through cooking. Season. (It won't be as sweet as that cooked in the husk.)*

CUCUMBERS — 2 medium = ¾ lb.

Peel and dice in ½-inch cubes. Add 2 Tbsp. water or cream and ½ tsp. salt (optl.), to 1 qt. glass dish. Add cucumbers. Microwave (high), covered, 6-7 minutes/lb., stirring halfway through cooking. Rest, covered, 5 minutes. Season.

EGGPLANT — 1 small = 1 lb.

Peel and dice in ½-inch cubes. Add 2 Tbsp. water and ½ tsp. salt (optl.), to 1½ qt. glass dish. Add eggplant. Microwave (high), covered, 6-7 minutes/lb., stirring halfway through cooking. Rest, covered, 5 minutes. Season.

● *May be pierced and cooked whole 6-7 minutes/lb.*

GREENS: Beet, Chard, Collard, Dandelion, Kale, Mustard, Turnip, and **Spinach** — 4 cups = 1 lb.

Wash and cook in water that clings to leaves in 2 qt. glass dish.

Microwave (high), covered, 6-7 minutes/lb. Rotate dish ¼ turn halfway through cooking. Rest, covered, 5 minutes. Season.

MIRLITONS (also known as Vegetable Pear) — Cook whole, wrapped in plastic wrap, pierced, 8-9 minutes/lb., turning over and rotating ¼ turn halfway through cooking. Rest 5 minutes. These are generally scooped out and combined with other ingredients. Refill to serve. We also like them as a substitute for potatoes, plain with butter, salt and pepper.

MUSHROOMS — Because mushrooms are porous, they cook very quickly — 4 minutes/lb. It is difficult to judge the weight because they vary a great deal in size. It's best to weigh for accurate cooking time. Heating a small amount of mushrooms for a garnish or accompaniment will require 1-2 minutes in butter. Clean, slice, and microwave (high) in 1 qt. covered glass dish 4 minutes/lb. 1-2 Tbsp. butter may be added before or during cooking, if desired.

ONIONS — 8 small or 2 large = 1 lb.

Clean and quarter or slice onions. Place in 1 qt. glass dish. Microwave (high), covered, 6-7 minutes/lb., rotating dish ¼ turn halfway through cooking. Rest, covered, 5 minutes. Season or add sauce.

● *Onions may be cooked whole if desired.*

PARSNIPS — 4 medium = 1 lb.

Split, remove core if desired, and wash. Add 2 Tbsp. water and ½ tsp. salt (optl.), to 1½ qt. glass dish. Add parsnips. Microwave (high), covered, 7-8 minutes/lb., rotating dish ¼ turn halfway through cooking. Rest, covered, 5 minutes. Season.

PEAS (GREEN) — 2 cups = 1 lb.

Shell peas. Add 2 Tbsp. water and 2 tsp. salt (optl.), to 1 qt. glass dish. Add peas. Microwave (high), covered, 5 minutes/lb., stirring halfway through cooking. Rest, covered, 5 minutes. Season.

PEAS (PODS) — Follow green pea directions.

PEAS (BLACK-EYED) — Dry peas are best cooked conventionally. After cooking, reheat in microwave. For microwave cooking, see dried peas (p. 91).

PEPPERS (GREEN OR RED) — 3 large = 1 lb.

Cut core from peppers and clean, allowing some water to cling. Arrange evenly in 2 qt. glass dish. Microwave (high), covered, 6-7 mintues/lb., rotating dish ¼ turn halfway through cooking. Rest, covered, 5 minutes. Season.

POTATOES (BAKED) — 2 small or 1 large = 1 lb.

Potatoes should be even in size and shape, otherwise small potatoes will overcook during cooking time for large. After scrubbing, pierce skins to allow steam to escape. Arrange potatoes 1-inch apart in a circle on roasting rack or bottom of oven. Microwave (high), rotating ¼ turn halfway through cooking, following timetable or 6-7 minutes/lb.:

1 medium	3½-4	minutes	High power
2 medium	6½-7	minutes	High power
4 medium	10-11	minutes	High power
6 medium	15-16	minutes	High power
8 medium	21-23	minutes	High power

For convenience in rotating, place potatoes on roasting rack or muffin pan. Remove potatoes when fork comes out with a "little resistance." Rest 5 minutes and test again for doneness.

• *Potatoes may be turned over when rotating to prevent becoming "soggy" on the bottom and cooking uneven. A rack allows more air circulation. I don't recommend cooking the potato on napkins or paper towels because of the danger of over-cooking and transferring too much heat from potato to the paper.*

• *Select potatoes that are round and not long and skinny.*
If you are preparing 1 potato for 2 servings, cook whole and cut in half after cooking is completed.

POTATOES (BOILED) — Peel and quarter potatoes, keeping pieces in a uniform size. In 1½ qt. glass dish, add ½ cup water and 1 tsp. salt (optl.). Add potatoes. Microwave (high), covered, as follows, stirring halfway through cooking:

2 medium	8-10	minutes	High power
4 medium	15-18	minutes	High power

Rest, covered, 5 minutes and test for doneness. (Reduce cooking time by boiling water first.) Season. Use as desired.

• *It may be more convenient to boil potatoes on the range surface. About the same cooking time is required for more than 4 potatoes.*

POTATOES — SWEET OR YAMS — 2 medium = 1 lb.
Potatoes should be even in size and shape (preferably oval, not long). After scrubbing, pierce skins to allow steam to escape. Arrange potatoes 1-inch apart on roasting rack or bottom of oven in a circle. Microwave (high) rotating ¼ turn halfway through cooking, following timetable or 6-7 minutes/lb.:

1 medium	3-4 minutes	High power
2 medium	5-6 minutes	High power
4 medium	7-8 minutes	High power
6 medium	8-9 minutes	High power

Place potatoes on rack or muffin pan for ease in rotating halfway through cooking. Remove potatoes when fork comes out with a "little resistance." Rest 5 minutes and test again for doneness.

• *Potatoes may be turned over when rotating to prevent becoming "soggy" on the bottom or cooking uneven. I don't recommend cooking the potato on napkins or paper towels because of the danger of over-cooking and transferring too much heat from potato to the paper.*

● *If you are preparing 1 potato for 2 servings, cook whole and cut in half after cooking is completed.*

PUMPKIN — Follow Hubbard Squash directions. (Below)

SPINACH — See Greens, p. 63.

SQUASH — ACORN, BUTTERNUT, DANISH — 1 small = 1 + lbs.
Pierce squash and place whole on dish or rack. Microwave (high) 6-8 minutes/lb. Rotate ¼ turn and turn over halfway through cooking as follows:

1 small	6 - 8 minutes	High power
2 small	12-14 minutes	High power

Rest 5 minutes; test for doneness. Halve, remove seeds and season.

● *Squash may be half cooked for easier piercing. (Don't forget to pierce!)*

SQUASH — HUBBARD — 6" x 6" piece = 1 + lbs.
Wash, allowing about ¼ cup water to cling to squash. Wrap in wax paper; place on glass dish. Microwave (high) 6-7 minutes/lb., rotating ¼ turn halfway through cooking. Rest, covered, 5-7 minutes. Season.

● *Squash may be cut in 1-inch cubes. (Precook 1-2 minutes to cut easier.) Add 2 Tbsp. water and 1 tsp. salt to 1½ qt. glass dish. Add squash. Microwave (high) covered, 6-7 minutes/lb., rotating dish ¼ turn halfway through cooking. Rest, covered, 5 minutes. Season.*

SQUASH - ZUCCHINI - 2 medium = 1 lb.
Pierce and cook whole or slice ¼-inch thick. Add 2 Tbsp. water and ½ tsp. salt (optl.) to 1 qt. glass dish. Add zucchini. Microwave (high), covered, 6-7 minutes/lb., stirring halfway through cooking. Rest, covered, 5 minutes. Season.

● *Skins may be left on to add color and texture.*

TOMATOES - 4 medium = 1+ lbs.
Wash and core tomatoes. Arrange evenly in 2 qt. glass dish. Microwave (high), covered, 4-6 minutes, rotating ¼ turn halfway through cooking. Rest, uncovered, 5 minutes. Season.

● *Caution: Avoid overcooking tomatoes. They loose shape and become juicy when overheated. Select ripe, firm tomatoes for cooking.*

TURNIPS - 2 medium = 1+ lbs.
Wash and cut in eighths. Add ¼ cup water and ½ tsp. salt, (optl.), to 1½ qt. glass dish. Add turnips. Microwave (high), covered, 6-7 minutes /lb., rotating ¼ turn halfway through cooking. Rest, covered, 5 minutes. Season.

FRESH VEGETABLE TIPS

● *These cooking times are as close to correct as possible. You will have some variation depending on texture, freshness, shape, etc. of each vegetable.* **Weight** *is the most accurate measure of cooking time, and practice is the best teacher to avoid overcooking!*

● *Many of these vegetables will be crisp-tender as some people prefer. If you like a softer texture, cook 1-2 minutes longer. Add another Tbsp. water for softer texture. Always "carry-over cook" before adding more cooking!*

●*If potatoes must be held for long periods, reheat before serving.*

●*Leave lid on the container during "carry-over cooking" unless the recipe suggests removing it.*

● *I don't recommend wrapping potatoes, squash, etc., in foil at the end of cooking because this traps moisture between foil and potato which can make the potato "soggy." It would be better to wrap in a terry cloth to absorb moisture, and at the same time, help to keep heat in the potato.*

FROZEN VEGETABLE COOKING CHART

ARTICHOKE - Hearts - 10 oz.

*Microwave (high) in package placed on paper plate 4-5 minutes rotating ¼ turn halfway through cooking. Rest 5 minutes. Season.

Or, place artichokes and 2 Tbsp. water in 1 qt. glass covered casserole. Follow directions above.

ASPARAGUS - Spears or Pieces - 10 oz.

*Microwave (high) in package placed on paper plate 6-8 minutes rotating ¼ turn halfway through cooking. Rest 5 minutes. Season.

Or, place asparagus and 2 Tbsp. water in 1 qt. glass covered casserole. Follow directions above.

● *For 9 oz. pouch, place pouch on a glass dish. Make a slash in the top. Microwave (high) 5-6 minutes as above.*

| 2-10 oz. pkgs. | 9-10 minutes | High power |
| 3-10 oz. pkgs. | 12-14 minutes | High power |

BEANS - GREEN OR WAX - 10 oz. carton or pouch

*Microwave (high) in package placed on paper plate 8-10 minutes rotating ¼ turn halfway through cooking. Rest 5 minutes. Season.

Or, place beans and 2 Tbsp. water in 1 qt. glass covered casserole. Follow directions above.

| 2-10 oz. pkgs. | 11-13 minutes | High power |
| 3-10 oz. pkgs. | 14-16 minutes | High power |

BEANS - LIMA - 10 oz. carton or pouch

Place beans and ⅓ cup hot water in 1½ qt. glass covered casserole. Microwave (high), 9-10 minutes, stirring or rotating ¼ turn halfway through cooking. Rest 5 minutes. Season.

| 2-10 oz. pkgs. | 14-16 minutes | High power |
| 3-10 oz. pkgs. | 18-20 minutes | High power |

BROCCOLI - Chopped or spears - 10 oz. carton or pouch

* Microwave (high) in package placed on paper plate 5-6 minutes chopped and 7-9 minutes spears, rotating ¼ turn halfway through cooking. Rest 5 minutes. Season.

*Or, place broccoli in 1 qt. glass covered casserole. Follow directions

*Slash or pierce package before cooking.

for package.

| 2-10 oz. pkgs. | 8-10 minutes | High power |
| 3-10 oz. pkgs. | 11-13 minutes | High power |

BRUSSELS SPROUTS - 10 oz. carton or pouch

*Microwave (high) in package placed on paper plate 6-8 minutes, rotating ¼ turn halfway through cooking. Rest 5 minutes. Season.

Or, place brussels sprouts and 2 Tbsp. water in 1 qt. glass covered casserole. Follow directions above.

| 2-10 oz. pkgs. | 8-10 minutes | High power |
| 3-10 oz. pkgs. | 11-13 minutes | High power |

CARROTS - Diced or whole - 10 oz. carton or pouch

*Microwave (high) in package placed on paper plate 6-8 minutes, rotating ¼ turn halfway through cooking. Rest 5 minutes. Season.

Or, place carrots in 1 qt. glass covered casserole. Follow directions above.

●*Whole carrots may require 2 Tbsp. water and 1-2 minutes more cooking. Diced carrots require 1-2 minutes less cooking.*

| 2-10 oz. pkgs. | 8-10 minutes | High power |
| 3-10 oz. pkgs. | 11-13 minutes | High power |

CAULIFLOWER - 10 oz. carton or pouch

*Microwave (high) in package placed on paper plate 6-8 minutes, rotating ¼ turn halfway through cooking. Rest 5 minutes. Season.

Or, place cauliflower in 1 qt. glass covered casserole. Follow directions above.

| 2-10 oz. pkgs. | 8-10 minutes | High power |
| 3-10 oz. pkgs. | 11-13 minutes | High power |

CORN - 10 oz. carton or pouch

*Microwave (high) in package placed on paper plate 5-7 minutes, stirring or rotating ¼ turn halfway through cooking. Rest 5 minutes. Season.

Or, place corn and 2 Tbsp. water in 1 qt. glass covered casserole. Follow directions above.

| 2-10 oz. pkgs. | 6-8 minutes | High power |
| 3-10 oz. pkgs. | 8-10 minutes | High power |

CORN ON THE COB

Before cooking defrost frozen corn on the cob in refrigerator overnight, wrapped tightly, or in 12x8-inch covered dish. Cob must also defrost. Wrap in wax paper or place in 12x8-inch glass, covered, casserole. Microwave (high) following table, turning over and rotating ¼ turn halfway through cooking:

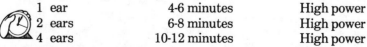

1 ear	4-6 minutes	High power
2 ears	6-8 minutes	High power
4 ears	10-12 minutes	High power

Rest 5 minutes. Season.

● *If cooked frozen, add 2-3 minutes per ear.*

* *Slash or pierce package before cooking.*

MIXED VEGETABLES - 10 oz. carton or pouch

*Microwave (high) in package placed on paper plate 5-7 minutes, rotating ¼ turn halfway through cooking. Rest 5 minutes. Season.
Or, place vegetables and 2 Tbsp. water in 1 qt. glass covered casserole. Follow directions above.

2-10 oz. pkgs.	8-10 minutes	High power
3-10 oz. pkgs.	11-13 minutes	High power

OKRA - 10 oz. carton

*Microwave (high) in package placed on paper plate 6-8 minutes, rotating ¼ turn halfway through cooking. Rest 5 minutes. Season.

ONIONS - FROZEN IN CREAM SAUCE - 10 oz. carton or pouch

*Microwave (high) in package placed on paper plate 5-7 minutes, rotating ¼ turn halfway through cooking. Rest 5 minutes. Season.
Or, place onions in 1 qt. glass covered casserole. Follow directions above.

2-10 oz. pkgs.	8-10 minutes	High power
3-10 oz. pkgs.	11-13 minutes	High power

ONIONS - FROZEN CHOPPED

Defrost in minutes (high) depending on amount for use in recipes.

PEAS AND CARROTS - 10 oz. carton or pouch

*Microwave (high) in package placed on paper plate 4-6 minutes, rotating ¼ turn halfway through cooking. Rest 5 minutes. Season.
Or, place peas and carrots in 1 qt. glass covered casserole. Follow directions above.

2-10 oz. pkgs.	6-8 minutes	High power
3-10 oz. pkgs.	8-10 minutes	High power

PEAS - BLACK-EYED - 10 oz. carton

Place peas and ¼ cup hot water in 1 qt. glass covered casserole.
*Microwave (high) 10-12 minutes, stirring halfway through cooking. Rest 5 minutes. Season.

2-10 oz. pkgs.	15-16 minutes	High power

PEAS - GREEN - 10 oz. carton or pouch

*Microwave (high) in package placed on paper plate 4-6 minutes, rotating ¼ turn halfway through cooking. Rest 5 minutes. Season.

2-10 oz./pkgs.	7 - 9 minutes	High power
3-10 oz./pkgs.	10-12 minutes	High power

PEAS - PODS - 10 oz. carton

*Microwave (high) in package placed on paper plate 4-6 minutes, rotating ¼ turn halfway through cooking. Rest 5 minutes. Season.
• *Or, place peas in 1 qt. glass covered casserole. Follow directions above.*

2-10 oz. pkgs.	7-9 minutes	High power

SPINACH - Leaf or chopped - 10 oz. carton or pouch

*Microwave (high) in package placed on paper plate 4-6 minutes, rotating ¼ turn halfway through cooking. Rest 5 minutes. Season.

Slash or pierce package before cooking.

Or, place spinach in 1 qt. glass covered casserole. Follow directions for package.

| 2-10 oz. pkgs. | 7-9 minutes | High power |
| 3-10 oz. pkgs. | 10-12 minutes | High power |

SQUASH - HUBBARD - 10 oz. carton

Place squash in 1 qt. glass covered casserole. Microwave (high) 5-7 minutes, stirring or rotating ¼ turn halfway through cooking. Rest 5 minutes. Season.

| 2-10 oz. pkgs. | 8-10 minutes | High power |
| 3-10 oz. pkgs. | 10-12 minutes | High power |

FROZEN VEGETABLE TIPS

- *Speed up the cooking time of frozen vegetables by removing from freezer at the start of meal preparation. At **room temperature**, they will require 1-2 minutes less cooking.*
- *I recommend **placing** frozen carton on a paper plate because dyes from some packages may stain the bottom of your oven.*
- *Cooking in the **freezing pouches** works very well. Each pouch must be slashed prior to cooking to allow steam to escape.*
- *Package **leftovers** and freeze for use later. Glass or heatproof plastic containers are best. Freeze in serving size packages.*
- *If you plan to cook a frozen bulky food, **defrost** first in the microwave (see p. 18). Most vegetables do not need defrosting before cooking. For large amounts, it's best to package in 2 small containers for better defrosting.*
- *Use your microwave as a convenience in **home freezing vegetables**. Select freshly picked vegetables. Microwave (high) 3-4 minutes per lb. and blanch in cold water. Drain. Pack and freeze immediately. Cooking times may vary but are usually ½ the cooking time of same fresh vegetables. You eliminate saturating vegetables with hot water before placing in cold so the end results are better. Blanch to 180°F.*

CANNED VEGETABLE TIPS

- **Pour liquid** *from canned vegetables prior to heating. (They heat faster without it.) You may want to save juices for soup or sauces.*
- *Canned vegetables have already been cooked; therefore,* **heat,** *not cook, before serving. Most canned vegetables heat in 2 minutes per cup (high) stirring or rotating ¼ turn halfway through cooking. You may prefer medium-high (70%) power.*
- *Canned vegetables should be **covered** during heating. Use wax paper, napkin, paper towel or an inverted saucer.*
- *A glass measuring cup is the ideal **utensil** for heating vegetables.*
- **Soups** *are heated like canned vegetables. Stir every ¾-1 minute or they become too hot on exposed surfaces and erupt in the center of the container. You may cover with a napkin. Mugs are ideal utensils for a serving of soup. They are also easy for children to manage.*

- *You may prefer to substitute canned beans and peas in recipes for* **dried**. *Because these heat so rapidly, they also make great foods to have on hand for emergencies — unexpected company, etc. (For dried beans, see p. 91 .)*
- *If desired, place 1-2 Tbsp.* **butter** *on top of canned vegetable prior to heating, or you may add at the end. A pinch of sugar also enhances flavor.*
- *Reheat to 150°F. with temperature probe.*

VEGETABLE RECIPES

PARTY-STYLE ARTICHOKES
A favorite for nibbling or lingering over dinner.

3 Tbsp. butter	Artichokes, number desired
Garlic salt	

In 1 cup glass measuring cup melt butter (high) 45 seconds. Add garlic salt to taste. Set aside.

Snip thistles off artichoke stems. Place on small glass plate. Pour butter mixture over artichoke and wrap in wax paper. Microwave (high) according to artichoke times (p. 61) rotating ¼ turn halfway through cooking. Rest 5 minutes covered. Serve hot or cold.

- *To cook more than 1, arrange in dish for artichoke size.*
- *For a special touch, slice lemons thinly, halve, and place one slice, flat side down, between leaves before cooking. This looks like a "flower," and adds lemon flavoring. It makes a nice centerpiece for a vegetable platter.*
- *Serve with melted butter, mayonnaise, or lemon sauce for dipping if desired. (When cooked with lemon, omit sauce.)*

Notes: _____

_____

BUTTERED ASPARAGUS — *A gorgeous green tempting dish.*

1-1½ lbs. thin fresh asparagus	½ tsp. salt
3 Tbsp. butter	¼ tsp. pepper
	½ tsp. dried marjoram

Slice asparagus diagonally in 2-inch pieces. In 1½ qt. glass casserole microwave (high) butter 45 seconds. Blend in salt, pepper, marjoram and asparagus. Microwave (high), covered, 6-8 minutes, stirring halfway through cooking. Rest 5 minutes. Serves 4-5.

Notes: _____

_____

GREEN BEANS AND BACON — *Bacon adds flavor to beans.*

1 (15½ oz) can French-cut green beans
2-4 slices diced bacon

½ tsp. salt
½ tsp. lemon pepper
1 hard-cooked egg, finely chopped, (optl.)

In a 1 qt. glass casserole, combine drained beans, bacon, salt and pepper. Microwave (high), covered, 5-7 minutes, stirring halfway through cooking. Rest 5 minutes before serving. Serves 4-6. Garnish with egg.

- *Use this classic recipe with most combinations of canned or fresh vegetables. Vary seasonings to suit your family favorites.*
- *Combine additional vegetables such as pearl onions, corn, etc. Good basic vegetable dish for leftovers.*

Notes: _____

_____

CREAMY GREEN BEANS

A cooking school favorite with a new taste.

1 (10 oz) pkg. frozen green beans
1½ oz. softened cream cheese

2 Tbsp. cream
¼ tsp. celery salt
¼ tsp. celery seed

Cook beans (p. 67). In a 1 qt. glass casserole, soften cream cheese (high) 30 seconds. Blend with cream, celery salt and celery seed. Stir in drained green beans. Microwave (high) 1 minute more. Serves 4.

- *Garnish with fried onion rings whole or broken in small pieces.*
- *An excellent* **CREAM CHEESE SAUCE** *for fresh vegetables.*

Notes: _____

_____

BAKED BEANS — *A good main dish for lunch.*

1 (15½ oz) can baked beans, or pork and beans
½ cup diced onion
3 Tbsp. brown sugar

1 Tbsp. Worcestershire sauce
¼ cup catsup or tomato sauce
½ tsp. dry mustard
4 slices diced bacon

In a 1½ qt. glass casserole, combine beans, onion, brown sugar, Worcestershire sauce, catsup and mustard. Sprinkle bacon on top. Microwave (high), covered, 8-10 minutes, rotating ¼ turn halfway through cooking. Rest 5 minutes. Serves 4.

- *For a dry baked bean, drain before combining with ingredients.*

● *This recipe doubles easily for a crowd. Substitute your favorite seasonings. Serve with Boston Brown Bread (p. 42) for a great meal.*

Notes: _____

_____

REFRIED BEANS
A favorite with a Mexican meal or serve as a dip.

3 slices diced bacon	1-3 drops hot sauce, optl.
1 (15 oz) can refried beans or mashed pinto beans	½ cup grated sharp cheddar cheese
	1 small package Dorito chips

Microwave (high) bacon 2-2½ minutes in 10" glass baking dish. Stir in beans and hot sauce. Spread evenly in dish. Top with grated cheese and chips. Microwave (high) 2-3 minutes, rotating dish ¼ turn halfway through cooking. Cheese should be evenly melted. Serves 4.

● *A good midnight snack. It may be served with tacos or other Mexican foods and easily doubles (even triples) for a* **BEAN DIP.**

Notes: _____

HARVARD BEETS — *A colorful vegetable that's always a treat!*

1 Tbsp. cornstarch	⅔ cup beet juice and water
1½ Tbsp. sugar	¼ cup vinegar
¾ tsp. salt	2 cups cooked, sliced or cubed beets

In 1½ qt. glass casserole blend cornstarch, sugar and salt with beet juice plus water to make ⅔ cup liquid. Bring to boil (high), 2-3 minutes, stirring every minute. After mixture boils, cook 1 additional minute. Add vinegar and beets. Microwave (high) 3-4 minutes, covered, stirring after 2 minutes. Rest 5 minutes. Serves 4.

● *When fresh or canned beets are a good buy, this recipe is excellent.*

Notes: _____

_____

PICKLED BEETS — *A pickled, homemade treat.*

1 (16 oz) can sliced beets, (save juice)	1 tsp. salt
¼ cup white vinegar	½ tsp. cinnamon
	¼ tsp. allspice

In 4 cup glass measuring cup, pour beet juice, vinegar, salt, cinnamon and allspice. Microwave (high) 3-5 minutes until mixture boils, stirring every minute. Add beets to juice. Store in covered container in refrigerator. Use as needed. Serves 4.

● *This recipe is good with canned okra and carrots, too.*

Notes: _____

_____

BROCCOLI-CORN SUCCOTASH — *A great colorful potluck dish!*

1 lb. fresh sliced broccoli	3 slices whole wheat bread
1 (1 lb) can cream-style corn	½ tsp. salt
2 eggs	¼ tsp. pepper
	2 Tbsp. melted butter

Cook broccoli, p. 62 . Drain well. Toast bread. In 3 qt. glass casserole combine broccoli, corn, eggs, 2 slices cubed toast, salt and pepper. Crush 1 toast slice and sprinkle over top. Drizzle with melted butter. Microwave (high) 6-8 minutes, rotating ¼ turn halfway through cooking. Rest, covered, 5 minutes before serving. Serves 6-8.

● *Frozen chopped broccoli may be substituted for fresh.*

CREAMED CABBAGE

Microwave cooking combines heated food well!

½ head shredded cabbage	1 cup cheese sauce

In 2 qt. casserole microwave (high) 2 Tbsp. water and cabbage 6-7 minutes/lb., covered, stirring halfway through cooking. Rest, covered, 5 minutes. Make cheese sauce (p. 100). Drain cabbage well. Stir in cheese sauce. Serves 4-6.

● *Once a fellow in class said he would never eat cabbage — but finished this!*

Notes: _____

CREAMY BRUSSELS SPROUTS

Frost fresh vegetables with a cheese sauce. Delicious!

1 lb. fresh Brussels sprouts	½ tsp. seasoning salt
1 (3 oz) pkg. cream cheese	3 Tbsp. finely chopped filberts (optl.)

Cook Brussels sprouts (p. 62). In 1 cup glass measure soften cream cheese (high) 15-30 seconds. Stir in salt. In 1 qt. dish blend cheese

over sprouts. Microwave (high), covered, 1 minute. Rest, covered, 5 minutes. Stir before serving. Sprinkle nuts on top. Serves 3-4.
- *Cream cheese really enhances the flavor of sprouts for a yummy variation. Use frozen if fresh aren't in season.*
- *Also good with green beans, peas, etc.*

CABBAGE CUSTARD — *A favorite if you like cabbage and custard.*

¾ cup butter	1 cup cream or evap. milk
6 cups shredded cabbage	½ tsp. nutmeg
4 beaten eggs	Salt and pepper

In 2 qt. glass casserole melt butter 1 minute. Blend with cabbage. To beaten eggs, add cream, nutmeg, salt and pepper to taste. Pour egg mixture over cabbage. Place in a dish of hot water. Microwave (high) 6-8 minutes, rotating ¼ turn halfway through cooking. Cook until center "jiggles like Jello." Rest 10 minutes before serving. Do not overcook! Serves 6-8.
- *May also be cooked in 6-cup ring mold for more even cooking.*

Notes: _____

_____

FANCY BROCCOLI AND CARROTS
Makes the sauce while cooking.

1 (10 oz) pkg. frozen chopped broccoli	3 Tbsp. flour
	¼ cup grated Parmesan cheese
1 (10 oz) pkg. frozen sliced carrots	¼ tsp. salt
	¼ tsp. pepper
½ cup cream	1 cup boiling water
	1 chicken bouillon cube

Defrost vegetables briefly to separate. In 1½ qt. glass casserole, combine cream, flour, cheese, salt and pepper. Pour over vegetables. Boil water in glass cup with bouillon cube. Pour over vegetables. Microwave (high), covered, 8-10 minutes, stirring halfway through cooking. Rest 5 minutes. Serves 6.
- *Substitute other vegetable combinations if desired.*

Notes: _____

_____

BAKED CARROTS — *Spices enhance the flavor of carrots.*

½ tsp. nutmeg	¼ cup water
½ tsp. salt	2 cups sliced carrots
1 Tbsp. sugar	3 Tbsp. butter

In 1½ qt. glass casserole mix nutmeg, salt and sugar with water. Add carrots and dot with butter. Microwave (high), covered, 8-10 minutes, stirring halfway through cooking. Rest 5 minutes. Serves 4-6.

Notes: _____

PARSLIED CARROTS — *A colorful carrot dish.*

2½ cups diagonally sliced carrots	¼ cup water
	½ tsp. lemon juice
1 Tbsp. finely chopped onion	2 Tbsp. butter
¼ tsp. salt	2 Tbsp. chopped parsley

In 1½ qt. glass casserole combine carrots, onion, salt, water, lemon juice and butter. Microwave (high), covered, 8-10 minutes, stirring halfway through cooking. Rest 5 minutes. Garnish with parsley just before serving. Serves 4-6.

● *Orange juice may be substituted for lemon juice in this recipe.*

Notes: _____

FROSTED CAULIFLOWER
A cooking school favorite which couldn't be easier!

1 med. head whole cauliflower	1-2 tsp. prepared mustard
½ cup mayonnaise	¾ cup shredded sharp cheddar cheese
¼ tsp. salt	Paprika (optl.)

With apple corer remove woody base from cauliflower. Leave whole; cook cauliflower (p. 62). In 2 cup glass measure mix mayonnaise, salt, and mustard. Microwave (high) 1 minute. Frost on cauliflower. Sprinkle with grated cheese. Microwave (high) 1 minute until cheese melts. Sprinkle with paprika. Serves 4-6.

● *1 (5 oz) jar sharp cheddar cheese may be substituted for grated. Heat jar 30 seconds to soften. Combine with mayonnaise mixture. Heat 1 minute. Spread on cauliflower.*

● *Place 1 generous slice of sharp cheddar cheese on top of cooked cauliflower. Rest, covered, 5 minutes. Sprinkle with paprika.*

Notes: _____

SWEET CELERY MEDLEY
A new variation for variety in your meals!

2 cups sliced celery	2 Tbsp. butter
2 leaves finely chopped lettuce	½ tsp. salt
½ cup finely chopped onion	1 (10 oz) pkg. frozen peas

In 2 qt. glass casserole combine celery, lettuce, onion, butter and salt. Microwave (high), covered, 4-6 minutes. Stir in frozen peas. Microwave (high), covered, 4-6 minutes. Rest, covered, 5 minutes. Serves 4-6.

Celery is often mixed in other foods but seldom served as the main vegetable. Cooked celery does not taste like fresh and is a welcome change.

SCALLOPED CORN — *A tradition in many homes.*

2 cups fresh or cooked corn	¾ cup evaporated milk
2 beaten eggs	½ cup cracker crumbs
1 tsp. salt	2 Tbsp. butter
Dash pepper	¼ cup thinly sliced green pepper

In 1½ qt. glass casserole combine corn, eggs, salt, pepper and milk. Sprinkle top with cracker crumbs; dot with butter. Place pepper strips on top. Microwave (high) 8-10 minutes, rotating ¼ turn halfway through cooking. Rest 10 minutes before serving. Serves 4-6.

Notes: _____

CREAMED PEAS — *Forms a perfect cream sauce!*
A favorite recipe from Barbara Pohlman in Cedar Rapids, Iowa.

2 Tbsp. butter	1½ Tbsp. Coffee Mate or Pream
2 Tbsp. flour	Salt and pepper to taste
	1 (1 lb) can peas, undrained

In 1 qt. glass casserole melt butter (high) 30-45 seconds. Blend with flour, cream substitute, salt and pepper. Add undrained peas. Microwave (high) 5-6 minutes, stirring every 2 minutes until hot and slightly thickened.
- *If using frozen peas add 1 (10 oz) box plus 1 cup water.*
- *Boiled onions are very good in this sauce!*

Notes: _____

EGGPLANT PARMESAN — *If you love eggplant, you'll love this!*

1 large peeled, sliced eggplant	1 cup Parmesan cheese
2 eggs	½ tsp. salt
1 cup mayonnaise	¼ tsp. pepper
1 medium chopped onion	1 tsp. butter
¼ cup chopped green pepper	1 slice whole wheat toast

In 2 cup glass casserole microwave (high), covered, eggplant 4-6 minutes. Drain well. In medium mixing bowl, blend eggs, mayonnaise, onion, green pepper, Parmesan cheese, salt and pepper. Combine with eggplant. Butter toast; crumble and sprinkle on top. Microwave (high) 4-6 minutes, rotating dish ¼ turn halfway through cooking until hot and bubbly. Rest, covered, 5 minutes. Serves 4-6.

● *Substitute zucchini or summer squash for eggplant.*

RATATOUILLE —
A fancy name for easy eggplant. A $ bargain, too!

1 med. peeled, diced eggplant	1 medium sliced zucchini
1 clove minced garlic	1 tsp. salt
1 small thinly sliced onion	¼ tsp. pepper
2 Tbsp. olive oil	½ tsp. oregano
1 sliced green pepper	1 (16 oz) can stewed tomatoes

In 3 qt. glass casserole microwave (high), covered, eggplant, garlic, onion and oil 4 minutes. Stir in green pepper and zucchini. Combine salt, pepper, oregano and tomatoes, pour over vegetables. Microwave (high), covered, 8-10 minutes. Rest, covered, 5 minutes. Serves 6-8.

● *Don't overlook this easy, inexpensive dish for serving company. It's colorful and tasty to many.*

SAUTEED MUSHROOMS — *Delicious on roast or steak.*

2 Tbsp. butter	3 Tbsp. chopped green onions
¼ tsp. tarragon leaves	½ lb. fresh sliced mushrooms
	Salt and pepper

In 1 qt. glass casserole, microwave (high) butter, tarragon and green onions 2-3 minutes. Add mushrooms. Microwave (high), covered, 2-3 minutes. Season with salt and pepper. Rest, covered, 5 minutes before serving. Serves 4.

Notes: _____

MUSTARD GREENS AND BACON
A southern dish delicious anywhere.

4 slices diced bacon	¾ lb. mustard greens
¼ cup finely chopped onion	Salt and pepper

In 3 qt. glass casserole microwave (high) bacon 2-3 minutes, stirring once. Add onion. Microwave (high), covered, 3-4 minutes, stirring once until bacon is crisp. Remove all but 1½ Tbsp. drippings.
Rinse and coarsely chop mustard greens. Blend evenly with onions. Microwave (high), covered, 2-3 minutes. Season to taste with salt and pepper. Rest, covered, 5 minutes before serving. Serves 3-4.
● *Fresh spinach may be substituted for mustard greens.*

Notes: _____

PICKLED VEGETABLES — *Make your own microwave pickles!*
Prepare your favorite vegetables for pickling — small asparagus spears, green or wax beans, sliced or small whole beets, tiny strips of carrots, cauliflowerets, and the American favorite, the cucumber in strips as well as slices. Microwave following directions for fresh vegetable (p. 61-66). Canned vegetables that are crisp-tender such as beans are also satisfactory. Avoid overcooking or they will become mushy when pickling liquid is added. Drain vegetable well; chill in refrigerator until use. Do not rest vegetables in liquid. A rack or paper towel in bottom of dish for chilling helps drain moisture from vegetable. Approximately 2 lbs. of vegetables fill 4 (1-pint) canning jars.

2 tsp. mustard seed	2 cups hot water
2 tsp. dill weed	2 cups white vinegar
1 tsp. dill seed	¾ cup sugar
4 cloves fresh garlic	2 Tbsp. coarse (salad) salt

Place ½ tsp. mustard, ½ tsp. dill, ¼ tsp. dill seed and 1 garlic in each jar. In 1½ qt. deep glass mixing bowl, combine water, vinegar, sugar and salt. Microwave (high) covered to boiling — about 4-6 minutes. Pour over vegetables; cover; chill overnight. Drain well. Store in refrigerator until needed. Serve cold.
● *Vegetables may be kept in the refrigerator for 2 weeks. If you plan to keep longer, pasteurize by a conventional method; then store at room temperature.*
● *These vegetables are a delight served on an hors d'oeuvres tray. They make nice meal accompaniments and an excellent hostess gift.*

Notes: _____

ONIONS a la CREAM — *An inexpensive, elegant, easy dish.*

1 cup cream or evap. milk	1 tsp. salt
¾ cup crushed soda crackers	¼ tsp. pepper
4 cups sliced Bermuda onions	2 Tbsp. butter

In a 2 cup glass measure, scald cream (high) about 2 minutes. Reserve ¼ cup crumbs. In 1½ qt. glass casserole, blend onions, remaining crumbs, salt and pepper. Pour hot cream over onions; sprinkle with crumbs; dot with butter. Microwave (high), covered, 10-12 minutes, rotating ¼ turn halfway through cooking. Rest, covered, 5 minutes. Serves 4-6.

Notes: _____

_____

BAKED WHOLE ONIONS

Achieve variety by serving a common vegetable in an unusual way.

4 small peeled onions	2 tsp. butter
(1 serving each)	Paprika

Slice top and bottom of onions. Arrange in 9-inch glass dish. Place ½ tsp. butter on each onion. Sprinkle with paprika. Microwave (high), covered, 6-8 minutes per pound. Rest, covered, 5 minutes. Serves 4.

● *When onions are sweet and fresh, this is a new vegetable welcome on any table.*

● *Fill onions with creamed corn, fresh peas, etc.*

Notes: _____

_____

SAVORY PEAS — *Peas and mushrooms blend well.*

1 (10 oz) pkg. frozen peas	1 Tbsp. finely chopped onion
4 med. fresh sliced mushrooms	½ tsp. salt
2 Tbsp. butter	¼ tsp. pepper

In 1 qt. glass casserole, microwave (high) peas, covered, 2-3 minutes. Blend with mushrooms, butter, onions, salt and pepper. Microwave (high), covered, 2-3 minutes. Rest, covered, 5 minutes. Serves 4.

● *Green beans or corn may be substituted.*

Notes: _____

_____

CHEESY MASHED POTATOES
Mashed potatoes may become a delicacy since baked potatoes are so easy! And this dish is fit for company!

4 medium potatoes	½ cup grated Parmesan cheese
⅓ cup milk	1 medium finely chopped
½ cup butter	green pepper
2 (3 oz) pkgs. cream cheese	4 diced green onions (tops too)
½ cup shredded cheddar cheese	Salt and pepper
	1 slice toasted, buttered bread

Cook potatoes (p. 64). Peel; whip; add milk. Soften butter and cream cheese (high) 45 seconds. Whip into potatoes with cheddar cheese, Parmesan cheese, green pepper, green onions, and salt and pepper to taste. Pour into 2 qt. glass casserole. Crumble toast and sprinkle on top. Microwave (high) 10-12 minutes, rotating ¼ turn halfway through cooking. Rest, covered, 5 minutes. Serves 8-10.

● *French fried onion rings may be crumbled on top.*

Notes: _____

_____

GRATED POTATO CASSEROLE
A variation of scalloped potatoes in less preparation time because mixing is done in blender.

1 cup milk (or evap. milk)	1 cup cubed sharp cheddar
3 eggs	cheese
1½-2 tsp. salt	½ coarsely cut green pepper
Dash pepper	1 small quartered onion
2 Tbsp. soft butter	4 med. peeled, cubed potatoes

Butter 2½ qt. glass casserole. Place all ingredients in blender, milk and eggs first. Blend at high speed until potatoes are coarsely chopped. (Don't over-blend.) Pour into casserole. Microwave (high), covered, 15-18 minutes, rotating ¼ turn every 4 minutes. Serves 6.

● *Also a good leftover dinner with tuna, ham, sliced or cubed roast beef, etc., added to casserole for one-dish meal. Increase cooking time for food added.*

Notes: _____

_____

● **Prepare instant mashed potatoes** *in glass measuring cup. Microwave (high) water, butter and salt until boiling. Add milk and potato flakes.*

EASY SCALLOPED POTATOES

No easier way to fix a time-consuming dish with excellent results.

4 med. peeled, sliced potatoes	¼ cup finely chopped onions
2 Tbsp. flour	1½ cup milk (or evap. milk)
1 tsp. salt	2 Tbsp. butter
	Paprika or parsley

In a 2½ qt. glass buttered casserole, arrange half the sliced potatoes. Sprinkle with half the flour, salt and onion. Repeat. Pour in milk; dot with butter. Microwave (high), covered, 15-18 minutes, rotating dish ¼ turn every 4 minutes. Rest, covered, 5 minutes. Garnish with paprika or parsley. Serves 4-6.

- *Sprinkle grated sharp cheddar cheese on top after cooking.*
- *Potatoes may boil over if they aren't in container large enough for milk to boil. Container should be about twice as large as amount of food. Buttering rim of dish may prevent this.*
- *Potatoes may be partially cooked alone before combining with other ingredients to prevent boiling over.*
- *For* **SUPER SPEEDY SCALLOPED POTATOES** *combine 1 can mushroom soup, ¾ cup evaporated milk and ¾ tsp. salt. Thinly slice 5 medium potatoes. In 2 qt. glass casserole, layer ⅓ potatoes, ⅓ soup mix, dot with butter and sprinkle with paprika. Repeat two times. Microwave (high), covered, 15-20 minutes, rotating dish ¼ turn halfway through cooking time. Sprinkle top with grated cheddar cheese. Rest, covered, 5 minutes. Serves 6-8.*

Notes: _____

_____

2ND DAY POTATOES — *An excellent use of leftover potatoes.*

4 medium cooked potatoes	½ tsp. dried marjoram
¼ tsp. salt	¼ cup finely chopped onion
1 Tbsp. minced parsley	1½ cups grated cheddar cheese
	¼ cup melted butter

Slice potatoes with skins. Arrange in 10-inch glass skillet. In medium mixing bowl, blend salt, parsley, marjoram, onion and cheese. Drizzle butter evenly over potatoes. Sprinkle with cheese mixture. Microwave (high) 3-5 minutes, rotating ¼ turn halfway through cooking until mixture is hot throughout. Serves 4-6.

- *If you don't have leftover potatoes, cook (p. 64). Cool.*

Notes: _____

_____

SPEEDY SPUDS

Betty Robnett and Gloria Brady, teachers at the House of Microwave, Spokane, Washington, find this a favorite in classes.

1 lb. frozen hash browns	½ tsp. salt
1 (10½ oz) can creamed chicken soup	¼ tsp. pepper
1 cup sour cream	5 oz. grated sharp cheddar cheese
¼ cup chopped onions	½ cup crushed corn flakes
2 Tbsp. melted butter	2 Tbsp. melted butter

In 1½ qt. casserole microwave (medium-low 30%) hash browns 10 minutes to thaw. Combine with soup, sour cream, onions, butter, salt, pepper and cheese. Mix corn flakes with melted butter. Sprinkle on top. Microwave (medium-high 70%) 14-16 minutes. Rest 5 minutes. Serves 4-6.

Mini-Time: High 3-4 minutes in step 1; high 10-12 minutes in step 2.

MICROWAVED HASH BROWNS — *With Browning Skillet.*

3 medium potatoes	½ cup chopped onion
2 Tbsp. butter	Salt and pepper to taste
	Grated cheddar cheese (optl.)

Cook potatoes (p. 64). Peel and dice. Heat browning skillet (high) 4 minutes. Add butter. Add onion and potatoes. Sprinkle with salt and pepper. Microwave (high) 3 minutes. Flatten with spatula and turn. Microwave 3-5 minutes until potatoes are soft. Sprinkle with grated cheese. Serves 3-4.

- *Without browning skillet, potatoes won't grill. 10-inch ceramic skillet may be heated on range as a substitute.*
- *Chopped green or red pepper adds color and flavor.*

COTTAGE FRIES: *Cook potatoes as above. Peel (optl.) and slice in ¼-inch slices. Follow directions above omitting onion.*

Notes: _____

TWICE-FILLED POTATO BOATS — *Eliminates filling at table.*

Potatoes, as desired	Salt and pepper
Butter	Sour cream, if desired
Grated sharp cheddar cheese	

Cook potatoes (p. 64). Cut slice from top of each. Carefully scoop out insides; mash. Add butter, grated cheese, salt, pepper and sour cream as desired. Pile mixture back into potato shells. Microwave (high), covered with napkin, 2 minutes. Garnish with parsley or chives.

- *Fix ahead and freeze for quick "planned-overs."*
- *For* **STUFFED DEVILED POTATOES** *add ¼ cup butter, ½ tsp.*

salt, ½ tsp. prepared mustard, ¼ tsp. paprika and milk (about ⅓ cup) to whip potatoes. Add cheese (optl.). Pile mixture into potato shells, microwave (high), covered, 2 minutes. Garnish with chives, bacon, parsley, paprika, etc. Serves 4.

Notes: _____

_____

GLAZED SWEET POTATOES — *A Thanksgiving goodie!*

1 (1 lb) can sweet potatoes	3 Tbsp. butter
⅓ cup brown sugar	1 cup miniature marshmallows (optl.)

In 1 qt. glass casserole cube sweet potatoes. Sprinkle with brown sugar; dot with butter. Microwave (high) covered, 5-6 minutes, spooning glaze over potatoes and stirring lightly halfway through cooking. Sprinkle with marshmallows. Rest, covered, 5 minutes. Serves 4-5.

● *Fresh sweet potatoes may be substituted for canned, p. 65 .*
● *Try* **FRESH BAKED SWEET POTATOES** *with butter and salt as a substitute for white.*
● *A very good* **ORANGE JUICE GLAZE** *combines the following:*

½ cup butter	¾ cup orange juice
¼ cup hot water	½ cup brown sugar
1 Tbsp. cornstarch	

Cook in 2 cup measure 1-2 minutes until boiling. Pour over sweet potatoes. Cook as directed above. Also delicious on gingerbread and cake.

Notes: _____

CREAMED SPINACH — *An interesting custard-type vegetable.*

2 (10 oz) pkgs. frozen chopped spinach	1 tsp. salt
2 cups small curd cottage cheese	⅓ cup grated Parmesan cheese
	2 beaten eggs
	Grated Swiss cheese

Cook spinach (p. 69). Blend spinach, cottage cheese, salt, Parmesan cheese and eggs. Pour ingredients into 6 cup ring mold. Microwave (high) 10-12 minutes, rotating dish ¼ turn every 4 minutes. Rest 5 minutes. Invert dish. Sprinkle with cheese. Serves 6-8.

● *Substitute broccoli for spinach, if desired, for* **CREAMED BROCCOLI.**

Notes: _____

FILLED SQUASH — *A delicious filling for squash.*

2 medium acorn squash	⅓ cup butter
2 cups drained canned or fresh cooked pearl onions	⅓ cup light molasses
	¼ tsp. salt
½ cup coarsely chopped walnuts	¼ tsp. cinnamon
	¼ tsp. nutmeg

Cook squash (p. 66). Halve lengthwise and remove seeds. Season cavity. Fill with onions and walnuts. In 2 cup glass measure, melt butter (high) 30 seconds. Add molasses, salt, cinnamon and nutmeg. Microwave (high) 1 minute. Spoon into squash. Microwave (high) 3-4 minutes, brushing with glaze and rotating ¼ turn halfway through cooking. Serves 4.

● *Mincemeat or cranberry sauce are also good with the squash. Cover with glaze for a special touch. The easiest filling is brown sugar or maple syrup and butter.*

Notes: _____

_____

SQUASH SKILLET

An interesting medley of a variety of vegetables.

2 Tbsp. water	1 small bunch fresh broccoli, split each stalk in ¼ths and cut in 1" pieces
½ tsp. salt	
2 small sliced zucchini squash	
2 small sliced yellow crookneck or pattypan summer squash	½ lb. fresh sliced mushrooms
	¼ tsp. lemon pepper
	2-3 Tbsp. butter

In 10" glass skillet combine water and salt. Add squash, broccoli, and mushrooms. Toss to blend. Sprinkle with pepper; dot with butter. Microwave (high), covered, 10-12 minutes, stirring halfway through cooking. Rest, covered, 5 minutes. Serves 4-6.

● *Vegetables will be crisp-tender. For more cooking, add 1-3 more minutes; rest, covered.*

● *A basic Oriental dish. Other vegetables can be added. Suggestions are bamboo shoots, small pieces of carrots, jicama, celery, water chestnuts, etc.*

● *For more color, add quartered tomatoes during last minute of cooking. Avoid overcooking. They loose shape and become mushy.*

Notes: _____

_____

APRIL'S SPECIALTY — *April is a very creative cook and a joy to have experimenting in our kitchen.*

4 peeled carrots, thinly sliced in 1-inch strips	3 sliced green onions (tops too)
2-3 Tbsp. butter	1 small finely chopped onion
	6 sliced mushrooms
	Parsley flakes

Cook carrots (p. 62). In 1½ qt. glass casserole melt butter (high) 45 seconds. Add onions. Microwave (high), covered, 3 minutes. Add carrots, mushrooms and parsley. Microwave (high), covered, 3-4 minutes, stirring halfway through cooking. Rest, covered, 5 minutes. Serves 4.

- *Part of the fun and convenience of having a microwave is family experimenting. My daughter loves creating dinner. She was never a vegetable "lover," but now eats most vegetables microwaved!*

Notes: _____

_____

ORIENTAL SKILLET — *A stir-fried combination.*

2 Tbsp. butter	6 fresh sliced mushrooms
½ cup chopped onion	½ tsp. salt
2 medium sliced zucchini	¼ tsp. curry powder
3 medium wedged tomatoes	¼ tsp. ginger
	Dash pepper

In 1½ qt. casserole melt butter (high) 30 seconds. Add onion and zucchini. Microwave (high), covered, 3 minutes, stirring once. Add tomatoes, mushrooms and seasonings. Microwave (high), covered, 3 minutes more, stirring once. Rest 5 minutes. Serves 4-6.

- *Zucchini is prettier if not peeled. Vegetables should be "crisp-tender."*

Notes: _____

BAKED TOMATOES

An interesting accompaniment for a light colored main dish.

4 medium firm ripe tomatoes	¼ tsp. oregano
¼ tsp. salt	¼ tsp. basil
¼ tsp. pepper	⅓ cup seasoned bread crumbs

Core tomatoes, removing tops. Arrange in 9" glass dish. Combine salt, pepper, oregano, basil and bread crumbs. Spread mixture on cut side tomatoes. Microwave (high), covered, 4-6 minutes, rotating ¼ turn halfway through cooking. Rest 5 minutes. Serves 4.

- *Be careful not to overcook or tomatoes will be mushy.*

CHINESE STIR-FRIED VEGETABLES

Stir-frying is simple in the microwave. Keep in mind colorful combinations with flavors that blend well together. You can clean out the vegetable drawer with a little of this and that. Your family won't get tired of the same old thing. The same cooking formula applies to all combinations. Cook 6-7 minutes per pound (high) for any amount of food.

2 Tbsp. butter	¼ lb. fresh sliced mushrooms
2 Tbsp. soy sauce	½ cup bean sprouts
1 (6 oz) pkg. frozen pea pods	Sesame seeds

Microwave (high) butter and soy sauce 1½-2 minutes. Stir in pea pods, mushrooms and bean sprouts. Microwave (high) 5-6 minutes, stirring halfway through cooking. Sprinkle with seeds. Serves 3-4.
●*When using a frozen vegetable, microwave (high) 2-3 minutes to separate vegetables before cooking.*

Notes: _____

_____

STEWED TOMATOES — *A favorite of my mom.*

¼ cup chopped onions	½ tsp. salt
2 Tbsp. melted butter	1 Tbsp. sugar
1 (1 lb, 12 oz) can tomatoes	½ cup cubed cheddar cheese
½ cup soda cracker crumbs	1 beaten egg
	½ tsp. paprika

In 2 qt. glass casserole saute onions in butter (high) 2 minutes. Add remaining ingredients. Microwave (high), covered, 6-8 minutes, stirring once. Rest 5 minutes. Serves 4-6.
●*Add cubed day-old bread to make casserole thicker.*

Notes: _____

_____

VEGETABLE MEDLEY — *A colorful combination.*

¼ cup butter	1 cup thinly sliced carrots
3 cups coarsely shredded cabbage	1 green pepper, cut in strips
	½ cup chopped onion
1 cup bias-cut 1" celery	1 tsp. salt
	Dash pepper

In 2½ qt. glass casserole melt butter (high) 30 seconds. Add remaining ingredients. Microwave (high), covered, 5-7 minutes, stirring once. Rest, covered, 5 minutes. Serves 6.

ZUCCHINI CUSTARD — *A cooking school favorite for 6 years.*

4-5 cups shredded and packed zucchini
1¼ tsp. salt
1 cup grated sharp cheddar cheese
¼ tsp. pepper
¼ tsp. garlic powder
¼ cup chopped parsley
¼ cup biscuit mix
4 well beaten eggs
1 Tbsp. butter

Sprinkle zucchini with salt, set aside for 1 hour. Place in colander; press out liquid. Thoroughly blend zucchini, cheese, pepper, garlic, parsley, biscuit mix and eggs. In 10" glass dish melt butter (high) 30 seconds. Add zucchini mixture. Microwave (high), uncovered, 10 minutes, stirring halfway through cooking. Rest 5 minutes. Top with chives. Serves 4-6.

●*Mixture may be cooked in microwave ring for more even cooking.*

Notes: _____

_____

Soup

Soups are convenient to prepare and serve directly from the microwave. Canned soups were among the first convenience foods we used, and are very easily heated in a serving bowl or mug (especially for children!) Packaged soup mixes contain dehydrated vegetables so more preparation time is needed to rehydrate. A 2- to 4-cup measure is a good utensil for soup preparation.

Cover soup with a napkin, wax paper, or an inverted saucer while heating to speed cooking. Some soups require stirring once or twice to distribute heat evenly. If not stirred, outer surfaces will heat more quickly than the center. Food in the center of the dish has a tendency to erupt or pop. Allow 2 minutes/cup heating time. You may prefer to make soups the day before and refrigerate overnight. This allows seasonings to penetrate broth and vegetables more evenly. If you have a temperature probe, heat milk-based soups to 140-150°F. and water-based to 160-170°F.

Notes: _____

_____

WEST COAST CHOWDER — *A delicious, hearty soup.*

6 diced bacon slices	1 cup water
½ cup chopped onions	2 (13 oz) cans evaporated
3 cups diced potatoes	milk
2 (7 oz) cans minced clams and liquid	Salt and pepper

In 3 qt. glass casserole microwave (high) bacon and onion 3-4 minutes. Add potatoes, clam liquid and water. Microwave (high) 15-18 minutes, stirring every 4 minutes. Add clams, milk, salt, and pepper to taste. Microwave (high) 5 minutes, stirring twice. Rest 5 minutes. Serves 4-6.

Notes: _____

VICHYSSOISE — *A fancy name for potato and onion soup.*

1 Tbsp. butter	4 (10 oz) cans chicken broth
1 medium minced onion	or 4 chicken bouillon cubes
3 minced leeks (or green onions)	and water
4 medium finely chopped potatoes	1 cup cream (or evap. milk)
	Salt and pepper to taste
	Chives or green onion tops

In 2½ qt. glass casserole microwave (high) butter, onion and leeks 3 minutes. Add potatoes and broth. Microwave (high) 12-15 minutes, stirring every 4 minutes. (Potatoes should be very tender.) Force the mixture through a sieve or process in blender; return to dish. Add cream, salt and pepper to taste. Microwave (high) 3-4 minutes until soup is very hot (140°F.), stirring as needed. Chill and garnish with chopped chives or green onion tops. Serves 4-6.

● *This soup is traditionally served cold, but equally good hot!*

Notes: _____

OYSTER STEW — *A delicious heated soup.*

¼ cup butter	1½ cups milk
1 tsp. Worcestershire sauce	½ tsp. salt
½ tsp. celery salt	Pepper to taste
1 pint fresh oysters, drained, saving juice	Minced parsley

In 3 qt. glass casserole combine butter, Worcestershire sauce, celery salt and oysters. Microwave (high) 2 minutes. Stir in oyster juice, milk, and salt. Microwave (high) 3-4 minutes until hot throughout (140°F.). Pepper to taste and sprinkle parsley on top. Serve hot to 4-5.

SPLIT PEA SOUP — *A yummy soup for a cold day.*

1 lb (2 cups) dry split peas	1 shank ham bone
1 diced carrot	2 cups cubed smoked ham
1 small cubed potato	2 qts. boiling water
1 small chopped onion	Salt and pepper to taste

In 3 qt. glass casserole combine all ingredients. Microwave (high), covered, 10 minutes. Reduce to medium (50%) for 20-30 minutes, stirring every 10 minutes. Rest, covered, 10 minutes. Test for doneness. Adjust seasoning. Serves 4-6.

● *Use either green or yellow peas or lentils. Add 1 slivered carrot.*

Notes: 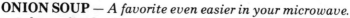 _____

ONION SOUP — *A favorite even easier in your microwave.*

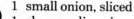

5 large sliced onions	1½ cups water
¼ cup butter	Toasted bread croutons (p.40)
2 (10 oz) cans beef broth (or make your own from bouillon cubes)	8 oz. grated Swiss cheese
	Parmesan cheese
	Salt and pepper to taste

In 3 qt. glass casserole combine onions and butter. Microwave (high), covered, 6-8 minutes, stirring halfway through cooking. Add broth and water. Microwave (high), covered, 5-7 minutes until steaming hot. Spoon into 4 soup bowls. Sprinkle with croutons and cheeses. Salt and pepper to taste. Microwave (high) 4-6 minutes until cheese melts, rearranging dishes halfway through cooking. Serves 4.

MOCK BOUILLABAISSE — *Quick version of a fish soup favorite.*

1 small onion, sliced	¾ soup can water
1 clove garlic, minced	2 cups cooked seafood (crab, lobster, shrimp, sole, etc.)
1 bay leaf	
¼ tsp. thyme	1 tsp. lemon juice
2 Tbsp. olive oil	Dash hot sauce
1 (10½ oz) can tomato soup	4 slices French bread, toasted

In 3 qt. glass casserole, combine onion, garlic, bay leaf, thyme and oil. Microwave (high) 3-4 minutes, stirring once. Add soup, water, seafood (any combination you like), lemon juice, and hot sauce. Microwave (high) 6-8 minutes, stirring every 2 minutes until boiling. Cook, covered, an additional 2 minutes. Rest, covered, 5 minutes. Ladle soup over toast in bowls. Serves 3-4.

● *Canned seafood may be substituted for fresh.*

Notes: _____

_____

TOMATO BISQUE — *A quick microwave soup!*

2 lbs. halved, **ripe** tomatoes   1 tsp. sugar
1 medium chopped onion   Salt and pepper
1 tsp. basil

In 2 qt. glass dish combine all ingredients except salt and pepper.
Microwave (high) 3-4 minutes, stirring once. Season. Serve hot to 3-4.
● *Puree in blender if desired before serving.*

HEATING CANNED SOUPS

1 (10 oz) can condensed soup
1 soup can water

In 4 cup glass measure, combine soup and water. Microwave (high),
covered, 3-5 minutes, stirring once or twice to distribute heat. Stir
once after removing from microwave. Pour into serving bowls or
mugs. Serves 2-3.

● *When heating in individual servings, use the following times:*

1-2 cup serving	1½-2½ minutes	140-170°F.	High
2-2 cup servings	2½-3½ minutes	140-170°F.	High
3-2 cup servings	4-6 minutes	140-170°F.	High
4-2 cup servings	6-8 minutes	140-170°F.	High

● *For **SOUP MIXES**, in 4 cup glass measure, prepare as directed on
envelope. Microwave (high), covered, 3½-5 minutes or until mixture
boils. Rest 5 minutes before serving. Serves 3-4.*
● *For **INDIVIDUAL SOUP MIX SERVINGS**, prepare in glass bowl
or mug as directed on package. Microwave (high), covered, 1½-2½
minutes, stirring once or twice. Serves 1.*

DRIED BEANS AND PEAS

In 3 qt. casserole add water and beans or peas. Microwave (high),
covered, until boiling. Microwave (medium 50%) as follows:

Water	Beans or Peas	Amount	After Boiling
6 cups	Great Northern Beans	12 oz. or 2 cups	1½-2 hours
4 cups	Pinto Beans	1 lb.	1½-2 hours
4 cups	Split Peas	1 cup	1-1½ hours

Stir every 30 minutes until tender.

● *Substitute canned beans and peas **and heat** in recipes for dry.*
● *Most home-made soups can be cooked in the microwave; however,
many will cook in about the same cooking time as the range. You
may prefer to cook soup on range top and use the microwave for
other foods to be served. (Remember, we have used the Electric Fry-
Pan, Slo-Cooker, etc. in combination with the range, and the microwave wasn't designed to do everything.) The main microwave
advantage is an easy "pot" to clean.*

Eggs

Eggs are a very delicate food and must be handled carefully. **NEVER** attempt to cook an egg **in the shell** in the microwave. This is one food that cannot be cooked! They explode from internal pressure created as they heat, making a horrible mess to clean! They can, however, be cooked many ways when removed from shell. Always undercook a little; they finish cooking during "carry-over cooking" time. If started at room temperature, they cook more evenly.

An egg has two distinct properties making it more difficult to cook than other foods. The yolk, high in fat, takes less cooking than the white. Because yolk is centered in the egg, and the center cooks more slowly than outside, a "fried" egg can be microwaved. If the yolk and white are mixed (scrambling) it cooks more evenly. Covering helps distribute heat better for "fried" eggs. If you have a medium-high (70%) or medium (50%) power, this helps eliminate the possibility of overcooking; however, it increases your cooking time. You can also place a cup of water in microwave with eggs. The water absorbs some energy, slowing cooking but increasing cooking time. When cooking a "fried" egg, pierce yolk through membrane with a fork in the shape of a cross. This will not make yolk run and will allow air to transfer from yolk, eliminating the possibility of exploding.

The popping sound when cooking eggs is caused by chemical properties of the egg and occurs whether cooking eggs in the microwave or conventionally. It is more apparent at certain seasons of the year as eggs are held in storage. Always cook an egg covered. Season eggs after cooking unless they are scrambled.

●*Egg* **substitutes** *may be used in most egg recipes.*

Notes: _____

_____

HARD-COOKED EGGS — Large eggs, number desired.
Break eggs into 6 oz. custard cups. Arrange in ring (may be cooked in baking papers in microwave muffin pan). Microwave (high), covered with plastic wrap, 20-25 seconds per egg, rotating ¼ turn halfway through cooking. **Maxi-Time:** medium (50%) 40-50 seconds per egg. Rest, covered, 2-3 minutes. Dice or slice for potato salad, egg salad, garnishes, etc.

Notes: _____

MICROWAVE BROWNING DISH FRIED EGGS
Butter   Microwave browning dish
Eggs

Preheat browning dish (high) 2-3 minutes. Melt butter on hot surface, spreading evenly. Break eggs onto hot dish. Pierce yolk with a fork. Microwave, uncovered, to desired doneness as follows:

1 to 2 eggs	1 to 1½ minutes	High power
3 to 4 eggs	1½ to 2 minutes	High power

- *Eggs may be turned over halfway through cooking time.*
- *For* **STEAMED EGGS,** *add 2 Tbsp. water to dish after cooking 30 seconds. Cover; Rest 2-3 minutes.*

MICROWAVE FRIED EGGS
1 tsp. butter per egg   Large eggs, number desired

In 10 oz. glass dish, melt butter (high) 30 seconds (omit if watching calories). Use a separate dish for each egg cooked. Break egg into dish; pierce yolk with a fork in shape of cross on top. Cover with plastic wrap. Cook as follows:

Amount	High Power	or Med. Pwr.
1 egg	20 seconds; rotate ¼ turn; 10-15 seconds	60-70 sec.
2 eggs	45 seconds; rotate ¼ turn; 15-20 seconds	2 minutes
3 eggs	1 minute; rotate ¼ turn; 25-35 seconds	3 minutes
4 eggs	1½ minute; rotate ¼ turn; 20-30 seconds	4 minutes

Rest eggs covered, 1 minute, before serving. Egg will have a soft yolk and cooked white. For a harder yolk, add a few seconds (up to 5) cooking time. **Maxi-Time:** Medium (50%) power, for time in chart, rotating dish ¼ turn halfway through cooking.

- *Plastic wrap is the best cover for cooking eggs. They cook very quickly, so plastic wrap does not melt as it may with foods high in fats.*
- *A firm egg can be chopped for use as hard-cooked eggs in salads, vegetables, sauces, etc.*
- *Leftover eggs can be reheated in about 10 seconds for late arrivals.*
- *Eggs cooked this way make a delicious egg sandwich.*

Notes: _____

POACHED EGGS
In a 10 oz. glass dish, heat ⅓ cup water (high) 30 seconds. Swirl water and drop egg into swirl. Cover with plastic wrap. Use cooking times above. For several eggs, they may be cooked in a ring dish in hot water.

- *Vinegar isn't necessary since the egg will firm well with microwave energy distribution.*

Notes: _____

SCRAMBLED EGGS — *Much better than conventionally cooked.*

1 tsp. butter per egg   Large eggs, number desired
1 Tbsp. milk or water per egg

In glass measuring cup, heat butter (high) 30-45 seconds. Add milk or water and eggs, blending lightly with fork. Cover; cook as follows, stirring one or two times during the last half of cooking:

Amount	High Power	OR	Medium Power (50%)
1 egg	30-45 seconds		1 - 1½ minute
2 eggs	1-1½ minutes		2 - 2½ minutes
4 eggs	2½-3 minutes		4 - 6 minutes
6 eggs	3½-4½ minutes		7 - 9 minutes
8 eggs	4½-5½ minutes		9 - 11 minutes

Remove from oven; stir. Rest, covered, 2-3 minutes. Season with salt and pepper.

- *For a light, fluffy egg, cook using shortest cooking time; add for drier egg.* **Do not** *add more cooking time until after resting time!*
- *Sour cream or water may be substituted for milk in recipe.*
- *Eggs should be moist but not runny when cooked.*
- *Mary Beth Cyvas from Houston, Tex., loves to substitute mayonnaise for water or milk in scrambled eggs.*
- *Bacon drippings may be substituted for butter; water for milk. Butter may also be omitted but eggs will have a tendency to stick to dish. Water instead of milk will give eggs more volume and produce a more tender egg.*

- **OMELETS**

  To make an **omelet** *or "souffle-like" egg, stir moving cooked edges to center of dish. Rotate dish ¼ turn for any other turning. Fill omelet with cheese, jelly, etc. and fold over before resting time. Separating and whipping egg white gives more volume to egg. This is a basic scrambled egg technique — cooked in pie plate instead of measuring cup, and rotated instead of stirred.*

  3 eggs, separated   1 Tbsp. butter
  2 Tbsp. water or milk

Whip egg whites until soft peaks form. Whip egg yolks with water or milk until well blended. Gently fold whites into yolks. In 9-inch glass pie plate melt butter (high) 1 minute. Pour eggs into dish. Microwave medium (50%) 4-5 minutes, rotating dish ¼ turn every minute until set. Fill with one of the following combinations or others of your choosing, and fold in half to serve. Serves 1-2.

- grated Swiss cheese and chopped green chilies
- chopped green onion and grated cheddar cheese
- chopped or sliced sauteed onions, chopped salami, and grated cheese
- fresh mushrooms and cheese (Cheddar or Swiss), and bacon bits

— fresh mushrooms, avocado slices, and quartered tomatoes. Tomatoes should always be added at end of cooking because heat makes them juicy.

Combinations may also be blended into eggs after first cooking time if desired.

Notes: _____

BROWNING SKILLET OMELET

2 eggs	½ tsp. salt
2 Tbsp. water	2 tsp. butter

Preheat browner (high) 2-3 minutes. In small bowl combine eggs, water and salt blending well. Swirl butter in skillet. Pour in egg mixture. Microwave (high) 1-1½ minutes. Fold in thirds. Serves 1-2.
● *Fill if desired with combination above.*

EGG FOO YONG — *An easy breakfast, lunch or dinner main dish.*

2 Tbsp. butter	6 well-beaten eggs
4 chopped green onions w/tops	½ tsp. salt
1 stalk thinly-sliced celery	½ tsp. pepper
1½ cups bean sprouts	1 (8½ oz) can drained bamboo
2 Tbsp. soy sauce	shoots

In 10-inch glass casserole, melt butter (high) 30 seconds. Add onion, celery, bean sprouts, and soy sauce; toss well, coating vegetables with butter and soy sauce. Microwave (high), covered, 4-5 minutes, stirring and tossing vegetables once or twice. Rest, covered, while blending eggs, salt and pepper. Blend vegetables, eggs and bamboo shoots. Heat microwave browning dish 3 minutes, or frying pan on range surface. Drop egg mixture onto hot pan. Microwave (high) 1-1½ minute. When golden brown, turn egg mixture over; microwave (high) 1-1½ minute on other side. Serve with Gravy (p. 100). Serves 4-6.
● *1 (1 lb., 12 oz) can Oriental vegetables may be substituted for fresh vegetables, or additional vegetables may be added.*
● *Cook ingredients 6-8 minutes for* **VEGETABLE CHOW MEIN**. *Add leftover meats chopped if available. (Omit eggs.)*

EGGS a la GOLDENROD — *Good for lunch.*

2 cups medium white sauce	1 tsp. salt
5 hard-cooked eggs	¼ tsp. pepper
	Toast points

Prepare medium White Sauce (p. 99). Cover. Cook eggs (p. 92). Dice 4 eggs and blend with sauce, salt and pepper. Reheat if needed. Spoon on toast points to serve. Sieve 5th egg on top. Serves 3-4.

EGGS BENEDICT — *Elegant but simple meal-in-one breakfast.*

Hollandaise sauce	4 slices Canadian bacon
2 split English muffins, toasted	1½ cups hot water
	4 eggs
	Paprika

Cook Hollandaise sauce (p. 101). Cover. On microwave safe serving platter arrange muffins with bacon slice on each. In 1 qt. casserole microwave (high) water 2½-3 minutes. Swirl water with spoon and break eggs into swirl. Pierce yolk with fork. Microwave (high), covered, 1½-2 minutes, rotating ¼ turn halfway through cooking. Rest, covered. Microwave (high) muffins and bacon 1-2 minutes until hot. With a slotted spoon place 1 egg on each bacon slice; drizzle Hollandaise on top. Sprinkle with paprika. Serves 4.

● *Sliced ham may be substituted for Canadian bacon.*

Notes: _____

POACHED EGGS AND HASH

A popular, easy breakfast in 3-4 minutes and no fussing. And the man in your life generally loves hash with eggs!

1 (1 lb.) can corned beef hash
4 eggs

In 6 cup ring mold evenly arrange hash. Divide mixture into fourths, indenting to bottom of pan every fourth. Break 1 egg into each indentation. Pierce yolk with fork. Microwave (high), covered with plastic wrap, 3-4 minutes, rotating dish ¼ turn halfway through cooking. Serves 4.

● *Yes, the corned beef hash does turn brown!*

● *If you have homemade corned beef hash, substitute 2 cups for canned.*

● *Add 1-2 Tbsp. mayonnaise to hash for a richer mixture.*

Notes: _____

Think Time — Not Heat!!

Cheese

Processed and natural cheeses are available in many forms and varieties for use either cooked or uncooked. Processed cheese blends more easily with other foods for cooking. For many uses cheese requires only melting, added near the end of cooking time. Avoid overcooking because it may become stringy, tough, and develop a grainy texture. Grated and shredded cheese cooks quicker than chunks, and is better for most microwaving. You may want to reduce energy to medium (50%) or medium-high (70%). Use cheese often as a garnish or extender when preparing foods.

QUICHE LORRAINE — *A popular, inexpensive main dish. Small pieces may be served as an appetizer.*

8 slices crisp-cooked bacon	1 (13 oz) can evaporated milk
1 9" baked pastry shell (p.179)	½ tsp. salt
1 cup shredded natural Swiss cheese	¼ tsp. sugar
	¼ tsp. cayenne pepper
¼ cup finely minced onion	Greep pepper strips, paprika
3 eggs	or chopped chives, for garnish

Layer crumbled bacon in bottom of pastry shell. Sprinkle with cheese and onion. Blend eggs, milk, salt, sugar and pepper. Pour over bacon mixture. Garnish. Microwave (high) 6-8 minutes, rotating dish ¼ turn once or twice. (Quiche should be cooked except center which will "jiggle like Jello.") Rest 10 minutes before serving. Serves 5-6.

Maxi-Time: medium-high (70%) 8-10 minutes.

- *Milk may be heated before combining ingredients for more even cooking. Less total cooking time will be needed.*
- *A combination — microwave and conventional cooking — may be used by following directions for Cherry Pie (p. 183). Pie may also be browned by placing under hot broiler 1-2 minutes if desired. The unbaked pie shell may be brushed with Worcestershire sauce for more browning, if desired.*
- *1 cup fresh crab or shrimp and ½ cup finely minced celery may be added in place of bacon to make* **SEAFOOD QUICHE.**
- *I often substitute Cheddar cheese for Swiss.*

Notes: _____

_____

CHEESE FONDUE

Good for a late supper or appetizer on a cold day.

1 lb. (4 cups) shredded Swiss cheese	Dash white pepper
¼ cup flour	¼ tsp. nutmeg
¼ tsp. salt	2 cups dry white wine
1/8 tsp. garlic powder	2 Tbsp. Kirsch, if desired
	French bread, cut in 1" cubes

In 2 qt. glass casserole, mix cheese, flour, salt, garlic powder, pepper, nutmeg and wine. Microwave (high), covered, 5-7 minutes, stirring once or twice during the last 2 minutes. Rest, covered, 5 minutes. Stir in Kirsch. Spear squares of bread in fondue. If cool, reheat 1-2 minutes. Serves 4-6.

Maxi-Time: medium-high (70%) 7-9 minutes.

Notes: _____

_____

CHEESE SOUFFLE

The microwave makes a fluffy, delicious cheese souffle. It won't brown on top but is very delicious and gorgeous to serve guests.

¼ cup flour	3 drops hot sauce
¾ tsp. salt	1½ cups (6 oz) grated sharp cheddar cheese
¾ tsp. dry mustard	
¼ tsp. paprika	6 eggs, separated
1 (13 oz) can evaporated milk	1 tsp. cream of tartar
	¼ cup grated cheddar cheese

In 1½ qt. glass casserole combine flour, salt, mustard, paprika, evaporated milk and hot sauce. Microwave (high) 4-5 minutes, stirring every 2 minutes until thick. Fold in cheese. Microwave (high) 1-2 minutes until cheese melts and sauce is smooth.

In large mixing bowl whip egg whites and cream of tartar until stiff but not dry. Set aside. In medium bowl whip egg yolks until thick. Slowly combine cheese sauce and egg yolks, beating until well blended. Fold gently into egg whites until just blended. Pour into 2½ qt. glass souffle dish. Microwave (medium 50%) 10 minutes, rotating dish ¼ turn halfway through cooking time. Microwave (medium-high 70%) 10-12 minutes, rotating dish ¼ turn halfway through cooking time. (Top will "puff" above dish and souffle will look "cooked" when done.) Sprinkle grated cheese on top. Serve immediately. Serves 6-8.

Maxi-Time: medium (50%) 25-30 minutes.

- *If you have a favorite cheese other than cheddar, substitute in recipe.*
- *Every time I've served this to guests, they want the recipe!*

RAREBIT — *Creamy cheese sauce traditionally served on toast.*

½ lb. diced cheddar cheese	½ tsp. Worcestershire sauce
1 Tbsp. butter	Drop hot sauce
¼ tsp. salt	¼ cup whole milk
½ tsp. dry mustard	1 egg yolk (optl.)

In 4 cup glass measure microwave (high) cheese and butter 2-3 minutes, stirring every minute until smooth. Stir in salt, mustard, Worcestershire sauce and hot sauce. Blend with milk and egg. Microwave (high) 2-3 minutes, stirring every minute until steaming hot. Serve on toast. Sprinkle with paprika. Serves 3-4.
Maxi-Time: medium (50%) 4-6 minutes in second step.

Notes: _____

_____

Sauces

Because sauces have all outside surfaces exposed in microwave, they cook evenly — thus eliminating lumping, sticking and scorching. I have recommended the use of a glass measuring cup throughout this book, but one of the most convenient uses is for making sauces. The handle remains cool, making it easy to stir often. Wax paper can be used as a lid. Use a larger container for milk sauces to prevent boiling over.

Flour or cornstarch as the base in sauces must be boiled to thicken. Egg yolk sauces must be stirred often to prevent overcooking near the outer surfaces. Boiling is not recommended or they may "curdle." What a pleasure to serve with meals!!

WHITE SAUCE

THIN	MEDIUM	THICK
1 Tbsp. butter	2 Tbsp. butter	3-4 Tbsp. butter
1 Tbsp. flour	2 Tbsp. flour	3-4 Tbsp. flour
½ tsp. salt	½ tsp. salt	½ tsp. salt
1 cup milk**	1 cup milk**	1 cup milk**

In a 2 cup glass measure melt butter (high) 30 seconds. Add flour and salt, blending to make a paste. Add milk gradually, stirring constantly. Microwave (high) 1 minute. Stir. Microwave (high) 1½-2½ minutes longer, stirring every 30 seconds until mixture boils. Stir well. Makes 1 cup.

** *Evaporated milk makes a richer sauce.*

CHEESE SAUCE — Cook medium white sauce. Add ¾ cup grated sharp Cheddar cheese, ¼ tsp. dry mustard, and dash paprika. Blend. Microwave (high) 1 minute. Stir well.

BECHAMEL SAUCE — Substitute ½ cup chicken stock and ¼ cup cream for milk in recipe for thin sauce. Season with 1 tsp. grated onion, 1/8 tsp. white pepper and dash thyme. Stir well.

MOCK HOLLANDAISE — To medium white sauce add 2 slightly beaten egg yolks, 1 Tbsp. lemon juice and 2 Tbsp. butter. Heat 1 minute.

BARBECUE SAUCE — *A delicious sauce to keep on hand.*

1 med. finely-chopped onion	1 Tbsp. Worcestershire sauce
2 Tbsp. finely-chopped green pepper	½ tsp. dry mustard
	2 Tbsp. brown sugar
1 clove minced garlic	½ tsp. salt
2 Tbsp. butter	2 drops hot sauce
1 (15 oz) can whole tomatoes	

In a 4 cup glass measure combine onion, green pepper, garlic and butter. Microwave (high) 2 minutes and add remaining ingredients, blending well. Microwave (high) 2 minutes. Makes 2 cups.

Notes: _____

GRAVY

3 Tbsp. flour	⅓ cup pan drippings
1⅓ cup liquid (water, milk or a combination)	Salt and pepper

Pour drippings into 2 cup glass measure. Let fat rise to surface, skim off, saving for recipe. Use remaining drippings as liquid in gravy. In 4 cup glass measure blend flour and liquid until smooth. Add drippings. Microwave (high) 2-3 minutes, or until liquid boils and thickens, stirring every minute. Salt and pepper to taste. Microwave (high) 1-2 minutes longer, stirring every 30 seconds.

●*Add liquid brown sauce for a browner gravy.*

ROUX

New Orleans recipes start with a roux. It's a delicious sauce (or brown gravy) for soups and stews in any part of the country!

½ cup oil	6 cloves minced garlic
½ cup flour	½ cup chopped parsley
1½ cups chopped onions	⅓ cup chopped green onions
½ cup chopped celery	Salt to taste

In 2 qt. glass casserole blend oil and flour. Microwave (high) 8-10 minutes, stirring once or twice until sauce is deep caramel color. Add onions, celery and garlic. Microwave (high) 3-4 minutes,

stirring halfway through cooking. Add parsley, onions and salt to taste. Microwave (high) 2-3 minutes more. Makes 2½-3 cups.
Thin with water or bouillon for gravy, soup or stew base.
Delicious with fresh mushrooms and roast beef!

Notes: _____

_____

BEARNAISE SAUCE
A rich, delicious sauce for meat or vegetables.

4 egg yolks	1 tsp. white wine
¼ cup minced onion	½ cup butter
1 tsp. cider vinegar	

On high speed of mixer or blender combine egg yolks, onion, vinegar and wine until smooth. In 1 cup glass measure melt butter (high) 1 minute. Slowly pour butter into mixture beating at high speed. Sauce will be thick. Makes ½ cup.

Notes: _____

_____

HOLLANDAISE SAUCE
The easiest way to make this delicious, difficult sauce.

¼ cup butter	2 beaten egg yolks
¼ tsp. salt	2 Tbsp. lemon juice
½ tsp. dry mustard	Dash cayenne pepper (optl)

In 2 cup glass measure melt butter (high) 45-60 seconds. Add salt, dry mustard, egg yolks, lemon juice, and cayenne, whisking thoroughly. Microwave (medium-50%) 1-2 minutes, stirring every 15-30 seconds until thickened. Whisk until light and thick. (Sauce "curdles" if overcooked.) Makes 2/3 cup.
●*If mixture separates, whip until smooth.*
● **SPEEDY-QUICK HOLLANDAISE:** *In 1 cup glass measure blend 1 Tbsp. milk or water and ½ cup mayonnaise. Microwave (high) 15-30 seconds. Stir in 1 tsp. lemon juice and dash dry mustard. Makes ½ cup.*

Notes: _____

_____

● *Make* **CARAMEL SAUCE** *from caramels. Combine 1 (14 oz.) bag caramels with 2 Tbsp. water or milk. Microwave medium-high (70%) 2-3 minutes stirring every minute.*

VANILLA SAUCE
Good served hot on ice cream, gingerbread and desserts.

3 Tbsp. soft butter	½ cup boiling water
½ cup sugar	Dash salt
2 slightly beaten egg yolks	1 tsp. vanilla

In 2 cup glass measure cream butter and sugar. Beat in egg yolks. Add boiling water and salt slowly. Microwave (high) 2 minutes, stirring well every 30 seconds. Do not overcook! Add vanilla. Makes 1 cup.

●*Rum flavoring may be substituted for vanilla in recipe.*

BUTTERSCOTCH SAUCE — *Delicious on ice cream!*

1¼ cup light brown sugar	¼ cup butter
½ cup light cream	1/8 tsp. salt
2 Tbsp. light corn syrup	1 tsp. vanilla

In 4 cup glass measure blend sugar, cream, corn syrup, butter and salt. Microwave (high) 4 minutes, stirring every minute. Stir in vanilla. Serve warm or cold. Makes 1½ cups.

PANCAKE SYRUP — *Making your own will save you $$.*

1 cup hot water	½ tsp. maple flavoring
1 lb. dark brown sugar	

In 2 qt. glass casserole boil water (high) 2½-3 minutes. Add brown sugar. Microwave (high) 2-3 minutes until sugar is dissolved, stirring frequently as mixture boils. Add maple flavoring. Makes 2 cups.

Notes: _____

RUM RAISIN SAUCE
Delicious on ice cream and cakes and a real winner to serve guests a **flamed** *dessert.*

1 Tbsp. cornstarch	1 tsp. cinnamon
⅓ cup sugar	½ cup raisins
¾ cup juice (orange, apple, etc.)	2-4 Tbsp. rum

In 4 cup glass measure combine cornstarch, sugar, juice, cinnamon and raisins. Microwave (high) 3-5 minutes until thick and bubbly, stirring every minute. In 1 cup glass measure microwave (high) rum 20-30 seconds. Ignite with match. Pour into sauce; stir until flame goes out. Makes 2 cups.

●*Also good served on sliced ham.*

Notes: _____

_____

HOT FUDGE SAUCE — *Delicious on ice cream!*

1 (6 oz) pkg. chocolate chips	2-3 Tbsp. water
1 Tbsp. butter	Dash salt
¼ cup light corn syrup	1 tsp. vanilla

In 2 cup glass measure combine chocolate chips and butter. Microwave (high) 3-4 minutes stirring every minute until smooth. Blend in corn syrup, water, salt and vanilla. Microwave (high) 1 minute until hot. Serve immediately. Makes 1 cup.

Notes: _____

_____

SWEETENED BUTTER SAUCE
Delicious with flank steak, ham or chicken.

¼ cup butter	2 Tbsp. soy sauce
¼ cup honey	¼ cup raisins (optl.)

In 1 cup glass measure combine butter, honey, soy sauce and raisins. Microwave (high) 1 minute. Stir to blend.
● *Add 1 tsp. cornstarch if thicker sauce is desired.*

Notes: _____

_____

CHERRY SAUCE — *for instant Cherries Jubilee!*

1 (1 lb) can dark sweet cherries with juice	1½ tsp. lemon juice
	Pinch salt
1 Tbsp. cornstarch	1 tsp. lemon peel

In 4 cup glass measure blend cherry juice and cornstarch. Microwave (high) 3-4 minutes, stirring every minute until thick and bubbly. Fold in cherries, lemon juice, salt and peel. Microwave (high) 1-2 minutes to heat throughout. Serve on desserts or ham. Makes 2 cups.
●*For CHERRIES JUBILEE, in 1 cup glass measure microwave (high) ¼ cup Brandy, Rum or Kirsch 20 seconds. Ignite and pour flaming over sauce. Serve on ice cream.*

Notes: _____

_____

Fish & Seafood

The microwave cooks fish better than any other way. Texture of fish is ideal. Fish cooks almost as fast as it heats, so overcooking must be carefully avoided! I prefer to defrost fish on high power 2-3 minutes per lb. Rest 10 minutes. Cook on high. Generally when fish flakes it's done. For microwave fish, it should flake easily with fork **after** "carry-over cooking" time. 4-6 minutes per lb. is very accurate timing for fish as a "rule of thumb." Add more time if foods are added to fish. Arrange in dish with thick portions to outside or fold under small ends of fillets.

Cover fish to cook. Poaching or steaming are conventional fish cooking techniques very adaptable in the microwave. Wax paper is a good cover for 12x8-inch dish. Parchment paper may be wrapped around each fillet in lieu of covering. A favorite of mine is to wrap fish in lettuce leaves during cooking. This traps steam and helps baste fish. Salmon fillets and roasts are excellent when cooked this way. Covering fish exceptions are those with crumb coatings which you wish to remain dry. When placed on rack, uncovered, breaded fish sticks, etc., cook very nicely and coating remains dry. For more browning, place under hot broiler element or infra-red element in microwave, if you have one, a few minutes. Overcooked fish is dehydrated, leaving a dry texture and strong flavor. To eliminate a fishy odor, brush with white wine after purchasing. This does not change taste when cooking. If fish is **frozen**, it must be defrosted before cooking. Be very careful not to over-defrost. Shield small sides.

BAKED FISH — *An easy, quick dinner!*

1 lb. fish fillets	⅓ cup Sauterne wine (optl.)
½ tsp. salt	2 Tbsp. butter
¼ tsp. pepper	1 large sliced tomato
1 small thinly sliced onion	½ thinly sliced green pepper
	1 Tbsp. Worcestershire sauce

In a 12x8-inch dish arrange fish, sprinkle with salt and pepper; cover with onion. Pour wine over fish, marinate 30 minutes, turning fish over after 15 minutes. In 1 cup glass measure melt butter, pour over fish. Cover with tomatoes and green pepper. Sprinkle with Worcestershire. Microwave (high), covered, 6-7 minutes, rotating dish ¼ turn halfway through cooking. Rest 5 minutes. Serves 4.

Notes: _____

HURRY-UP FISH STICKS

1 lb. pkg. frozen breaded fish sticks   Tartar sauce
1 lemon, cut in thin wedges

In 12x8-inch glass dish with rack, arrange fish sticks evenly over top. Microwave (high) 2 minutes, rotate dish ¼ turn. Microwave (high) 2 minutes. Remove from oven 5 minutes. Return to microwave; cook (high) 2 minutes. (Broil if desired.) Serve hot with tartar sauce and lemon. Serves 4.

EASY BREADED FISH — Dip fillets in bottled French dressing. Roll in crushed Ritz cracker or Cornflake crumbs. Arrange on microwave rack in 12x8-inch glass dish. Microwave (high) 4-6 minutes/lb., rotating dish ¼ turn halfway through cooking time. Serve.

Notes: _____

SPEEDY TUNA CASSEROLE

Jeannette Riley, a Portland Home Economist, loves recipes like this her girls can fix.

1 (7 oz) can tuna, drained
1 (10½ oz) can condensed chicken soup
1 (10½ oz) can chicken-noodle or chicken rice soup
1 (5 oz) can evaporated milk
1 (10 oz) pkg. frozen peas
1 (5 oz) can Chow Mein noodles or 1 cup quick raw rice

In 3 qt. glass casserole combine tuna, chicken soup, chicken noodle soup, evaporated milk, peas and ½ can noodles. Blend well. Microwave (high), covered, 10 minutes, stirring halfway through cooking. Sprinkle remaining noodles on top. Microwave (high) 3-5 minutes until mixture is heated and noodles are crisp. Serves 4-5.

● *Cooked chicken or turkey may be substituted in this recipe.*
● *Chopped hard-cooked eggs may be added.*

Notes: _____

YE OLDE TUNA CASSEROLE
We all have a favorite recipe for this standby. This is mine.

4 cups (8 oz) noodles	½ tsp. celery salt
1 (7 oz) can tuna fish, drained	1 tsp. Worcestershire sauce
1 (10½ oz) can mushroom or celery soup	¼ cup cornflake crumbs or buttered toast crumbs
	Paprika or chives

Cook noodles (p. 48). In 1½ qt. glass casserole flake tuna; mix with noodles, soup, celery salt, and Worcestershire sauce. Top with crumbs; sprinkle with paprika and chives. Microwave (high), covered, 8-10 minutes, rotating dish ¼ turn halfway through cooking. Rest 5 minutes. Serves 4-6.

- *Leftover peas, green beans, etc., may be added 3-4 min. before done.*
- *Celery or onions may be sauteed and added to casserole for more texture.*
- *Curry is a favorite seasoning in this recipe.*

Notes: _____

FISH FILLETS ALMONDINE
This recipe taught my husband to request fish.

⅓ cup slivered almonds	1 Tbsp. lemon juice
2 Tbsp. butter	Lemon, cut in thin wedges
1½ lbs. (6 serving size) fish	Paprika

Toast almonds in microwave (p. 196). In 10'' glass skillet melt butter (high) 30 seconds. Coat fillets in butter; arrange around outside of dish. Sprinkle with lemon juice, toasted almonds, and paprika. Microwave (high), covered, 6-8 minutes, rotating ¼ turn halfway through cooking. Rest, covered, 5 minutes. Serve with lemon wedges. Serves 4-6.

- *Almonds complement fish fillets. If available use abalone. Yum!*

Notes: _____

BAKED FISH AND RICE — *A delicious one-dish fish meal.*

1½ cups quick-cooking rice	2 Tbsp. lemon juice
¼ cup onion, chopped	1¼ cup water
1 tsp. salt	1 lb. fresh fish fillets
1 Tbsp. parsley flakes	2 Tbsp. butter
¼ tsp. poultry seasoning	Paprika

In 2 qt. glass casserole blend rice, onion, salt, parsley, poultry seasoning, lemon juice and water. Arrange fish evenly over rice. Dot with butter; sprinkle with paprika. Microwave (high), covered, 10-12 minutes, rotating dish ¼ turn halfway through cooking time. Rest, covered, 5 minutes. Serves 4-5.

Notes: _____

LOBSTER TAILS — *For special occasions and budgets!*

  2 lobster tails (about 8 oz each)   ¼ cup melted butter
                                         2 Tbsp. lemon juice

Split each tail lengthwise (heavy scissors help!), to bottom. Open and lift tail on top of shell leaving bottom connected. Brush with butter. Arrange in shallow glass dish. Microwave (high), covered, 4-6 minutes, rotating dish ¼ turn halfway through cooking. Meat will be firm and translucent; shells will be pink. Rest 5 minutes.

- *4-8 oz. tails require 9-11 minutes cooked following same method.*
- *Serve with* **clarified butter** *and lemon juice. To* **clarify***, melt butter; cool in deep container. Skim butterfat from top.*

Notes: _____

FRESH TROUT

A fisherman's family loves microwaved trout!

  Fresh trout   Melted butter

Clean fish well. Arrange in 12x8-inch glass dish with narrow ends toward center. Brush with melted butter. Microwave (high), covered, 2 minutes per pound. Turn over and rotate. Microwave (high) 2-3 minutes per pound. Rest, covered, 5 minutes. Serve with lemon wedges.

- *If using temperature probe, cook to 170°F.*
- *Shield head and tail of whole fish to prevent overcooking*

Notes: _____

FILLETS OR STEAKS: **Any** fish may be microwaved easily without adding other ingredients. Microwave (high) 4-6 minutes/lb., covered, rotating ¼ turn halfway through cooking.

- *Add herbs such as parsley, basil, oregano and thyme. (I have a favorite wonderful mixed herbs I purchased for $5 in dept. store that can be fresh ground as needed.) Lemon juice or wine also enhances flavor. Weight watchers will love their microwave for fish!*

SHRIMP KABOBS — *Elegant to serve family or guests.*

1½ lbs. large shrimp, peeled	¾ tsp. dry mustard
1 clove minced garlic	¾ tsp. salt
1 small chopped onion	2 Tbsp. oil
1 tsp. dried basil	2 Tbsp. lemon juice

Combine all ingredients; marinate 1 hour. On wooden skewer, thread 3 shrimp. (May alternate with whole cherry tomatoes.) Arrange on roasting rack in 12x8-inch glass dish. Brush with marinade. Microwave (high), covered, 8-10 minutes, rearranging and rotating ¼ turn halfway through cooking. Serve with rice. Serves 4-6.

- *Ingredients may also be combined. Microwave (high), covered, 6-8 minutes, stirring halfway through cooking. Rest, covered, 5 minutes.*

Notes: _____

SHRIMP CREOLE

A favorite recipe from our New Orleans friends. A great company recipe to serve guests.

3 Tbsp. butter or oil	¼ tsp. pepper
¾ cup chopped onion	2 (8 oz) cans tomato sauce
½ cup chopped green pepper	1 tsp. Worcestershire sauce
½ cup diagonally sliced celery	1 tsp. lemon juice
½ cup chopped mushrooms	2 bay leaves
3 Tbsp. flour	1½ lb. medium shrimp, peeled
¾ tsp. garlic salt	Hot sauce to taste

In 3 qt. glass casserole microwave (high) butter, onion, green pepper, celery and mushrooms 3-5 minutes, stirring once or twice. Stir in flour, garlic salt and pepper. Microwave (high) 1-2 minutes to make sauce. Add tomato sauce, Worcestershire sauce, lemon juice and bay leaves. Microwave (high) 3-5 minutes until boiling. Stir in shrimp and hot sauce. Microwave (high), covered, 6-8 minutes, stirring halfway through cooking. Rest, covered, 5 minutes. Serve over rice. Serves 5-6.

- *For more vegetables in sauce, add as desired.*

Notes: _____

- **Open the shells of stubborn seafood such as clams and oysters:** *microwave (high) 4 at a time 10-15 seconds. Remove from oven when open a crack.*

SHRIMP CASSEROLE — *For variety, serve shrimp in a casserole.*

¼ cup butter	2 Tbsp. chopped parsley
½ cup sherry or broth	2 Tbsp. finely chopped onion
⅓ cup dry bread crumbs	¼ tsp. pepper
¼ tsp. garlic powder	¼ tsp. nutmeg
	1½ cup small fresh shrimp

In 1 qt. glass casserole melt butter (high) 45 seconds. Blend with sherry, bread crumbs, garlic, parsley, onion, pepper and nutmeg. Sprinkle shrimp evenly over top. Microwave (high), covered, 4-5 minutes, rotating ¼ turn halfway through cooking. Rest 5 minutes. Serve on rice. Serves 4.

Notes: _____

BAKED SALMON STEAKS — *Delicious to serve hot or cold.*

4 1"-thick salmon steaks of equal size	Salt
	Lemon pepper
2 Tbsp. butter	1 small thinly sliced onion
2 Tbsp. lemon juice	Paprika
	8 washed lettuce leaves

In 10" glass casserole, arrange salmon equally in four corners (narrow ends toward center of dish). In glass cup melt butter (high) 30 seconds. Add to lemon juice. Pour equally over salmon. Salt and pepper. Arrange onion slices on steaks, sprinkle with paprika. Top each steak with damp lettuce leaf to cover. Microwave (high) 5-7 minutes, rotating dish ¼ turn halfway through cooking. Rest 5 minutes, covered. Serve hot or cold. Serves 4.

- *To serve, arrange steaks on fresh lettuce leaves, garnish with thinly sliced lemon. Sprinkle with paprika if desired.*
- *We're glad we live in the Northwest where salmon is plentiful and we can serve this often.*
- *Substitute Halibut Steaks for Salmon if desired.*

Notes: _____

SALMON ROAST: Substitute 2 lb. roast for steaks. Follow directions above cooking 10-12 minutes, turning roast over and rotating ¼ turn halfway through cooking. Serves 6. (Hot or cold.)

Notes: _____

Think Time — Not Heat!!

SALMON LOAF — *A yummy salmon loaf in a ring.*

1 (1 lb.) can salmon	¼ tsp. salt
2 lightly beaten eggs	2 Tbsp. finely chopped onion
1 cup soft bread crumbs	2 tsp. lemon juice
¼ cup evaporated milk	1 (2 oz) jar pimientos, diced
½ cup finely diced celery	Chives

In medium mixing bowl combine salmon, eggs, bread crumbs, milk, celery, salt, onion, lemon juice and diced pimiento. Arrange in 6 cup plastic ring dish. Decorate top with pimiento strips, sprinkle with chives. Microwave (high) 7-9 minutes, rotating ¼ turn halfway through cooking. Rest 5 minutes. Serve with creamed peas or **dill sauce**. Serves 4-5.

• **SALMON PATTIES**: Shape mixture into 6 patties. Arrange on rack in 12x8-inch glass dish. Microwave (high) 6-8 minutes, rotating ¼ turn halfway through cooking. Serves 4.

Patties may be grilled on preheated browning dish.

DILL SAUCE: In 2 cup glass measure, mix 1 can celery soup and ½ tsp. dill weed. Microwave (high) 2-3 minutes, stirring every minute, until heated. Serve warm.

Notes: _____

DEVILED CRAB

A tangy taste is very complimentary to seafood, especially our fresh Northwest Dungeness crab!

1 (10½ oz) can cream of mushroom soup	1 Tbsp. minced onion
	1 Tbsp. lemon juice
1 lb. fresh crabmeat **or** 2 (7 oz) cans crab, drained	2 tsp. Worcestershire sauce
	¾ tsp. prepared mustard
2 Tbsp. finely chopped celery	2 Tbsp. buttered bread crumbs
	Paprika

In medium mixing bowl combine soup, crab, celery, onion, lemon juice, Worcestershire sauce and mustard. Spoon equal amounts of mixture into 4 scallop shells or ramekin dishes. Sprinkle with buttered crumbs and paprika. Microwave (high) 7-9 minutes, re-arranging ¼ turn halfway through cooking. Serves 4.

• **SCALLOPS** *are excellent as a substitute.*

SCALLOPS a la MICROWAVE

A tasty seafood even more delicious when microwaved!

1½ lb. scallops	½ tsp. salt
1 tsp. dried basil	1 thinly sliced lemon
¼ tsp. thyme	Paprika

In 2 qt. glass casserole add even size scallops. (If too large, you may cut.) Combine basil, thyme and salt; sprinkle over scallops. Microwave (high), covered, 7-9 minutes, stirring halfway through cooking. Rest, covered, 5 minutes. Serve with lemon and sprinkle with paprika. Serves 4-5.

Notes: _____

SCALLOPED OYSTERS
This is a favorite of an oyster "lover," including my husband. It is also a tradition for our Thanksgiving dinner!

- ¾ cup dry seasoned bread crumbs
- ⅓ cup melted butter
- 1 pint fresh oysters, drained but saving liquor
- ½ tsp. salt
- ¼ tsp. pepper
- ½ tsp. Worcestershire sauce
- ⅓ cup finely diced celery
- 2 Tbsp. minced parsley
- 1 cup liquid, half oyster liquor and half cream or milk
  Parsley, minced

Combine bread crumbs and butter, spread ⅓ of mixture in 2 qt. glass casserole. Layer oysters over crumbs. Combine salt, pepper, Worcestershire sauce, celery, parsley and liquid; pour over crumbs. Top with leftover crumb mixture; sprinkle with parsley. Microwave (high) 10 minutes, rotating ¼ turn halfway through cooking. Rest 5 minutes. Serves 4-6.

Notes: _____

OYSTER PUDDING — *A new way to serve oysters.*
- 6 slices buttered white bread
- 6 slices American cheese
- 1 pint fresh oysters, drained but saving liquor
- Milk
- 2 beaten eggs
- 1 tsp. salt
- ¼ tsp. pepper

Cube bread with serrated knife. Arrange half cubes evenly in 10-inch glass dish. Top with cheese slices. Arrange oysters on cheese, top with remaining bread cubes. Add milk to oyster liquor to make 1½ cups. Combine with eggs, salt and pepper. Pour over ingredients. Microwave (high) 10-12 minutes, rotating ¼ turn halfway through cooking. Test with knife to come out clean. Rest 5 minutes. (Be careful not to overcook outside edges.) Serves 4-6.
Maxi-Time: medium-high (70%) 15-17 minutes.
● *Dish may be inverted for serving. Be certain pudding is set!*

Notes: _____

MAGIC: *When* **reheating** *fish dishes, be careful not to overcook! They reheat very quickly. It is best to reheat covered with a sauce.*

GEFILTE FISH

The most requested of all Kosher recipes traditionally served at the Friday night Sabbath meal.

6 cups water	½ lb. fresh red snapper
2 sliced carrots	2 eggs
2 medium chopped onions	2 Tbsp. Matzo Meal (or fine
1 Tbsp. salt	cracker crumbs)
¼ tsp. pepper	2 Tbsp. cold water
½ lb. fresh salmon	¾ tsp. salt
½ lb. fresh cod or sturgeon	¼ tsp. pepper

In 3 qt. glass casserole combine water, 1 sliced carrot, 1 chopped onion, salt and pepper. Microwave (high), covered, 10-12 minutes until mixture boils. Microwave (medium 50% or less to simmer) 15 minutes to make court bouillon. With food processor or meat grinder finely grind fish, 1 onion and 1 carrot. In large bowl combine fish, eggs, matzo meal, water, salt and pepper. Blend with mixer on high until well mixed and airy. Shape into oval balls using approximately ¼ cup for each. Drop into hot broth. Microwave medium-high (70%) 8-10 minutes. Drain. Serve hot or cold with horseradish. Serves 5-6.

- *Onion can be browned (almost burned!) on range to give more flavor to fish. Do this before grinding.*
- *Balls should be shaped soft and light — not compressed hard.*
- *Combinations of fish will vary in different regions of the country. We use these in the Northwest. A friend in Ohio makes hers with Whitefish, Carp and Pike. Use what is available to complement each other in your area.*
- *If fresh fish isn't available, use frozen. Thaw before preparing recipe and pat dry to remove excess moisture.*
- *A mixture of powers is used. If your oven has only high, it's best to prepare this on top of range.*

Notes: _____

_____

- *Fix* **CRUMB MIX,** *p. 144, to use for breading your own fish with homemade, handy convenience.*

Beef

Try a variety of beef cuts in your microwave. You will be pleased with results! It's very important to read and follow directions carefully You may also learn to convert many of your family favorites (p. 24). Since there is no dry heat, meat will retain more juice. Dry surface with paper towel to prevent steaming. Elevate on roasting rack for dry roasting results. Cook veal like beef.

Tender cuts of meat cook better than less tender which need moisture and long, slow cooking to soften connective tissue. If you have a medium (50%) or medium-high (70%) setting on your oven, you will achieve better results with less tender cuts. To time slower cooking, see chart (p. 14). Amount of energy is decreased by one-half to one-fourth. (Consult your manual for more information.) Meat tenderizers or high acid foods, e.g. wine, pineapple juice, tomato juice, etc., also tenderizes meat. Marinate overnight if possible for good results.

Meats cooked longer than 10 minutes will **brown** like cooking conventionally. Cured meats such as ham, bacon, etc., require less cooking time to brown. Searing, grilling or frying will not be achieved unless microwave browning dish is used (p.129) or conventional cooking is combined with microwave cooking in a glass ceramic dish.

Room **temperature** meats cook more evenly than those removed directly from refrigerator. Thaw frozen meats and allow a resting time to equalize temperature before cooking. All meats must be **completely** thawed before cooking.

Thermometers are available for use inside the microwave. "Regular" thermometers may be placed in meat **at the end** of cooking time to test internal temperature. "Carry-over cook" 10-15 minutes. If more cooking is needed, remove thermometer and return to microwave. A temperature probe can also measure internal temperature of food.

Barbecuing has a tendency to toughen outer surfaces of many foods. Use barbecue in combination with microwave to produce juicy, tender, flavorful barbecued foods. Precook a short period (about 3 minutes per lb.) in microwave. Place on hot barbecue grill to sear. Excellent results will be achieved, especially for thick cuts of meat such as Chateaubriand or London Broil. (Fried chicken too!) Grilling is necessary only to sear outer surfaces of food.

"Carry-over cooking" is very important for cooking meats. Because most meats are dense, temperature continues to equalize during this time. If foods need more cooking at the end of "carry-over cooking" time, return to microwave for additional cooking needed. Always select the shortest time in a recipe! If overcooked, your meat will be tough. If meat main dish is cooked covered, leave lid on for additional carry-over cooking or resting time.

ROASTING TIPS: The same basic techniques apply for all roasts. Important points to keep in mind are:

Select roasts even in shape. If meat has a large portion of bone, e.g. ham, prime rib, etc., "shield" bone or shank with foil during first half of cooking time to prevent overcooking. A perfect ball is the best shape. Odd-shaped meats can often be compressed and tied to a more even shape which will microwave better.

If roast is **unevenly shaped**, "shield" pointed edges and corners with foil before cooking to prevent overcooking. (Hold foil in place with a toothpick.) Remove foil halfway through cooking.

Invest in a slotted rack designed for microwave use. **Place roasts** on rack to keep out of cooking juices so meat won't steam. Begin with fat side down. Prop it in place with glass measuring cup if it doesn't rest evenly. If you don't have a rack periodically remove juices from the dish so they won't absorb energy. If you wish to use an inverted saucer be certain to remove saucer IMMEDIATELY when roast is taken from the oven or it may create a vacuum and seal to the dish. Remember, plastic racks made especially for the microwave CANNOT be used in the conventional oven! It's very hard to microwave meats without a rack for excellent results.

Roast must be rotated and turned over ¼ turn halfway through cooking time. You will obtain more even cooking by turning roast to a side for the last half of cooking. (Notice that the roast looks pink in the center of both ends alerting you to change position.) If your family has members who like meat both rare and well, do not rotate and that's what you will get. Half the roast will cook well and half rare.

Cooking times for beef are:

	High	Med.-high (70%)	Medium (50%)	Temperature
Rare	6-7 min/lb	8-10 min/lb	12-14 min/lb	120° incr. to 135°F
Med.	7-8 min/lb	10-12 min/lb	14-16 min/lb	130° incr. to 145°F
Well	8-9 min/lb	12-14 min/lb	16-18 min/lb	155° incr. to 170°F

Increase in temperature occurs during "carry-over cooking." Allow 15 minutes for roasts (enough time to finish cooking meal).

Salting meat prior to cooking has a tendency to draw moisture, drying it out and may cause uneven cooking. It also promotes more shrinkage. Other seasonings such as garlic, pepper, etc., may be added before cooking if you wish. If desired, salt near or at the end of cooking. A browning glaze can be made with a mixture of Kitchen Bouquet, paprika, butter, soy sauce or Worcestershire sauce if desired. Roast may be basted with a bulb baster for a crisper outside.

Cover only those roasts you wish to steam. Even wax paper will trap enough steam to soften meat texture instead of drying as is preferred with most roasts. If you object to wiping splatters out of the oven, make a tent of wax paper over roast. (The microwave is easy to clean after cooking!)

PRIME RIB OR ROLLED RIB ROAST

You'll never miss a perfect roast when microwaving a rib. I prefer cooking on high power.

    1 Prime or Rolled Rib Roast (allow 2 servings per lb.)
    4 cloves garlic (optl.)

Tie roast compactly. Cut garlic in half. Pierce 8 holes in roast, place ½ bud in each. Mark with toothpick if removal desired before serving. Shield. Place on microwave rack in 12x8-inch glass dish. Microwave (high) for degree of doneness desired (p. 114), rotating dish ¼ turn and turning roast over ¼ turn halfway through cooking. Baste with drippings if desired. Cover with a tent of foil. Rest 10-15 minutes. Check with meat thermometer if desired. Remove garlic. Serve.

BEEF ROAST

My very favorite cut of roast is the CHUCK, CROSSRIB, POT ROAST (also called English, Newport, Chef Cut, Boston) for its flavor and tenderness. I've cooked thousands at schools with nothing but raves!! It's inexpensive and has no waste. It ties into a perfect "ball-shape" for microwaving. I cook it like a prime rib — not a pot roast!

    1 boneless roast (3-6 lbs)

Tie and shield. Place fat side down on microwave rack in 12x8-inch glass dish. Figure cooking time by weight for high power (p. 114.) Divide time in half. Microwave (high) for first half of time. Turn roast over. Microwave at reduced power (chart p. 14) as follows for last half of time:

    Sirloin Tip or Chuck Crossrib — medium (50%)
    Rump Roast — medium low (30%)

Cover, if desired, while resting 10-15 minutes. Make gravy from drippings (p. 100.) Slice thinly across grain of meat. Reheat for serving if needed.

• *Weight cooking time is more accurate than a probe or thermometer.*

- *For more roasting information consult chart p. 114 and power chart p. 14.*

POT ROAST

A tight cover and lower power is the secret of tenderizing pot roast. And best of all, no cooked-on pan to wash! Begin with 10-15 minutes on high. Reduce to medium (50%) or medium-low (30%) 1-1½ hour.

3 lb. chuck pot roast	¾ tsp. salt
1 (5/8 oz) pkg. gravy mix or flour	1 Bay leaf
	4 medium sliced carrots
1 cup water	2 medium sliced onions
	2 lrg. potatoes cut in ½" cubes

In 12x8-inch glass dish, coat roast on both sides with gravy mix or flour. Add water, salt and bay leaf. Microwave (high), covered, 10 minutes. Rotate and turn roast over. Microwave medium (50%), covered, 35-40 minutes. Add carrots, onions and potatoes. Microwave medium (50%), covered, 35-40 minutes. Rest, covered, 15-20 minutes. (Do not lift lid!) To serve, slice diagonally across grain of meat. Serves 4-6.

- *Roast may be tenderized with commercial tenderizer prior to cooking if desired (not necessary for a tender roast — only flavor).*
- *For a larger roast cook medium (50%) another 30 minutes to 1½ hour total time.*
- *For a **tomato base sauce**, combine ½ cup tomato paste and ½ cup water in place of gravy mix and water. Dredge roast in flour. Follow recipe as above.*
- *For a **creamy brown gravy sauce**, combine 1 envelope onion soup mix and 1 (10½ oz) can mushroom soup. Dredge meat in flour. Follow recipe as above.*
- *For temperature probe, cook to 170°F.*
- *If part of roast is out of the liquid, turn over halfway.*
- *1-3 inches is the best thickness for cooking. Remove bone before cooking. Searing is not necessary for browning.*
- *A tight cover is important for steaming meat and vegetables. We like roast prepared in clay cooker which can go directly to table. A cooking bag also makes a good container. Secure with rubber band — not metal ties.*
- *This recipe takes the same time as simmering on top of range; however, it does not heat up kitchen or create a burned pan to wash.*

Notes: _____

_____

Think Time — Not Heat!!

SWISS STEAK — *Delicious, tender tomato base main dish.*

2 lb. round steak, ½" thick, (Ask butcher to tenderize)
3 Tbsp. flour
¼ tsp. pepper
½ tsp. thyme
1 envelope onion soup mix
1 stalk celery, diagonally sliced ¼" thick
1 medium thinly sliced onion
¼ cup water
1 (8 oz) can tomato sauce

Cut steak in serving pieces. Mix flour, pepper and thyme. Dredge meat coating both sides. Arrange meat in 12x8-inch glass dish. Cover evenly with soup mix, celery and sliced onion. In 2 cup measure blend water and tomato sauce; pour over meat. Cover with plastic wrap, venting 1 small corner. Microwave (high) 10 minutes. Reduce to medium (50%) 20-25 minutes. Rotate dish ¼ turn; rearrange pieces for even cooking. Microwave medium (50%), covered, 20-25 minutes. Rest, covered, 15 minutes. Serves 4-6.
● *Substitute your favorite swiss steak recipe if desired.*

FAVORITE FAMILY STEW

Clare Acker who teaches microwave cooking at the Creative Cooking School in Portland, Ore., gave me this delicious family recipe. It's a favorite for generations that always gets returns for seconds at cooking schools. It takes 5 hours in conventional oven at 250°F. or 90 minutes in the microwave!

1½ lbs. stew meat
MSG
2 medium 1" sliced carrots
2 medium sliced onions
1 cup sliced celery
4 medium cubed potatoes
1 (10½ oz) can tomato soup
½ cup water
1 Tbsp. sugar
1 Tbsp. salt
¼ tsp. pepper
2 Tbsp. tapioca pudding mix

In 4 qt. casserole or Country Cooker, microwave (high) stew meat sprinkled with MSG, 8-9 minutes, stirring once or twice until pink color is gone. Layer with carrots, onions, celery and potatoes. In 2 cup glass measure combine tomato soup, water, sugar, salt, pepper and tapioca. Stir to blend; pour on vegetables to cover. Microwave medium-low (30%) 90 minutes. Don't lift the lid. Don't stir. Don't peek. Serves 6-8.

MICRO SHAKE POT ROAST

Moisten 3 lb. chuck roast with water. Sprinkle generously with meat Micro Shake. Pierce with a fork at ½-inch intervals. Place in 12x8-inch glass dish. Add 1½ cups water. Microwave (high), covered, 5 minutes. Microwave (medium-50%), covered, 30 minutes. Turn meat over. Add vegetables as desired. Microwave (medium-50%), covered, 30-40 minutes. Rest, covered, 10-15 minutes. Serves 5-6.

CORNED BEEF DINNER

A delicious boiled dinner cooked with "planned-overs" in mind.

3 lb. corned beef
4 cups water
2 bay leaves
1 tsp. peppercorns

3 medium peeled ½" cubed potatoes
4 medium carrots, diagonally sliced ½" thick
1 medium wedged cabbage

In 3 qt. casserole combine corned beef, water, bay leaves and peppercorns. Microwave (high), covered, 1 hour, rotating ¼ turn halfway through cooking. Turn corned beef over; add potatoes and carrots. Microwave (high), covered, 15-20 minutes, rotating dish ¼ turn halfway through cooking. Add cabbage. Cook (high), covered, 12-15 minutes. Rest, covered, 10 minutes. Test for doneness. Remove any finished ingredients, arrange on serving platter; return others to microwave to finish cooking. Be careful not to overcook, especially the meat! Slice corned beef diagonally very thin across grain to serve. Sauce may be served as is or thickened with flour and seasoned. Serves 6-8.

Maxi-Time: Medium-high (70%) 1½ hour in step one. Finish on high.

● *A nice one-dish dinner with leftovers for lunch or Chip Beef recipe below or Hash recipe (p. 96).*

Notes: _____

_____

CREAMED CHIP BEEF

A versatile sauce to use with leftover meats and seafood.

3 Tbsp. butter
3 Tbsp. flour
1½ cup milk

4 oz. dried chip beef or thinly sliced corn beef
Salt and pepper

In 4 cup glass measure melt butter (high) 45 seconds. Blend in flour. Add milk gradually, stirring constantly. Microwave (high) 4 minutes, stirring every minute. When sauce is thick and smooth, add beef. Season. Serves 4.

● *Serve over hot biscuits, muffins, toast, etc.*

● *Sauce can be used for other creamed dishes —* **CREAMED TUNA, CREAMED SHRIMP, CREAMED CRAB, CREAMED LAMB,** *etc. Texture can be added to sauce with chopped celery, green pepper, water chestnuts, etc. Add color with pimiento, paprika, parsley, chives, green onions, etc. Grated sharp cheddar cheese may be sprinkled on top. Individual servings can be reheated.*

Notes: _____

STEAK-IN-A-BAG — *A delicious new way to prepare steak!*

2 lbs. sirloin steak, ¾-1" thick	1 tsp. salt
2 Tbsp. garlic spread	2 tsp. lemon pepper
2 Tbsp. salad oil	1 cup coarse seasoned bread crumbs

Dry steak with paper towel. Make a paste of garlic spread, oil, salt and pepper. Spread both sides of steak. Press bread crumbs into paste. Place in brown paper bag, tuck opening under. Microwave (high) 6 minutes. Turn steak over and rotate ¼ turn. Microwave (high) 6-8 minutes. Rest 5 minutes. Remove steak from bag. Serve diagonally sliced. Serves 4-6.

- **Do not** *use* **recycled** *paper bags as they may have metal filings which could cause arcing.*
- *Substitute flank steak for sirloin in this recipe.*
- *Make your own* **GARLIC SPREAD** *and store in refrigerator for use on bread, meats: Boil 5 peeled garlic cloves in ½ cup water in 2 cup glass measure (high) 2-3 minutes or until garlic is soft. Pour off water. Mix garlic cloves and ½ cup butter in blender until very well blended. Store in refrigerator until needed. (If you don't have blender, mash garlic with bottom of glass, mix well with fork.)*

Notes: _____

ORIENTAL DINNER — *A tasty, easy stir-fry main dish.*

2 Tbsp. salad oil	1 cup diagonally sliced celery
1½ lbs. round steak, tenderized and thinly sliced diagonally across the grain	¼ cup soy sauce
	2 beef bouillon cubes
	¼ cup hot water
2 medium thinly sliced onions	2 Tbsp. cornstarch
1 cup thinly sliced jicama or water chestnuts	2 Tbsp. cold water

In 10" glass skillet heat oil (high) 1 minute. Add meat. Microwave (high) 3-4 minutes, stirring once. Add onions, jicama, celery, soy sauce and bouillon cubes dissolved in hot water. Microwave (high), covered, 10-12 minutes, stirring every 3 minutes until vegetables are crisp-tender. Remove vegetables and meat. Thicken sauce with cornstarch and cold water. Microwave (high) 1-2 minutes, stirring every 30 seconds until sauce is thick. Adjust seasonings. Pour sauce on meat. Serves 4-6.

- *To slice meat easily, place in freezer 30 minutes.*
- *Bamboo sprouts may be added at the end of cooking time; heat 2 more minutes. Stir well. Green pepper or canned Oriental vegetables may be substituted.*

Notes: _____

STIR-FRY TOMATO BEEF
A cooking school favorite and picture pretty!

2 lbs. sirloin, round, flank or chuck steak
2 Tbsp. sugar
½ cup soy sauce
1 clove minced garlic
¼ tsp. ginger
3 Tbsp. salad oil
2 large green peppers, cut in strips
3 green onions, 1" slices w/tops
2 lrg. tomatoes, cut in wedges
1 Tbsp. cornstarch
¼ cup water

Slice steak diagonally across grain in 1/8-inch thick slices. (Freeze 30 minutes to slice easier.) In 2 cup glass measure combine sugar, soy sauce, garlic and ginger. Pour over meat in medium bowl; marinate 30 minutes, turning meat after 15 minutes.

Preheat browning skillet (high) 6 minutes or fry pan on range until very hot. Remove meat from marinade, reserving extra. Add oil and meat. Microwave (high) 5-6 minutes stirring halfway through cooking. Add green peppers and onion. Microwave (high) 3-4 minutes, stirring halfway through cooking. Top with tomato wedges. In 1 cup glass measure combine cornstarch, water, and remaining marinade. Microwave (high) 1-2 minutes, stirring once or twice until thick. Pour over stir-fry. Microwave (high) 1-2 minutes more. Rest 5 minutes. Serve on cooked rice. Serves 6-8.

LIVER AND ONIONS
Cookie Edwards, an assistant at my classes, has requested this recipe. A word of caution — do not overcook liver! If in doubt, cook less time and allow a resting time before more cooking to reach doneness you prefer. We like ours a little pink inside.

1 lb. calves or beef liver
3 Tbsp. flour
1 tsp. salt
¼ tsp. pepper
6-8 slices diced bacon
2 medium, thinly-sliced onions

In paper sack coat liver with flour, salt and pepper. In 10-inch glass skillet microwave (high) bacon and onions 8-10 minutes, stirring once or twice until bacon is crisp. With slotted spoon, remove onions and bacon. Add liver. Microwave (high), covered, 5-6 minutes, turning over and rotating dish ¼ turn halfway through cooking. Return onions and bacon to dish on top of liver. Microwave (high), covered, 1-2 minutes more or until heated throughout. Rest, covered, 5 minutes. Serves 3-4.

Maxi-Time: Medium-high (70%) 7-9 minutes in step 2. Medium-high (70%) 2-3 minutes in step 3.

● *You may prefer to brown liver in step 2 in 10-inch glass skillet on range surface. Finish in microwave.*

Notes: _____

MUSHROOM STUFFED FLANK STEAK
A delicious recipe from a student.

¾ cup dry bread stuffing
1 (3-oz) can sliced mushrooms
2 Tbsp. melted butter
1 Tbsp. grated parmesan cheese
1 flank steak (about 1¾ lbs),
  scored on both sides

1 envelope brown-gravy mix
¼ cup dry red wine
2 Tbsp. minced green onions
  (tops too)
1 Tbsp. salad oil
1 clove minced garlic
¼ cup apricot preserves

Combine stuffing with drained mushrooms, butter and cheese. Spread over flank steak; roll like jelly roll. Fasten with wooden skewers. In 2 cup measure prepare gravy mix according to package directions. Microwave (high) 4-6 minutes, stirring once. Add wine and onions. In 12x8-inch glass dish combine oil and garlic. Microwave (high) 2 minutes. Coat steak in oil. Pour gravy over meat. Cover with plastic wrap. Microwave medium (50%), 30-35 minutes, rotating ¼ turn halfway through cooking. Rest 10 minutes. Remove meat from sauce; add preserves. Microwave (high) 2-3 minutes to dissolve. Serve sauce over meat. Serves 4-6.

BEEF STROGANOFF — *A favorite delicious main dish.*

2 Tbsp. flour
1½ tsp. salt
¼ tsp. pepper
1 lb. sirloin steak, thinly sliced
  diagonally across grain
¼ cup salad oil

½ cup minced onion
1 clove minced garlic
¼ cup water
1 (10 oz) can mushroom soup
8 fresh sliced mushrooms
1 cup dairy sour cream

Mix flour, salt and pepper; dredge meat in mixture. Pound mixture into both sides of meat. In 9" glass baking dish, heat oil (high) one minute. Add meat. Microwave (high) 3-4 minutes stirring frequently to brown meat. Add onion and garlic. Microwave (high) 2-3 minutes. Stir in water, soup, and mushrooms. Microwave (high) 4-5 minutes, covered, stirring twice. Test beef for tenderness. Slowly blend in sour cream; heat (high) 1 minute. Serve on cooked noodles or rice. Serves 4-6.

Maxi-Time: Medium-high (70%) meat in step 2, 4-6 minutes stirring several times. Finish on high.

●*Substitute ground beef for steak. Omit flour and salad oil. Garnish with chopped parsley, chives or green onions.*

MICRO SHAKE (R) may be used in place of seasonings in most beef, pork, or lamb recipes. It enhances browning and reduces shrinkage. Flavors are: Natural Meat, Onion and Garlic, and Natural Chicken.

SOUTH-OF-THE-BORDER CASSEROLE

If purple ribbons were awarded for recipes, this would be grand prize. It has been the favorite at cooking schools for 9 years! And it couldn't be easier!

2 Tbsp. butter
1 small chopped onion
1 (6 oz) pkg. corn chips (4 cups)
2 cups grated sharp Cheddar cheese

1 (1 lb) can chili without beans
1 (1 lb) can kidney beans, drained
1 (12 oz) can Mexicorn, drained

In 12x8-inch glass casserole add butter and onion. Microwave (high) 3 minutes, stirring once. Reserve 1 cup corn chips and 1 cup cheese. Blend remaining chips, cheese, chili, beans and corn with onions. Microwave (high), covered, 8-9 minutes, rotating ¼ turn halfway through cooking. Sprinkle with reserved cheese. Microwave (high), uncovered, 3 minutes. "Ring" remaining corn chips around edge. Rest 5 minutes. Serves 8.

● *An emergency dinner because ingredients can be kept on hand. It is great for a potluck dinner or serving a crowd that arrives unexpectedly. Omit corn chips if you don't have on hand.*

Notes: _____

Ground Beef

Ground beef is a regular food in many homes. It is a regular for microwave cooking too! It's economical, tender, readily available and flexible as a substitute for other cuts in many recipes. Other ground meats — pork, lamb, veal, and turkey, may be substituted for ground beef. I prefer to pre-brown and drain fat before using. It's easy to do if a plastic collander is placed in glass dish. Crumble ground beef in collander. Add onions, celery, green pepper, etc., to saute. Microwave (high) 5-6 minutes/lb. Pour off drippings. Regular ground beef should be browned first. Lean ground beef has less fat for recipes where pre-browning isn't possible (meatloaf). Meat may be browned in quantity and frozen for later use.

GROUND BEEF PATTIES

Season ground beef. (Mix salt into meat rather than sprinkled on top.) Shape into ¼-lb. patties, making a thumbprint indentation in center of each. Arrange evenly on microwave rack in 12x8-inch glass dish. Baste with mixture of soy sauce, brown sauce and water or sprinkle with microwave browner if desired. Cook, rotating ¼ turn halfway through cooking as follows:

1	patty	-	1-2 minutes	High Power
2	patties	-	2-3 minutes	High Power
4	patties	-	4-5 minutes	High Power
6	patties	-	6-7 minutes	High Power

- *If you have a favorite seasoning for patties, pre-mix and keep on hand for convenience in preparing.*
- *A large number of patties may be prepared in advance and frozen until used. Store in freezer no more than 3 months.*

Notes: _____

MEATY SPAGHETTI SAUCE — *A favorite spaghetti sauce.*

1 lb. lean ground beef	1 (6 oz) can tomato paste
2 finely chopped small onions	1 tsp. salt
1 minced clove garlic	¼ tsp. pepper
3 Tbsp. minced parsley	½ tsp. oregano
½ cup finely chopped celery	½ tsp. basil
1 (1 lb) can whole tomatoes	¼ tsp. thyme
	Water, to thin

In 2 qt. glass casserole brown ground beef (high) 3-4 minutes, stirring to crumble. Add onions, garlic, parsley and celery. Microwave (high), covered, 5 minutes stirring once. Add tomatoes, tomato paste, salt, pepper, oregano, basil, and thyme. Microwave (high), covered, 20 minutes, stirring several times. Rest, covered, 5 minutes. Serves 4.

- *Serve over or mix with cooked spaghetti. Sprinkle with grated Parmesan cheese.*
- *If you prefer* **meatless sauce,** *omit ground beef; add 2 Tbsp. olive oil to saute vegetables.*
- *Seasonings in recipe blend better if prepared the day before and refrigerated overnight. Reheat to serve.*
- *Prepare* **SLOPPY JOES** *by adding 1-2 Tbsp. chili powder and 1 (1 lb) can kidney beans to sauce. Serve on hamburger buns.*

Notes: _____

MICRO SHAKE HAMBURGER PATTIES — Place patties on slotted roasting rack in 12x8-inch glass dish. Microwave (high), covered with wax paper, 5-6 minutes per pound, turning center to outside halfway through cooking time. Rest 5 minutes.

CHILI

I had a letter from a fellow in Seattle, Wash., who bought a microwave because of eating this recipe!

½ cup chopped onion
¼ cup chopped green pepper
1 lb. lean ground beef
1 (1 lb) can tomato sauce
1 (1 lb) can whole or stewed
   tomatoes
1 (1 lb) can drained kidney
   beans
1½ tsp. salt
1½-2½ tsp. chili powder
¼ tsp. pepper
½ tsp. dry mustard
¼ tsp. M.S.G.

In plastic collander in 2 qt. glass casserole, combine onion, green pepper, and crumbled ground beef. Microwave (high) 6 minutes, stirring every 2 minutes. Pour off drippings. Transfer to glass. Add tomato sauce, tomatoes, beans, salt, chili powder, pepper, mustard, and M.S.G. Microwave (high), covered, 10-12 minutes, stirring halfway through cooking. Rest, covered, 5 minutes. Serves 4-6.

STUFFED TOMATO CUPS — *If you have a garden, try this.*

4 large ripe firm tomatoes
   Dried basil leaves, crushed
½ lb. lean ground beef
¼ cup finely chopped onion
⅔ cup herb-seasoned croutons
½ tsp. salt
¼ tsp. Worcestershire sauce
   Parmesan cheese

Top tomatoes, scoop out pulp. Chop tops and pulp; drain. Flute edges of tomato; drain. Season inside with salt and dried basil. Microwave (high) ground beef and onion in plastic collander in 1 qt. glass dish 3-4 minutes, stirring once. Drain fat. Stir in tomato pulp, croutons, salt and Worcestershire sauce. Stuff tomatoes with mixture. In 9-inch glass dish microwave (high), covered, 8-10 minutes, rotating ¼ turn halfway through cooking. Sprinkle 1 tsp. grated Parmesan cheese on each tomato. Rest, covered, 5 minutes before serving. Serves 4.

● *Good for brunch or light dinner.*

Notes: _____

UPSIDE-DOWN PIZZA — *Easy for children to make.*

1 lb. ground beef
1 small chopped onion
½ cup finely chopped celery
¼ cup chopped green pepper,
   optl.
1 (10½ oz) can tomato soup or
   sauce
½ tsp. salt
1½ cups biscuit mix
⅓ cup milk
½ cup grated Cheddar cheese

In plastic collander in 10-inch round glass dish crumble ground beef, onion, celery, and green pepper. Microwave (high) 6-8 minutes, stirring once or twice. Pour off drippings; blend with soup and salt. In small mixing bowl combine biscuit mix and milk. Roll into 10-inch circle on floured board. Place dough on top of beef mix. Microwave (high), covered, 8-10 minutes, rotating dish ¼ turn halfway through cooking. Rest, covered, 5 minutes. Invert casserole onto serving dish. Sprinkle with cheese. Serves 3-4.

● *Omit ground beef and substitute sliced pepperoni or ground sausage in recipe.*

SPANISH STYLE RICE
A cooking school favorite, this is a little different version, and it's yummy! My daughter fixes this often!

3 cups cooked rice	½-1 tsp. garlic salt
1 lb. lean ground beef	½ tsp. cumin
1 Tbsp. butter	1-2 Tbsp. chili powder
1½ cup chopped celery	½ tsp. oregano
1 cup chopped green pepper	¾ cup sour cream
1 cup chopped onion	2-3 wedged tomatoes

Cook rice (p. 51). Crumble ground beef in collander in 2 qt. glass casserole. Microwave (high) 5-6 minutes, stirring twice. Drain fat. Stir in butter, celery, green pepper, and onion. Microwave (high) 6-8 minutes, stirring every 2 minutes. Blend garlic salt, cumin, chili powder and oregano into sour cream. Add with rice to beef. Place tomato wedges on top. Microwave (high), covered, 3 minutes; stir. Microwave (high), uncovered, 3 minutes. Rest 5 minutes. Serves 6-8.

● *A good way to use leftover rice.*
● *Top casserole with crushed corn chips for variation.*

Notes: _____

_____

TACOS — *A quick, inexpensive main dish.*
Precook 1 lb. ground beef (high) 5-6 minutes/lb. Drain. Sprinkle on tortilla with grated cheese, shredded lettuce, chopped tomato and a dash of hot sauce. Heat on roasting rack (high) ½-1½ minutes (depending on amount of filling) rotating dish ¼ turn halfway through cooking.

● *Substitute tuna for ground beef.*
● *Ground beef may be frozen pre-cooked to use for snacks.*
● *A rubber band may be used to hold tacos shut.*

● **Crepes** *and* **tortillas** *roll easier when heated in a damp towel 20-30 seconds.*

MEAT LOAF RING

Your family can enjoy this often because it's easy and inexpensive.

1 lb. lean ground beef	¼ tsp. pepper
1 beaten egg	1 tsp. garlic salt (or 1 clove minced garlic)
6 crushed soda crackers or ¼ cup dry bread crumbs	¼ cup chopped green pepper
1 small minced onion	¼ cup chopped celery
1 Tbsp. minced parsley	½ cup tomato juice
¾ tsp. salt	¼ cup catsup

Thoroughly combine all ingredients except catsup. Pack lightly into 9'' glass dish making a well in center. Place empty glass, right side down, in center of dish. Microwave (high) 6 minutes, rotating ¼ turn halfway through cooking. Drizzle catsup over top. Microwave (high) 5 minutes longer, rotating ¼ turn halfway through cooking. Rest 5 minutes. Remove glass; baste off drippings. Serves 5-6.

Maxi-Time: Medium-high (70%) 9-10 minutes in step 1. Medium-high (70%) 7-9 minutes in step 2.

● *May be cooked with temperature probe to 160-170°F.*

● *If desired, sauce for meatloaf can be served in center of ring. If you use loaf pan, rest 5 minutes, after cooking 8 minutes to allow heat transfer. Return to oven and finish cooking time. Test center with meat thermometer to determine doneness.*

● *In classes we combine ingredients in plastic bag and squeeze for easy mixing. Paper towel may be crumbled in center to absorb drippings. Dilute catsup by ½ water if you have no tomato juice on hand.*

Notes: _____

QUICK BEEF PIE — *A pretty ground beef dish.*

1½ lbs. ground beef	1 (1 lb) can drained green beans
1 med. finely chopped onion	¼ tsp. pepper
1 (10½ oz) can tomato soup	1½ cup seasoned mashed potatoes
½ tsp. salt	½ cup shredded Cheddar cheese

In plastic collander in 10-inch glass skillet, crumble beef; add onion. Microwave (high) 6-7 minutes, stirring halfway through cooking. Drain fat. Add soup, salt, green beans and pepper. Microwave (high) 3-4 minutes, stirring halfway through cooking. Press into sides of pan. Drop potatoes in mounds around edge of hot mix. Sprinkle with cheese. Microwave (high), 3-4 minutes, rotating dish ¼ turn halfway through cooking. Rest 5 minutes before serving. Broil if desired. Serves 5-6.

● *A good use for leftover potatoes.*

Notes: _____

BEEFY CABBAGE ROLLS
A delicious cabbage roll recipe from a student.

10 cabbage leaves	½ tsp. salt
1 lb. lean ground beef	¼ tsp. dry dill weed
2 beaten eggs	¼ tsp. pepper
½ cup milk	1 (10 oz) can tomato soup
1 cup cooked rice	¼ cup catsup
	⅓ cup finely chopped onion

Microwave (high), covered, cabbage leaves 2-3 minutes until slightly limp. Drain. In collander in 9-inch glass dish, microwave (high) crumbled beef 3-4 minutes, stirring once. Drain fat. Blend with egg, milk, cooked rice, salt, dill weed and pepper. Place ½ cup mixture in center of each cabbage leaf; fold sides in; roll ends, securing with toothpick. Mix soup, catsup, and onion. Pour over cabbage rolls in 12x8-inch dish. Microwave (high), covered, 10-12 minutes, rotating dish ¼ turn and basting rolls every 4 minutes. Drizzle catsup on each roll. Rest, covered, 5 minutes. Serves 4-6.

● *Heavy center vein of cabbage leaves may be cut out if desired.*
● *A good "fix ahead" dish to keep in the freezer for "emergencies."*

Notes: _____

SWEDISH MEATBALLS — *A very good meatball recipe.*

½ cup milk	¾ tsp. salt
½ cup dry seasoned bread crumbs	¼ tsp. pepper
	1 Tbsp. Kitchen Bouquet
1 lb. lean ground beef	½ cup chopped onion
1 beaten egg	1 Tbsp. dried chives

Pour milk over crumbs, soak 15 minutes. Blend ground beef, egg, salt, pepper, Kitchen Bouquet, onion, and crumb mixture. Shape into 1" meatballs; arrange on roasting rack in 12x8-inch dish. Microwave (high) 8-10 minutes, rotating dish ¼ turn halfway through cooking. (Rearrange meatballs if cooking unevenly.) Rest, covered, 5 minutes; make gravy or roux (p.100). (We love this cooked in roux.) Pour gravy over meatballs; top with dried chives. Serves 4-6.

● *If you prefer larger meatballs, shape larger and arrange evenly on dish. Maximum cooking time may be needed.*
● *Substitute leftover cooked rice for bread crumbs if desired.*

Notes: _____

GROUND BEEF MEDLEY — An inexpensive ground beef meal!

1 lb. ground beef
1 medium finely chopped onion
1 small finely-chopped green pepper
1 cup uncooked elbow macaroni
1 cup tomato juice
1 (1 lb) can whole corn, drained
1 cup water
½ cup catsup or tomato paste
½ tsp. chili powder
½ tsp. salt
¼ tsp. pepper
½ envelope onion soup mix

In collander in 3 qt. glass casserole, microwave (high) ground beef, onion and green pepper 4-6 minutes, stirring twice. Pour off drippings. Blend with macaroni, tomato juice, corn, water, catsup, chili powder, salt and pepper. Microwave (high) covered, 8-10 minutes, stirring halfway through cooking. Sprinkle top with soup mix. Microwave (high), covered, 6-8 minutes. Rest, covered, 5-10 minutes. Serves 4-6.

● *Add vegetables as desired to this recipe.*

POTATO-BEEF GOULASH — *An easy meal in one dish.*

1 lb. lean ground beef
¼ cup minced onion
1 (10½ oz) can mushroom soup
2 med. thinly-sliced potatoes
1 (8 oz) can whole corn w/liquid
2 tsp. Worcestershire sauce
½ tsp. salt
¼ tsp. pepper

In 2 qt. glass casserole, blend all ingredients well. Microwave (high), covered, 15-18 minutes, stirring every 5 minutes. Rest, covered, 5-10 minutes. Serves 3-4.

Notes: _____

BEEF TIMBALES — *A nice dish in individual servings.*

1 lb. lean ground beef
½ cup cream or milk
1 beaten egg
½ cup quick-cooking oatmeal
2 Tbsp. minced green pepper
2 Tbsp. minced celery
½ tsp. salt
Dash pepper
2 tsp. prepared horseradish
1 tsp. prepared mustard
⅓ cup chili sauce

Combine beef, milk, egg, oatmeal, green pepper, celery, salt, pepper and horseradish. Blend; divide equally into 6, 6-oz. glass custard cups. Press a "thumbprint" in center of each. Mix mustard with chili sauce; spoon into cups. Arrange dishes in a circle. Microwave (high) 8-10 minutes, rotating ¼ turn halfway through cooking time. Rest 3-4 minutes. Serve inverted on cooked rice or noodles. Serves 4-5.

● *For ease in turning, place dishes on round dish or rack and turn dish.*
● *Make small meat loaves using this same technique.*

Notes: _____

QUICK CHOW MEIN — *A quick version that's very easy.*

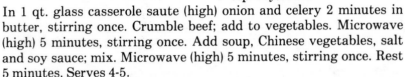

½ cup chopped onion	1 (10 oz) can mushroom soup
½ cup diagonally sliced celery	1 (12 oz) can mixed Chinese vegetables
1 Tbsp. butter	½ tsp. salt
1 lb. lean ground beef	1 tsp. soy sauce

In 1 qt. glass casserole saute (high) onion and celery 2 minutes in butter, stirring once. Crumble beef; add to vegetables. Microwave (high) 5 minutes, stirring once. Add soup, Chinese vegetables, salt and soy sauce; mix. Microwave (high) 5 minutes, stirring once. Rest 5 minutes. Serves 4-5.

● *Serve over chow mein noodles, rice or fried rice.*

Notes: _____

● *Cooked rice makes a perfect base for many ground beef recipes. To save last minute preparation, pre-cook a large amount of rice and store in 1 cup portions in freezer until needed.*

Browning Dish

Browning dishes are available for most ovens. Consult your dealer for information. Use to sear, grill, fry, or "stir-fry" foods needing intense heat on the surface. 6-8 minutes (high) is maximum preheat time. A little butter will enhance browning. Do not use a spray coating. Flatten foods with a spatula for better surface contact. Side 1 gives greater browning. Do **not** use this dish in your conventional range. **Handle hot dish carefully!** (Use hot pads.) Set hot dish **only** on heatproof surfaces! Use as a casserole in microwave without preheating if desired. Clean with a paste of baking soda. Use high power for preheating and cooking.

Notes: _____

_____

ORIENTAL STIR-FRIED STEAK — *A good company dish, too!*

1 lb. sirloin steak, cut diagonally in thin strips	1 Tbsp. teriyaki sauce or marinade
½ tsp. sugar	¼ cup sliced onions w/tops
¼ cup dry sherry	1 cup fresh sliced mushrooms
2 Tbsp. soy sauce	1 (8½ oz) can drained bamboo shoots

Combine steak, sugar, sherry, soy sauce and teriyaki. Marinate in refrigerator 1 hour, stirring occasionally. Saving marinade, drain meat on paper towel. Heat browning dish 6 minutes (high). Place meat on hot dish and top with onions, mushrooms, and bamboo shoots. Microwave (high) 4 minutes, stirring every minute. Add marinade mixture. Microwave (high) 1 minute more or until desired doneness. Serve hot on rice. Serves 4.

Notes: _____

GRILLED STEAK — *Good for 1-2 servings.*

Heat browning dish 5-6 minutes (high). Cooking time varies depending on size and thickness of steak. Room temperature meat cooks more evenly. Cooking time for 1 steak, 6-8 oz., ½"-¾" thick is:

Rare	1 min. 1st side + 1 min. 2nd side	High Power
Med.	1½ min. 1st side + 1 min. 2nd side	High Power
Well	2 min. 1st side + 1 min. 2nd side	High Power

To cook more than one steak at a time, add additional 30 seconds per steak, per side. If cooking more than browning dish will accommodate at one time, reheat browner 1-1½ minutes between each use. Wipe excess fat from surface with paper towel.

To cook **potato with steak**: cut potato in half lengthwise; butter cut side. Place on grill cut side down before preheating (high) 6-8 minutes. Turn potatoes over; add steak (high) 1½-2 minutes. Turn steak over. Cook 1-3 minutes to desired doneness. Serves 1-2.

- *DO NOT COVER hot browning dish. A paper towel or napkin may get too hot. Smoking and spattering will occur. A lid forms moist heat and will not give good browning. Lids with browning dishes are for use as a casserole without preheating.*

Notes: _____

- **Do not use browning dish on the surface or oven of your range!**

Lamb

After acquiring a taste for lamb, it will become a treat in the weekly menu. It is a tender meat with a delightful flavor when properly cooked. Overcooking increases flavor, often produces an offensive odor, and will dry and dehydrate the meat, making it unpalatable. Generally most lamb is cooked well done. Dry surfaces with paper towel to prevent steaming. Allow 8-9 minutes/lb. cooking time (high), or 15-16 minutes/lb. on medium (50%). Temperature will be 165-170°F. Lamb may be substituted in most pork recipes.

ROAST LEG OF LAMB — *A very simple roast!*

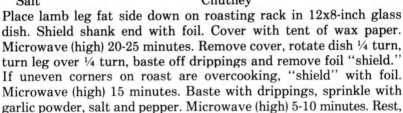

5 lb. leg of lamb	Pepper
Garlic Powder	Peach or pear halves
Salt	Chutney

Place lamb leg fat side down on roasting rack in 12x8-inch glass dish. Shield shank end with foil. Cover with tent of wax paper. Microwave (high) 20-25 minutes. Remove cover, rotate dish ¼ turn, turn leg over ¼ turn, baste off drippings and remove foil "shield." If uneven corners on roast are overcooking, "shield" with foil. Microwave (high) 15 minutes. Baste with drippings, sprinkle with garlic powder, salt and pepper. Microwave (high) 5-10 minutes. Rest, covered with foil, 15 minutes. Serve with Peach Boats. Serves 6-8.

- *Roasting lamb is similar to roasting beef or pork. Leftover lamb is good served either hot or cold. When served the first time,* **it must be hot!** *Reheat in microwave after slicing if necessary.*
- *PEACH BOATS: Drain 1 lb., 13 oz., can peach halves. In 9-inch glass baking dish arrange peach halves up. Fill each half with 1 Tbsp. chutney. Microwave (high) 5 minutes, rotating ¼ turn halfway through cooking. Arrange with lamb on serving platter. PEAR BOATS: Heat pears 3 minutes (high). Add mint jelly. Serve.*

Notes: _____

_____

- *Leftover cooked lamb may be added to casseroles. (See Shepherd's Pie). It is also good served with Barbecue Sauce or Lamb Curry.*
- *You may prefer browning cubes on the range or in browning dish.*
- *For* **LAMB STEW** *brown cubes (high). Combine with ingredients. Microwave medium-low (30%), covered, for 1½ hours.*
- *Mint and currant jelly are often served as accompaniments with lamb. When heated, jelly turns to liquid which is ideal for basting.*

CHUTNIED LAMB CHOPS—*Peaches give chops nice fruity taste.*

4 lamb shoulder chops, 1½'' thick	¼ tsp. salt
	¼ tsp. pepper
1 (8 oz) can sliced cling peaches (save ½ cup juice)	½ cup chutney (or apricot preserves)
2 Tbsp. sugar	1 Tbsp. cornstarch
1 Tbsp. lemon juice	2 Tbsp. peach liquid

In 8'' sq. glass dish arrange chops evenly with bone ends in center. Microwave (high), covered, 8-10 minutes, rotating dish ¼ turn halfway through cooking. Remove chops to paper towel. Drain fat. Add chops to dish. Blend ½ cup peach liquid, sugar, lemon juice, salt, pepper and chutney. Arrange peach slices on chops; spoon chutney mixture on each. Microwave (high), covered, 6-8 minutes, rotating dish ¼ turn halfway through cooking. Remove chops; keep covered. Blend cornstarch with peach liquid and lamb juices. Microwave (high) 1½-2 minutes, stirring every 30 seconds until smooth and thick. Spoon on chops. Serves 4.

Maxi-Time: Medium-high (70%), covered, 12-14 minutes; medium-high (70%), covered, 9-10 minutes in step 2.

● *Other fruits or jellies may be substituted for peaches.*

Notes: _____

SHEPHERD'S PIE — *A favorite of the meat and potatoes man.*

1 (10 oz) pkg. frozen carrots	8 fresh sliced mushrooms
1 (10 oz.) pkg. frozen green beans	¼ cup chopped onion
	Salt and pepper to taste
2 Tbsp. salad oil	1½ cups hot mashed potatoes
1 Tbsp. flour	¼ cup melted butter
2 cups cooked, cubed lamb	Parsley, chives, paprika
1 (10 oz) can mushroom soup	

Precook frozen vegetables (p.67,68). Heat salad oil in hot browning dish or conventional range. Dredge lamb in flour; sear in hot dish. In 2 qt. glass casserole, combine lamb, soup, mushrooms, onions, carrots and green beans. Salt and pepper to taste. Blend evenly. Mound mashed potatoes in a ring around edge of dish. Microwave (high), covered, 4-5 minutes. Pour butter over potatoes. Top with parsley or chives and paprika. Microwave (high) 4-6 minutes, uncovered, rotating ¼ turn halfway through cooking. Rest, covered, 5 minutes. Serves 4-6.

● *A great "planned-over" lamb dish. Vary vegetables to suit family taste. Also a good use of leftover mashed potatoes.*
● *If desired, place casserole under hot broiler a few minutes.*

Notes: _____

Pork

Pork is a good choice for microwaving. Since pork needs to be well done, cook 8-10 minutes/lb. (high) or 15-16 minutes/lb. (medium 50%). For a precooked product, such as ham or hot dogs, cook 4-6 minutes/lb. (high). For temperature, cook to 170°F. Quality of cut as well as proper cooking determine tenderness. Select well marbled cuts. Dry surface with paper towel to prevent steaming.

GLAZED FRESH HAM
Select evenly shaped ham. For shank, shield with foil during first half of cooking. Begin cooking fat side down, 8-10 minutes/lb. (high) or 15-16 minutes/lb. (medium 50%) on roasting rack in 12x8-inch dish. Halfway through cooking remove shield, turn fat side up and rotate ¼ turn.

- *If ham has rind attached, 15 minutes before cooking is completed, cut off rind and most of outer fat layer.*
- *Drain juices from bottom of dish. They absorb energy and increase cooking time. Reserve 5 minutes for glazing.*

HONEY-MUSTARD GLAZE — *A favorite of mine.*
½ cup prepared mustard	2 tsp. dark brown sugar
½ cup honey	

Blend ingredients. Baste evenly over ham. Microwave (high) 5-8 minutes. Rest, covered with foil, 15 minutes before slicing.

- *Most jellies — apple, berry, etc. plus a small amount of brown sugar make good glazes.*

Notes: _____

BUTTERMILK GLAZED HAM STEAK — *a la Eggs Benedict.*
½ cup buttermilk	¼ tsp. pepper
1 1-inch thick center slice ham	2 egg yolks
1 tsp. dry mustard	1 cup buttermilk
1 tsp. flour	Paprika

Generously brush buttermilk on both sides of ham slice. Cut in serving pieces. Place on rack in 12x8-inch glass dish. Microwave (high) 7-8 minutes, rotating ¼ turn halfway through cooking. In 2 cup glass measure blend mustard, flour, pepper and egg yolks. Stir in 1 cup buttermilk. Microwave (high) 2-3 minutes, stirring every 30 seconds until mixture thickens. Spoon over ham on serving dish. Sprinkle with paprika. Reheat (high) 1-2 minutes, if needed. Serves 6-8.

- *Serve for dinner, breakfast, brunch or a midnight supper.*

FULLY COOKED HAM

Mini-Time: Place ham on roasting rack in 12x8-inch glass dish. Microwave (high) 5-7 minutes/lb., turning ham over and rotating dish ¼ turn halfway through cooking. Cover ham with tent of wax paper (optl.) Rest, covered, 10 minutes. Serve.

Maxi-Time: Medium (50%) 10-12 minutes/lb.

Temp-Cook: Microwave to 115-120°F. internal temperature.

GLAZED COOKED HAM

2-3 lb. precooked ham	1 (8 oz) can sliced pineapple
	8 maraschino cherries

Cut pineapple in halves. Arrange diagonally on ham to decorate. Place maraschino cherry in the center of each fruit half. Microwave (high) 5-7 minutes per lb., rotating ¼ turn halfway through cooking. Rest, covered, 10 minutes.

● *A wonderful dinner for unexpected guests because ingredients can be kept on hand. It is fast and no work to prepare! Serve hot or cold.*

Notes: _____

HAM SLICES

Arrange ham slices on plastic roasting rack in 12x8x2-inch shallow glass dish. Microwave (high), covered with wax paper, rotating dish ¼ turn halfway through cooking. Edges will begin to sizzle. Avoid overcooking or slices will dry out.

1 slice, 1-1½ min.	High power	3 slices, 3-3½ min.	
2 slices, 2-2½ min.	High power	4 slices, 4-4½ min.	

● *Ham slices should be approximately the same size and shape. If not, place small in center.*

● *Substitute Canadian bacon. Use same timing.*

● *Ham slices may be glazed with fruit preserves or marmalade during last few minutes of cooking, if desired.*

Notes: _____

ONE DISH HAM CASSEROLE

After a recipe testing, we had an abundance of cooked ham. This was a favorite recipe!

8 oz. uncooked noodles	1 (10 oz) pkg. frozen peas
2 cups (about ½ lb.) cubed cooked ham	¾ cup milk
	¾ tsp. dry mustard
1½ cups grated cheddar cheese	2½ cups water
1 (10½ oz) can mushroom soup	

In 3 qt. glass casserole blend noodles, ham, ¾ cup cheese, soup, peas, milk, mustard and water. Microwave (high), covered, 15-20 minutes, rotating ¼ turn halfway through cooking. Sprinkle with remaining cheese. Rest, covered, 5-10 minutes. Serves 5-6.

● *If noodles are pre-cooked, microwave (high) 6-8 minutes, stirring once. Finish as above. For probe, cook to 150°F.*

BARBECUED RIBS — *Dinner in 25 minutes instead of 3 hours!*

2 lbs. meaty spareribs   Water
(country-style O.K.)   Barbecue sauce (p. 100)

In 12x8-inch glass dish, arrange ribs with meat toward outer edge and bone in center. Add ¼ cup water. Microwave (high), covered, 5-7 minutes. Pour off water. Rotate ¼ turn and rearrange. Repeat 2 times, rearranging ribs for even cooking. Baste ribs with barbecue sauce. Microwave (high), uncovered, 4-5 minutes more or until sauce "cooks" on ribs. Rest, uncovered, 5 minutes. Serves 4-5.

● *This method may seem unusual, but it works! Water provides moist heat. To prevent ribs from cooking in too much fat, I drain it off. Ribs are very tasty and tender and fast! Beef ribs may be used.*

Notes: _____

PORK LOIN

An apricot preserve glaze is basted on roast during last half of cooking. Omit for a very tasty plain pork roast. Cook pork well done, 8-9 minutes/lb. (high) or 15-16 minutes/lb. (medium 50%).

1 center-cut pork loin roast   2 Tbsp. apricot preserves
(3-5 lbs.)   ¼ tsp. garlic powder
¼ cup sherry

Tie roast compactly, if needed. Shield. Arrange fat side down on microwave rack in 12x8-inch glass dish. Microwave (high) by weight, rotating dish ¼ turn and turning over ¼ turn halfway through cooking.

In glass measuring cup combine sherry, preserves and garlic powder. Baste roast once or twice during last half of cooking. Cover with tent of foil. Rest 10-15 minutes. Check with meat thermometer (170°F.). Serve with remaining preserves. Serves 6-8.

● **MICRO SHAKE PORK LOIN ROAST —** Moisten roast with water. Sprinkle liberally with natural or flavored Micro Shake. Place fat side down on roasting rack in 12x8-inch glass dish. Microwave (high), covered with wax paper, 5 minutes. Microwave (medium-50%) 11 to 14 minutes per pound, turning roast over and rotating ¼ turn halfway through cooking. Rest, covered, 10-15 minutes.

PORK CHOP CASSEROLE
I've had many letters about how good this is!

4 (½" thick) rib or loin pork chops	½ tsp. salt
1 small thinly sliced onion	1 (10½ oz) can condensed celery soup
3 Tbsp. brown sugar	1 (1 lb) can applesauce

In 10" glass skillet arrange chops in corners. Layer with onion, brown sugar and salt. Top with soup. Microwave (high), covered, 12-14 minutes rotating ¼ turn halfway through cooking, or until pork chops are done. Rest, covered, 10 minutes. In 2 cup glass measure heat applesauce and spoon hot onto casserole prior to serving. Serves 4.

Notes: _____

BREADED PORK CHOPS
Pork Chops
Crumb mix p. 144 (or cornflake crumbs, Shake 'n Bake, etc.)
Coat chops with mix. Arrange on rack in 12x8-inch glass dish. Microwave (high) 8-10 minutes per lb., uncovered, rotating ¼ turn halfway through cooking. Broil 1-2 minutes if desired.
Browning dish may be used to sear chops prior to cooking.
STUFFED PORK CHOPS — *In 10" glass skillet arrange chops evenly. Prepare stuffing (p. 142). Spoon stuffing onto each chop. Top with additonal chops. Sprinkle each chop with brown sugar. Microwave (high) covered, 10 minutes per lb., including stuffing, using method above.*

Notes: _____

PORK CHOP AND RICE BAKE
Clare Acker, Amana Home Economist in Portland gave me this favorite recipe from her cooking schools.

½ cup long grain rice	Salt and Pepper
½ cup water	1 medium sliced onion
Salt and pepper	1 (10½ oz) can golden mushroom soup
4 (1½ lb) pork chops	

In 4 qt. casserole or Country Cooker, arrange rice evenly over bottom. Cover with water. Salt and pepper to taste. Arrange pork chops with meaty portions toward outside edges on rice. Salt and pepper. Arrange sliced onion rings evenly over chops. Spoon mushroom soup over top. Microwave (medium 50%), covered, 45 minutes, rotating ¼ turn halfway through cooking time. Serves 4.
●*If desired add 2 more pork chops and an additional 15 minutes cooking.*

FRANKS AND BEANS — *An easy, favorite one dish meal.*

2 tsp. butter
1 medium sliced onion
¼ cup dark corn syrup
¼ cup dark brown sugar
2 tsp. prepared mustard
1 tsp. Worcestershire sauce

¼ tsp. ground ginger
1 (1 lb) can drained pork and beans
1 (1 lb) can drained kidney beans
1 lb. scored frankfurters

In 10'' glass skillet combine butter and onion. Microwave (high), covered, 2-3 minutes. Add corn syrup, brown sugar, mustard, Worcestershire sauce and ginger. Microwave (high) 1 minute. Add beans and franks. Microwave (high), covered, 5-7 minutes, stirring twice. Serves 4.

● *Without the franks, these are good BAKED BEANS.*

Notes: _____

LAYERED SPAM AND SWEET POTATO CASSEROLE
A can of this and that and dinner's on!

1 (1 lb) can sweet potatoes
1 (8 oz) can crushed pineapple
1 (1 lb) can chunked Spam

¼ cup brown sugar
½ tsp. dry mustard
2 Tbsp. butter

In 1 qt. glass casserole slice half the sweet potatoes. Layer with half pineapple, then half the Spam. Repeat again. Mix brown sugar and mustard. Sprinkle over top. Dot with butter. Microwave (high), covered, 5 minutes, rotating ¼ turn halfway through cooking time. Rest 5 minutes. Serves 6.

● *Leftover ham may be substituted.*

Notes: _____

SAUERKRAUT AND HOT DOGS — *Good for sausage lovers!*

1 (1 lb, 10 oz) can sauerkraut
1 thinly sliced onion
¼ cup brown sugar
1 tsp. caraway seeds

½ cup beer or broth
1 Tbsp. flour
1 lb. (1'' chunks) hot dogs
1 diced baking apple

In 12x8-inch glass dish blend sauerkraut, onion, brown sugar, caraway seeds, beer, flour, hot dogs and apple. Microwave (high), covered, 8-10 minutes, stirring halfway through cooking. Rest, covered, 5 minutes. Serves 6-8.

● *Substitute other favorite sausage for the hot dogs.*

Notes: _____

BACON

Arrange bacon on plastic roasting rack or 1-2 layers of crumpled paper towel in 12x8-inch glass dish. (For several slices, layer paper towel between each layer of bacon.) Cover with paper towel to prevent splattering. Cook to desired crispness as follows:

1 slice, 1-1¼ min.	High power	4 slices, 4-4½ min.
2 slices, 2-2½ min.	High power	6 slices, 5½-6 min.
3 slices, 3-3½ min.	High power	8 slices, 6-7 min.

Rest 2-3 minutes before adding more cooking time to achieve desired crispness.

To separate bacon slices, microwave (high) 30 seconds before pulling off slices.

- *A slotted plastic roasting rack will hold 1 lb. of bacon for cooking. Rearrange halfway through cooking time. When I cook bacon I don't separate slices until halfway through cooking time. They have shrunk and are easier to arrange on rack. I place those near outside edge near center and vice versa. (No need to separate since microwave cooks all food at once.) Baste off drippings halfway. Cook (high) 8-9 minutes per lb.*

- *Cooking time varies a great deal depending on thickness, starting temperature, brand, curing process and degree of doneness desired. Bacon will become crisp during the "carry-over cooking" time.*

- *A paper plate is convenient for 1-2 slices of bacon. There is too much grease for more.*

Notes: _____

SAUSAGE LINKS

    1 lb. precooked sausage links

Arrange sausage on plastic roasting rack in 12x8-inch glass baking dish. Cover with paper towel. Microwave (high) 4-5 minutes. Rearrange. Microwave (high) 2-3 minutes or until heated throughout.

- *For raw sausage links, add 3-4 minutes cooking time. Cook* **patties** *like hamburger. One pound takes 7-8 minutes/lb. (high) or 10-12 minutes/ lb. medium-high (70%).*

Poultry

Poultry cooked in the microwave will be among the most juicy and tender you have ever eaten! Natural browning occurs as the food heats. For foods cooked less than 10-15 minutes, you may want to improve the color with paprika, browning sauce, soy sauce, etc. Dry surface with paper towel to prevent steaming. Because most poultry is unevenly shaped you will need to take special care to arrange on the plate for even cooking or to "shield" uneven corners. Pour off juices and save for use in sauces. (I freeze in ¼-cup cubes to defrost later.)

Chicken parts may be easily precooked to add to recipe. *Cover* to cook evenly. A wax paper tent helps to trap steam and will not prevent natural browning. Cover during the first half of the cooking time. Uncover during the last half for more crispness. Timing is often determined by the age and tenderness of the bird. Be careful not to overcook! Select the **shortest** cooking time and add to it if needed. Giblets may remain in the cavity when roasting a bird. Substitute cooked turkey in most chicken recipes.

ROAST CHICKEN — *This is wonderful!*
A 3 to 5 lb. chicken requires cooking 6-7 min./lb. on high **or** 9-10 min./lb. on medium high (70%). "Shield" protruding parts with foil. Sprinkle with paprika or brush with barbecue sauce during last half of cooking time. Place breast down on rack in 12x8-inch glass dish. Microwave, covered or in cooking bag, for half the cooking. Remove foil. Place breast up, rotate ¼ turn, baste with pan drippings (remove extra drippings). Microwave, covered, for remaining cooking time or to 190°F. Rest, covered, 10 minutes. Broil if desired. Serves 5-6.
- *For stuffing, add 6 minutes per lb. of stuffing.*
- *For a drier roasted chicken, place uncovered on roasting rack during last half of cooking.*

Notes: _____

CORNISH HENS: 1 lb. hen requires cooking 6-7 minutes/lb. (high). Shield, tie legs and wings close to body with string. Brush with Teriyaki sauce. Place breast down on rack in 12x8-inch glass dish. Microwave, covered, half the cooking time. Remove foil, place breast up, rotate ¼ turn, cut string, baste with pan drippings. (Remove extra drippings.) Microwave, uncovered, for remaining cooking time to 175°F. Rest, covered, 10 minutes. Sear under hot broiler if desired. Serves 1 person.
- *For stuffing, add 6 minutes per lb. more cooking time. Seasoned or wild rice is excellent for stuffing.*

Notes: _____

ROAST DUCK: 4-6 lb. duck requires cooking 6-7 minutes/lb. (high). Shield, tie legs and wings close to body with string. Place breast down on rack in 12x8-inch glass dish. Microwave, covered, half the cooking time. Remove foil, place breast up, rotate ¼ turn, cut string, baste with browning sauce. (Remove extra drippings.) Microwave, uncovered, for remaining cooking time or to 180°F. Rest, covered, 15 minutes. Broil if desired. Serves 4-6.

● *For stuffing, allow 6 minutes/lb. extra cooking time.*
● *Fruit stuffings or glazes enhance flavor of duck.*

Notes: _____

ROAST GOOSE: 10-12 lb. goose requires cooking 6-7 min./lb. (high). Use directions for Roast Duck. Watch for overcooking near uneven corners. Shield if needed. For stuffing, add 6 minutes/lb. extra time.

Notes: _____

ROAST TURKEY: Cook on high **or** medium (50%) 11-12 min./lb. Read tips p. 141 before cooking first bird. Review as needed.

8 to 10 lb. turkey requires cooking 7-8 min/lb. (high).
10 to 14 lb. turkey requires cooking 6½-7½ min/lb. (high).

Stuff. Tie legs and wings close to body with string. Shield protruding parts with foil. Place breast down on rack in 12x8-inch glass dish. Figure cooking time.

8-12 lbs. - Rotate ¼ turn and turn over when half cooked.
12-15 lbs. - Divide total cooking time by 4 and cook ¼ time, breast down, covered; ¼ time, right side down, covered; ¼ time, left side down, covered; and last ¼ time, breast up, uncovered. Shield top of breast. (Bird must be rotated ¼ turn with each change in position.) Remove pan drippings each time. (They absorb energy and increase cooking time.) Baste with drippings after every turn. You may also baste with browning sauce, diluted with butter and paprika. Remove foil, cut string and uncover during last phase of cooking. Shield overcooking parts. Meat thermometer should register 165°F. in breast and 170°F. in thigh. Rest, covered, 15-20 minutes. If needed, return to oven for more cooking. Allow 2 servings/lb.

● *Turkey can be cooked in a cooking bag if desired.*
● *To* **combine with conventional cooking,** *allow 5-6 min./lb. and finish conventionally at 350°-375°F. for 30-60 minutes, breast up, until temperature reaches 175°F. Remove from oven. Rest until temperature reaches 185°F. The oven also gives a crisper skin. This method frees microwave for last minute cooking. Be certain to remove wax paper, plastic rack and foil shields.*

To cook **TURKEY BREAST**, *select 4-5 lb. evenly shaped breast. Microwave (high) 7-8 minutes/lb. to 175°F. following directions for turkey.*

POULTRY ROASTING TIPS
The hollow center makes turkey a good microwave shape. It must be turned so all sides are up since more cooking occurs in this area (near source of energy). This isn't as necessary for small birds.

- **Select** *a hen rather than a tom for a more even shape. 10 lbs. is the ideal weight.*
- *Completely* **defrost** *before cooking (p. 18). Rotate during defrosting time. Shield wing tips, legs, and breast bone during defrosting and cooking.*
- *Tie legs and wings close to body to make an even* **shape.** *Cut strings and allow legs to stand away near the end of timing so meat on inside of thigh cooks evenly.*
- **Stuffing** *may be used; add additional 6 minutes/lb. of stuffing to cook. Pack lightly in bird. Instead of metal skewers, tuck a slice of bread into the cavity to hold stuffing. Skewer neck with toothpicks. Allow ¾ cup stuffing/lb. bird.*
- *If possible, use a slotted rack designed for microwaves;* **place on rack** *to keep out of cooking juices. (If using inverted saucer, remove it* **immediately** *after taking food from oven.)*
- **Baste** *with pan drippings.* **Remove** *extra drippings as they accumulate. If not removed, they absorb energy and increase cooking time. Save drippings for gravy (p. 100). (A bulb baster is a good investment for this.)*
- *If you have a* **tray** *in the bottom of your oven with an edge, you may use it for cooking. Most hold 16-20 oz. of liquid. Remove drippings before too full to handle!*
- *Avoid* **salting** *the outside surface. Do not use salted butter or margarine for basting. Salt will dry skin and may cause it to split.*
- *If you plan to cook turkey on a* **serving platter,** *test the dish (p. 9). (Dishes with gold or silver bands cannot be used.)*
- *It is not necessary to remove* **metal band** *holding legs. Be certain metal does not touch sides of oven.*
- *Poultry cooks more evenly and prevents splatters if* **covered** *during part of the cooking. Wax paper is a good cover.*
- **Test for doneness** *with a meat thermometer. Do not use mercury thermometer in microwave. If necessary to cook longer, remove thermometer before returning food to the oven. Microwave safe thermometers are also available.*
- **Rotate** *¼ turn halfway through for even cooking.*
- *Cover with foil after* **removing from microwave** *to trap heat during "carry-over cooking."*

- *If **additional browning** is desired, place under broiler element a few minutes before serving or combine with conventional oven (p. 140). Usually this is not necessary.*
- *The **pop-up indicator** is not a true test of doneness. Usually it will not pop-up during cooking, but during resting.*
- *A **large turkey** is difficult to manage. The ideal size is 10-12 lbs. For a large crowd, it would be more practical to cook two smaller turkeys. For more than 15 lbs. it may be started in the microwave, finished conventionally.*
- **Giblets** *may be left in cavity, simmered in microwave, or on range top. Combine with water to cover, add onion and celery slices and salt for flavor. Bring to boil, reduce to simmer (medium 50%), covered, until tender (about 1 hour). Use broth for stuffing and gravy. (Do the day ahead to free microwave.)*

POULTRY STUFFING — *The best stuffing I've ever eaten!*

1 cup chopped onion	1½-2 tsp. poultry seasoning
1½ cup chopped celery	1½ tsp. ground sage
¾ cup butter	½ tsp. celery salt
1 lb. chopped fresh mushrooms	½ tsp. salt
8 cups dry bread cubes (about	½ tsp. pepper
14 slices cut in ½-inch cubes)	1-1½ cup liquid (from cooking giblets or water)

In 4 cup glass measure add onion, celery and butter. Microwave (high) 4-5 minutes, stirring once. Add mushrooms. Microwave (high) 1½ minutes. Combine with bread, poultry seasoning, sage, celery salt, salt, and pepper. Toss with liquid to moisten. Pack loosely into bird or cook separately, 6 min./lb. Stuffs 10-12 lb. bird.

- *Adjust liquid for dry or moist stuffing.*
- *Bread may be dried in the microwave (p. 40).*
- *Leftover stuffing may be frozen. Use later for Stuffed Pork Chops (p. 136), etc.*

Notes: _____

_____

CHICKEN a la KING — *A "planned-over" recipe!*

¼ cup butter	1 tsp. sugar
½ cup chopped green pepper	½ tsp. salt
½ cup fresh sliced mushrooms	1 tsp. Worcestershire sauce
1 (10 oz) can creamed chicken soup	2 cups cooked, cubed chicken

In 4 cup glass measure combine butter, green pepper and mushrooms. Microwave (high) 2-3 minutes, stirring once. Add soup, sugar, salt and Worcestershire sauce. Microwave (high) 2 minutes. Blend in chicken, microwave (high) 5 minutes, stirring once. Serve on toast or biscuits. Serves 4-6.

● *Add your favorite vegetables (green peas, etc.) to this recipe.*
● *It's easy to cook extra chicken or turkey for* **TURKEY a la KING.** *Combine with cooked noodles for a meal in one dish!*

Notes: _____

_____

FRIED CHICKEN

Everyone has an opinion concerning the quality of good Fried Chicken. Some like lots of thick crust, others no crust; some golden or light, others almost burned; some juicy, others dry. To microwave Fried Chicken, use basically the same technique as with conventional cooking. If you prefer chicken fried or seared on top of the range, then covered or placed in oven to finish cooking, fry or sear on top of the range or browning dish before microwaving. If you enjoy chicken cooked conventionally without pre-browning, the same results are achieved in the microwave. Allow 8-9 minutes/lb. cooking time. Pre-cook to combine in recipes. A crumb coating crisps the skin. Our family likes Fried Chicken coated with cornflake crumbs as follows:

1 (2½-3 lb) fryer chicken, in serving pieces or fryer parts	¼ cup butter
1 cup cornflake crumbs	Paprika

Wash and pat dry chicken. Coat with crumbs. (A plastic or paper bag makes this job easier!) In 1 cup glass measure melt butter (high) 45 seconds. On rack in 12x8-inch glass dish arrange chicken pieces with large ends toward corners and edges and small pieces in the center with giblets tucked underneath. Pour a small amount of melted butter over each piece. Sprinkle with paprika. Microwave (high), covered, 10-12 minutes. Turn chicken over, recoat each piece with butter and paprika. Rotate dish ¼ turn. Microwave (high) 10-12 minutes more. Rest, covered, 5 minutes. Serves 4-6.

● *If you cover chicken, the skin will be slightly soft. For a drier skin, do not cover. (Skin may be removed before adding crumbs.)*
● *For additional browning broil a few minutes.*
● **Another delicious version** *is to combine ¼ cup mayonnaise, 1 envelope onion soup mix, ½ cup Russian salad dressing and 1 cup apricot preserves. Omit rack. Baste chicken pieces. Microwave (high), covered, 15 minutes. Rearrange, baste again, and rotate dish ¼ turn.*
(over)

Microwave (high), uncovered, 10-15 minutes more. Rest, covered, 10-15 minutes.

- For **BARBECUED CHICKEN,** *omit cornflake crumbs in recipe above. Cook as directed, pouring off juices and basting with barbecue sauce (p. 100) during the last 10 minutes of cooking.*

- For juicy **Speedy Barbecued Chicken** *grilled over coals, pre-cook chicken in the microwave 3-4 minutes/lb. (high). Place over hot coals. Baste with Barbecue Sauce (p. 100) and grill until well browned. Turn over and repeat. Your chicken will not be dry using this technique! (Avoid overcooking small pieces.)*

CRUMB MIX — *A homemade version of "Shake 'n Bake."*

2 cups fine bread crumbs	1 tsp. salt
½ cup cornmeal	1 Tbsp. seasoned salt
⅓ cup instant minced onion	¾ tsp. pepper
2 Tbsp. parsley flakes	½ tsp. oregano

Mix thoroughly in plastic or glass jar. Substitute for crumb coating on poultry and fish. Store covered. Makes 3 cups.

Notes: _____

HURRY-UP CHICKEN AND DUMPLINGS — *Good for leftovers!*

2 Tbsp. butter	1½ cups cooked, cubed chicken
1 small thinly sliced onion	1 (10 oz) pkg. frozen peas
½ small chopped green pepper	1 (8 oz) can refrigerator
1 (10½ oz) can mushroom soup	biscuits
½ cup whole milk	Parsley flakes

In 2 qt. glass casserole combine butter, onion and green pepper. Microwave (high) 2-3 minutes. Combine with soup, milk and chicken. Microwave (high), covered, 5-6 minutes, stirring once. Stir in frozen peas. Microwave (high), covered, 5-6 minutes, stirring once. Arrange biscuits evenly in ring around edge of casserole; sprinkle with parsley. Microwave (high), uncovered, 3-4 minutes, rotating dish ¼ turn halfway through cooking. Rest, covered, 5 minutes. (Dumplings should be cooked but soft.) Serves 3-4.

- *Leftover turkey may be substituted for chicken.*

Notes: _____

CHICKEN AND RICE SUPREME — *An easy family meal.*

1¼ cup uncooked long-grain rice
1 small thinly sliced onion
1 (10½ oz) can mushroom soup
1 soup can water
1 large green pepper, ¼" cubes
1 tsp. salt

2-3 lb. fryer chicken (serving pieces or parts)
2 Tbsp. melted butter
Paprika
2 finely chopped green onions

In 3 qt. glass casserole, blend rice, onion, soup, water, green pepper and salt. Arrange chicken with large ends around edges and small in the center over rice. Brush each piece with butter. Sprinkle with paprika and green onions. Microwave (high), covered, 30 to 35 minutes, rotating ¼ turn halfway through cooking. Rest, covered, 10 minutes. Check rice and chicken for doneness. Add a few minutes more if needed. Serves 4-6.

● *A cooking school favorite, also a great emergency meal because most ingredients can be kept on hand.*
● *Substitute other vegetables or add leftovers.*

Notes: _____

_____

CHICKEN CORDON BLEU — *For the Gourmets!*

6 boned chicken breasts w/skin
6 thinly sliced pieces cooked ham
6 thin slices Monterey Jack cheese
2 Tbsp. flour

¼ cup butter
¼ lb. grated Mozzarella cheese
¼ cup milk
8 medium sliced mushrooms
¼ cup dry white wine

Flatten chicken breasts until thin. Place ham and cheese slice on each (cheese tucked inside). Roll and pin edges together with a toothpick. Dust with flour on each side. In a 10-inch glass skillet, melt butter (high) 45 seconds. Coat chicken sides with butter. Arrange large ends toward outside of dish. Microwave (high), covered, 6-8 minutes. Turn chicken over with large sides near edge. Rotate dish ¼ turn. Microwave (high), covered, 8-10 minutes. Rest 10 minutes. Remove chicken from dish; blend in cheese and milk. Microwave (high) 1-1½ minutes, stirring often until boiling. Add mushrooms and wine, blending until smooth. Pour over chicken. Serves 4-6.

Notes: _____

_____

ORIENTAL CHICKEN BREASTS

A yummy dish to serve guests. Prepare in quantity for a crowd.

¼ cup minced celery
½ cup minced onion
1 (8 oz) can minced water chestnuts, well drained
1 lb. lean pork sausage
¼ cup milk

1 cup bread crumbs
1 egg
1 Tbsp. Teriyaki sauce
½ tsp. ground ginger
2-3 drops hot sauce
6-8 boned chicken breasts
Sesame seeds

In collander in 2 qt. glass dish combine celery, onion, water chestnuts and sausage. Microwave (high) 4 minutes, stirring once. Pour off drippings. Blend with milk, bread crumbs, egg, Teriyaki sauce, ginger and hot sauce. Flatten chicken breasts. Divide mixture and spread on chicken. Roll and secure with toothpick. Make Sweetened Butter Sauce (p. 103). Pour over chicken in 12x8-inch glass pan. Sprinkle with sesame seeds. Microwave (high), covered, 25-30 minutes, rotating dish ¼ turn and basting halfway through cooking. Rest, covered, 5 minutes. Serve with rice. Serves 6-8.

Notes: _____

HOT CHICKEN SALAD — *An easy favorite!*

2-3 chicken breasts in bite-size pieces
1 (10½ oz) can creamed chicken soup
1 Tbsp. Worcestershire sauce
2 Tbsp. minced onion
1 cup diced celery

3 diced hard cooked eggs
⅓ cup nuts
½ cup mayonnaise
¾ tsp. salt
¾ tsp. curry powder
1 cup crushed potato chips
Paprika

In 2 qt. glass casserole stir-fry chicken (high) 4 minutes. Blend in remaining ingredients except potato chips and paprika. Microwave (high), covered, 5-7 minutes. Rotate dish ¼ turn; sprinkle with chips and paprika. Microwave (high), uncovered, 5-7 minutes. Rest 5 minutes. Crisp top under broiler if desired. Serve on toast or toasted English muffins. Serves 6-8.

- *Soup is one of the best convenience foods on hand! Make this recipe with any canned, creamed soup.*
- *For additional texture add sliced water chestnuts, bamboo shoots, green pepper, bean sprouts, etc. Substitute cooked turkey for* **HOT TURKEY SALAD.**

Notes: _____

CHICKEN-CHEESE ONE DISH — *Good for budget stretching.*

1 (10 oz) pkg. frozen chopped broccoli, cooked and drained or fresh cooked
1 (10½ oz) can creamed chicken soup
1 egg
1 cup shredded cheddar cheese
2 cups diced cooked chicken
¼ cup cornflake crumbs
¼ cup slivered almonds

In 2 qt. glass casserole combine broccoli, soup, egg, cheese and chicken. Sprinkle with crumbs and almonds. Microwave (high) 10-12 minutes, rotating ¼ turn halfway through cooking. Rest, covered, 5-10 minutes. Serves 5-6.

●*Leftover turkey and other vegetables may be substituted.*

Notes: _____

CHICKEN LIVER STROGANOFF — *A fast variation!*

3 Tbsp. butter
¾ cup chopped onion
1 lb. halved chicken livers
½ lb. fresh sliced mushrooms
¼ tsp. pepper
1 tsp. salt
¼ cup dry white wine
1 cup dairy sour cream
2 Tbsp. chopped parsley

In 10-inch glass skillet microwave (high) butter and onion 3 minutes, stirring once. Add chicken livers. Microwave (high) 2 minutes, stirring once. Blend in mushrooms, pepper and salt. Microwave (high) 4-6 minutes, covered, stirring several times. Blend wine and sour cream. Pour over chicken mixture. Sprinkle with parsley. Heat (high) 1 minute. Serve on cooked rice or noodles. Serves 4-6.

● *If chicken livers are small, pierce with a fork so steam can escape to prevent popping.*
● *Blend sour cream into hot mixture slowly to prevent curdling.*
● *Saute chicken livers on pre-heated browning dish 5-6 minutes, stirring once or twice if desired.*

Notes: _____

MICRO SHAKE ROAST CHICKEN OR TURKEY —

Moisten 3-4 lb. chicken with water. Sprinkle liberally with Chicken Micro Shake. Tie and shield. Place breast down on slotted roasting rack in 12x8-inch glass dish. Microwave (high), covered with wax paper, 7-8 minutes per pound, turning over halfway through cooking time. Rest, covered, 10 minutes.
*Substitute turkey for chicken if desired. Directions are the same.

CHICKEN VEGETABLE STEW — *Delicious with dark meat!*

¼ cup salad oil	2 Tbsp. flour
8 drumsticks or 16 wings, halved	½ tsp. salt
	¼ tsp. pepper
1 medium sliced onion	3 carrots, quartered and sliced in 2-inch pieces
1 cup water	
2 chicken bouillon cubes	3 medium quartered onions
	⅓ cup Burgundy wine or broth

In 12x8-inch glass dish, heat oil (high) 1 minute. Saute chicken until evenly heated (high) 6-8 minutes, stirring once or twice. Use browning dish if desired. Add onion; microwave (high) 1 minute. In 2 cup glass measure boil water and bouillon cubes (high) 2½-3 minutes. Stir in flour, salt and pepper. Combine carrots and onions with chicken. Pour sauce over mixture, coating evenly. Microwave (high), covered, 15-20 minutes, rearranging halfway through cooking. Add wine. Microwave (high) 1-2 minutes. Rest 5 minutes. Serves 4-6.

• *Chicken breasts or a fryer may be substituted; however, the combination is very good with dark meat. If using cooked chicken, make sauce and cook (high) 8-10 minutes.*

Notes: _____

_____

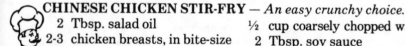

CHINESE CHICKEN STIR-FRY — *An easy crunchy choice.*

2 Tbsp. salad oil	½ cup coarsely chopped walnuts
2-3 chicken breasts, in bite-size pieces	2 Tbsp. soy sauce
	1 Tbsp. lemon juice
2 Tbsp. butter	1 tsp. ground ginger

In 10" glass skillet heat oil (high) 45 seconds. Add chicken. Stir-fry (high) 4 minutes. Add remaining ingredients. Stir-fry (high) 3-4 minutes more. Rest, covered, 5 minutes. Serve on soft or chow mein noodles or rice. Serves 4-5.

• *This basic recipe can be used in many ways for an oriental dinner. Vegetables such as pea pods, celery, green pepper, bamboo shoots, water chestnuts, etc. may be added for variation (p. 87).*

• *Pork or beef may be substituted. As a "planned over dinner" use either leftover meat, poultry, or shrimp.*

Notes: _____

_____

Candy

Candy-making is very easy in the microwave since the energy cooks all surfaces evenly. Stirring blends ingredients. High power is used for speedy results. Several candy recipes require heating basic ingredients and blending while warm. As they cool they solidify to a typical candy consistency. Candy cooking at a hard boil stage will require more careful watching but no worry of burning a pan. Longer cooking is required as syrup becomes very hot. Select a container that can stand intense temperatures and allow mixture extra room for boiling. Candy thermometers cannot be placed in the microwave. Testing must be done by removing candy and using either a cold water test or a thermometer. **Always** remove thermometer before more cooking.

MAGIC VELVET FUDGE
I've been told this is a match for Van Duyn's!

3 (6 oz) pkgs. chocolate chips	2 tsp. vanilla
1⅔ cup sweetened condensed milk (p. 195)	⅓ cup powdered sugar
	Pinch of salt
	½ cup chopped walnuts

In 1½ qt. glass casserole, microwave (high) chips, 2 minutes, rotating ¼ turn halfway through cooking. Stir until smooth. Blend in milk, vanilla, powdered sugar and salt. Add nuts, blending well. Pour into 12x8-inch dish lined with wax paper. Chill until firm. Makes 1½ lb.

- *Substitute 1 (14 oz) can sweetened condensed milk for homemade if desired.*
- *Add miniature marshmallows for a* **ROCKY ROAD CANDY.**
- *Sifted powdered sugar blends more evenly.*
- *Adults seem to prefer this creamy fudge.*

Notes: _____

QUICKIE SUGAR FUDGE — *Your children will love this!*

1 lb. box powdered sugar	Pinch salt
½ cup cocoa	¼ lb. butter
¼ cup milk	1 tsp. vanilla
	½ cup chopped walnuts (optl.)

In 1 qt. glass casserole, add powdered sugar, cocoa, milk, salt and butter. Microwave (high) 2 minutes. Stir evenly. Add vanilla and nuts, blending well. Line a pie plate with wax paper. Pour fudge into plate; chill until firm. Makes 1 lb.

- *Children seem to prefer this fudge which is more "sugary." Add miniature marshmallows if desired.*

WHITE ALMOND BARK — *One step candy.*
1 lb. white or dark chocolate
1 cup whole almonds

In 2 qt. glass dish microwave (high) chocolate 2-3 minutes. Stir in nuts, toasted if desired (p. 196). Spread thinly on wax paper. Chill until firm. Break in pieces. Makes 1 lb.
Maxi-Time: Medium (50%) 4-6 minutes.

● *For* **PEANUT CLUSTERS** *substitute dark chocolate for white and peanuts for almonds. Cook as above. Drop by spoonfuls on wax paper. Chill. Makes 5 dozen. (Add raisins if desired.)*

PEANUT BRITTLE
Pat Harms, Overland Park, Ks., made this every day at lunch in December for co-workers. She says the recipe can't be beat!

1 cup sugar	1 cup roasted, salted peanuts*
½ cup light corn syrup	1 tsp. vanilla
1 tsp. butter	¾ tsp. baking soda

In 2 qt. glass batter bowl, blend sugar and syrup. Microwave (high) 6-8 minutes or until syrup turns a light brown color. Stir in butter, peanuts and vanilla, mixing well. Microwave (high) 1-1½ minutes. Place bowl on a cloth hot pad as it will be very hot! Gently stir in baking soda until light and foamy. Pour onto buttered cookie sheet. Working quickly, cool partially by lifting edges with spatula so mixture won't stick. When firm but still warm, turn over. Pull mixture thin. When cool, break into small pieces. Makes 1 lb.

●*If raw peanuts are used, add to sugar syrup mixture with ⅛ tsp. salt before cooking. Peanuts will brown in syrup. If salted redskin Spanish peanuts are used, there is more color contrast in the finished brittle.*

Notes: _____

_____

TAFFY — *Invite friends for a pull!*

2 cups sugar	¼ cup water
¼ cup vinegar	1 tsp. vanilla
	Food coloring (optl.)

In 2 qt. glass dish combine sugar, vinegar and water. Microwave (high) 8-10 minutes, stirring after 6 minutes. Measure temperature at 280°F. (soft crack). Add vanilla. Divide equally on 3 well-buttered glass plates. Cool until warm. Grease hands. Pull, working in food coloring until taffy dulls (it will be too stiff to pull). Twist into rope. Cool. Pound with knife into small pieces. Makes 1 lb.

● *If mixture is too cool to pull as desired, reheat 1-2 minutes to re-soften.*

NEVER-FAIL DIVINITY

Vivian Freeman, a candy expert in Portland, Ore., says this is her favorite! Use an electric mixer or you'll really have a sore arm! It's delicious.

3 egg whites	3 Tbsp. light corn syrup
2 cups white sugar	Food coloring (optl.)
½ cup water	1 cup chopped walnuts or pecans

With mixer beat egg whites until stiff; set aside. In 4-cup glass measure combine sugar, water and corn syrup. Microwave (high) 7-9 minutes to 236°F. (soft ball), stirring once or twice. Remove ⅓ cup of this syrup; add slowly to egg whites, beating continuously at medium speed.

Continue cooking remaining syrup (high) 3-5 minutes to 264°F. (soft crack), stirring once or twice. Slowly add to egg whites, beating at medium speed. When all syrup is added, continue beating 12-15 minutes, until it turns dull. Remove beaters, fold in food coloring (optl.) and nuts. Spoon onto wax paper. When set, store in covered container. Makes about 60 drops.

Notes: _____

TOFFEE — *Easy candy to make with very little attention.*

1 cup butter	2 Tbsp. water
1⅓ cups sugar	1½ tsp. vanilla
1 Tbsp. light corn syrup	½ cup chocolate chips
	½ cup finely chopped walnuts

In 2 qt. glass casserole combine butter, sugar, corn syrup and water. Microwave (high) 10-12 minutes, stirring once or twice to 300°F. (hard crack). Blend with vanilla. Pour into 12x8- or 13x9-inch pan. Sprinkle with chocolate chips. After 2 minutes spread evenly. Sprinkle with nuts, pressing into chocolate. Chill until cool. Break into uneven pieces to serve. Makes about 1 lb.

Notes: _____

Magic: Soften uncovered sundae toppings 15-30 seconds.

CARAMEL APPLES — *Good fruit and candy combo.*

14 oz. bag caramels	5 medium apples, washed and
2 Tbsp. hot water	dried
	5 wooden sticks

In 2 qt. deep glass bowl add caramels and water. Microwave (high) 2½-3½ minutes until caramels melt, stirring occasionally. Meanwhile, insert sticks into stems of apples. Dip each apple into hot mixture, turning to coat. Place on buttered wax paper to cool. Reheat mixture if it becomes too stiff. Makes 5 caramel apples.

● *For leftover caramel, reheat a minute and pour onto buttered wax paper. Place a whole pecan every inch. Divide into squares by scoring with a knife before cool. You have instant* **CARAMEL CHEWS***!*

Notes: _____

CHOCOLATE BITES

This cooking school favorite came from Sally Clay in St. Louis, Mo.

1 (6 oz) pkg. chocolate chips	2 cups chopped walnuts
1⅔ cup homemade condensed	Dash salt
milk (p. 195)	

In 1½ qt. glass casserole microwave (high) chocolate chips 2 minutes. Blend with milk, walnuts and salt. Spoon onto wax paper to harden. Makes 36.

● *1 (14 oz) can sweetened condensed milk may be used.*
● *Substitute nuts of your choosing.*

Notes: _____

QUICKIE PEANUT BUTTER BITS — *Almost too easy.*

1 (12 oz) pkg. butterscotch bits	5 heaping cups cornflakes
½ cup chunky peanut butter	

Place butterscotch bits and peanut butter in large, deep glass mixing bowl. Microwave (high) 2½-3 minutes, stirring once. Blend until smooth. Pour cornflakes into bowl, blending lightly but thoroughly. Drop by teaspoons on wax paper. Cool. Makes 5 dozen.

● *Substitute 12 oz. chocolate morsels for* **QUICKIE CHOCOLATE BITS.**

Notes: _____

PRALINES

A truly southern specialty! We always look forward to Christmas and a gift from Lorraine Flora. She shared this recipe this year, too!

¾ cup buttermilk	¼ tsp. salt
2 cups sugar	2 Tbsp. butter
2 cups pecans, halved	1 tsp. baking soda

In 4 qt. glass casserole blend buttermilk, sugar, pecans, salt and butter. Microwave (high) 12-14 minutes, stirring every 4 minutes. Add baking soda, stirring to foam. Microwave (high) 1-2 minutes to darken mixture. Whip with wooden spoon until mixture turns dull (1 minute). Spoon onto wax paper to harden. Makes 5 dozen.

● *Yum! You can't wait to try one!*

Notes: _____

GELATIN FINGER SNACKS

An easy treat for your kids in any flavor. Not a candy but a good snack.

1 cup boiling water	2 envelopes Knox ®
2 (3 oz) pkgs. flavored gelatin	unflavored gelatin

In 1-cup glass measure microwave (high) water 2½-3 minutes until boiling. In large bowl combine water, flavored gelatin, unflavored gelatin and 1 cup cold water. Stir until completely dissolved. Pour into buttered 12x8-inch dish. Chill until firm. Cut in 1-inch squares to serve. Makes about 50.

● *Good to have on hand for the neighbor's kids, too!*

Notes: _____

_____

Cakes

Microwave baked cakes are moist and tender if not overcooked. They do not develop browning during cooking, but when covered with a topping, sauce, icing or fruit no one knows! Line cake dishes with paper towel or wax paper for easy removal (unless served in baking dish). I don't recommend greasing and sugaring dish because both foods heat quickly instead of passing energy directly into batter. After resting 10 minutes, loosen edges with a knife for easy removal when inverted. Fill cake pans no more than ½ full because of expansion that occurs. Cakes will have more volume. Make cupcakes with remaining batter. Allow cake batter to rest 10 minutes after preparing so leavening can "work" and top will be more even. For cakes with large amounts of liquid, reduce liquid by ¼. If your cooking pattern gives you difficulties cooking the center of food, invert another glass baking dish on the shelf and bake in raised position, or place drinking glass in center. Cakes may need rotating more than once during cooking. Opening the door will not cause cake to fall! It is very convenient to dovetail cake-making with other kitchen activities (such as clearing a table, etc.) because they demand some attention. Cool cakes on flat surfaces or leave in oven after baking to help cook the bottom. The cake is lighter so refrigerate to frost easier.

Cakes cook best in round dishes. If using square, "shield" corners. Ring or "donut" dishes are even better. A glass may be placed in center of round dish or bowl. (3 qt. large or mixer bowl with glass in center is perfect for 2 layers.) Medium and high combinations make the cake more even on top. Begin on medium (50%). Raise to high during the last minutes of cooking. If your oven has no "hot spot," you can cook on high with good results. With a hot spot, combining energy is best. Bundt-type cakes are preferred on high since there is more volume. I always make 2-layer cakes in this pan. A mixer isn't necessary — just blend ingredients well. Adding ¼ cup oil to a 1-layer cake mix (⅓ cup—2 layer) cooks it more evenly. 2 Tbsp. sugar + 1 tsp. vanilla may be used as a topping in the bottom of cake pans. It is not necessary to sift flour.

I've heard of more failures with cakes than other microwave foods (except maybe meat). Both failures are caused by overcooking! Rotating is also important! Follow directions carefully! Cakes are easy — not difficult!

MAGIC: *An easy snack is to prepare a cake mix. Store in tightly-covered pitcher in refrigerator. Pour batter as desired to make cupcakes. Batter will keep one month.*

COCONUT TOPPED OATMEAL CAKE — *A cooking favorite!*

1¼ cup water	2 beaten eggs
1 cup quick cooking oats	1 tsp. vanilla
½ cup butter	1⅓ cup flour
1 cup brown sugar	1 tsp. baking soda
1 cup granulated sugar	1 tsp. cinnamon
	½ tsp. salt

In 4-cup glass measure, boil water (high) 2½-3 minutes. Add oats. Rest 15 minutes. Cream butter and sugars until fluffy. Stir in oat mixture. Blend in remaining ingredients. Pour batter into 12x8-inch glass dish. Microwave (high) 10-12 minutes, rotating ¼ turn halfway through cooking. Meanwhile make topping.

Maxi-Time: Medium (50%) 10 minutes in step 1. Rotate ¼ turn. High 5-7 minutes.

COCONUT TOPPING

½ cup brown sugar	¼ cup butter
⅓ cup milk	½ cup chopped nuts
1 cup flaked coconut	

In 4-cup glass measure, combine ingredients. Microwave (high) 2-3 minutes, stirring halfway through cooking. Spread on cake.

Notes: _____

CAKE MIXES: Prepare mix as directed on package. If directions include a large amount of water in addition to eggs, you may reduce the water by ¼. Leave it for high altitudes. If no oil in batter add ⅓ cup. Line two 8" glass dishes with paper towel or wax paper. Pour batter in dish, filling **no more** than ½ full. Plastic microwave pans allow more volume. Rest batter 10 minutes. Cook 1 layer at a time (high) 5-6 minutes/layer (**Maxi-Time:** medium (50%) 5-7 minutes. High 2-3 minutes), rotating dish ¼ turn, once or twice. Test with a toothpick. Cool 5-10 minutes before removing from pan. *Review introduction for more information.

- *To make* **1 large (12x8-inch)** *cake, follow directions above. Pour batter into glass dish. Microwave (high) 9-11 minutes, (***Maxi-Time:** *medium (50%) 8 minutes. High 4-6 minutes), rotating once or twice.*
  - *Rectangle butter dish lid may be placed in center for even cooking.*
- *Square dishes hold more batter than round and will require 2-3 more minutes/pan.*
- *Use 6 cup ring mold for 1 layer cake for good results. 2 layer batter may be prepared in 12 cup plastic bundt pan.*
- *Cake mixes with pudding added are excellent.*
- *Use extra batter for small or cupcakes.*

CUPCAKES: Prepare cake batter. Place baking papers in 6 cup plastic muffin pan, glass custard cups or drinking cups. Fill half full with batter. Arrange cupcakes in a circle. Cook as follows, rotating ¼ turn halfway through cooking.

Amount	High	Medium (50%)
1 cupcake	- 20-30 seconds	40-60 seconds
2 cupcakes	- ¾-1¼ minutes	1-1¾ minutes
4 cupcakes	- 1½-2 minutes	3-4 · minutes

- *Place cupcakes on a plate to turn easier. (Not necessary for muffin pan.)*

MAGIC: *Ice cream cones make good cupcakes for little and big kids!*

Notes: _____

BUNDT CAKE — *A 12-cup bundt pan holds batter for 2-layer cake.*
1 (18¼ oz.) Bundt cake mix

Follow package directions reducing water by ¼ cup. Pour into ungreased bundt pan. Rest 10 minutes. Microwave (high) 8-10 minutes, rotating ¼ turn every 4 minutes. Test for doneness. (Cake should be pulling away from sides of pan.) Rest 10 minutes. Loosen in center and around edges with a knife. Invert on serving dish. Cool before frosting. Serves 10-12.

- *Any 2-layer cake batter may be cooked in Bundt pan. I prefer ¼-⅓ cup of oil added to the batter (if not in recipe) for more even cooking. A spirit (wine or sherry) may be substituted for water.*

- *For* **PUDDING BUNDT CAKES** *add 1 (18.3 oz) cake mix, 1 (3 oz) pkg.* **instant** *pudding mix, or flavored gelatin, ½ cup oil, ¾ cup water and 4 eggs. Follow directions above.*

- *For a* **PUMPKIN SPICE CAKE,** *substitute 1 (10½ oz) can tomato soup for liquid in spice cake mix. Bake in Bundt pan. Frost with Cream Cheese Frosting (p. 162).*

Notes: _____

SNACKIN' CAKE MIXES — In 8-inch round glass baking dish prepare batter as directed on package. Microwave (high) 8-10 minutes, rotating dish ¼ turn halfway through cooking. Test with a toothpick. (6 cup ring mold is excellent dish.)

Notes: _____

MAGIC: *Leftover toppings and icings can be refrigerated. Make them "spreadable" by reheating a few seconds.*

JEAN'S YUMMY CAKE

Jean Fortenbery, P. R. Director for Friedman's Microwave Ovens is one of the best, most creative cooks I've ever met. She suggested ingredients for this excellent, yummy cake.

1 (1 lb, 3 oz) pkg. cake mix	2 eggs
1 (22 oz) can pie filling	½ cup sour cream (optl)

In large mixing bowl blend ingredients. Rest 10 minutes. Spoon into 12-cup plastic bundt pan. Microwave (high) 9-12 minutes, rotating ¼ turn every 4 minutes. Rest 10 minutes. Loosen sides and middle. Invert on serving dish. Drizzle with complementary flavor of frosting. Serves 10-12.

- *Select spice mix with apple filling, chocolate mix with cherry filling, lemon or orange mix with peach filling or 1 (1 lb) can whole cranberry sauce, or gingerbread with brandied mincemeat.*
- *We like to frost with FLAMING RUM SAUCE (p. 102.)*
- *Cake can be cooked, covered, on A-3 automatic sensor setting.*

Notes: _____

LA CARROT CAKE

A nutrition filled goodie! Think of all the vitamin A you are getting with dessert! A real winner! And "no-fail!"

3 eggs	1¼ tsp. baking soda
1½ cups sugar	2½ tsp. cinnamon
1 cup oil	1¼ tsp. cloves
1 tsp. vanilla	2½ cups (4-5 whole) grated carrots
1½ cups flour	¾ cups coarsely chopped walnuts
¾ tsp. salt	

In large mixing bowl combine eggs, sugar, oil and vanilla. Blend in flour, salt, baking soda, cinnamon and cloves. Fold in carrots and nuts. Pour into 12-cup bundt pan. Microwave (high) 12-14 minutes, rotating ¼ turn every 4 minutes. Rest 10 minutes. Loosen sides and center; invert on serving plate. Frost with Cream Cheese Frosting (p. 162).

- *I make this instead of fruitcake for friends during the holidays.*

Notes: _____

FROSTED FUDGE CAKE — *Always a winner.*

1 (6 oz) pkg. chocolate chips	¾ cup sugar
2 Tbsp. water	3 Tbsp. shortening
⅔ cup sweetened condensed milk (p. 195)	⅔ cup milk
	1 egg
1 tsp. vanilla	1 tsp. vanilla
1⅓ cups biscuit mix	½ cup chopped nuts

In 4 cup glass measure melt chocolate (high) 2 minutes. Blend with water, milk and vanilla. Pour into 8-inch round glass dish lined with wax paper. In small bowl combine biscuit mix, sugar, shortening, milk, egg, and vanilla. Pour over chocolate. Microwave (high) 6-8 minutes, rotating ¼ turn halfway through cooking. Cool 5 minutes. Invert on serving dish. Sprinkle with nuts. Serves 6-8.
Maxi-Time: Medium (50%) 6 minutes in step 2, high, 3-5 minutes.

Notes: _____

PINEAPPLE UPSIDE-DOWN CAKE — *Couldn't be easier!*

2 Tbsp. butter	5 maraschino cherries
½ cup brown sugar	1 (9 oz) pkg. yellow cake mix - (one-layer)
1 (8 oz) can sliced or crushed pineapple, undrained	

In 8-inch round glass dish, melt butter (high) 30 seconds. Blend with brown sugar. Pack in bottom of dish. Drain pineapple juice into cup for liquid in cake. Arrange pineapple over sugar mixture; place cherries randomly over pineapple. Prepare mix following package directions, substituting pineapple juice for water. Pour batter over pineapple. Microwave (high) 5-7 minutes, rotating dish ¼ turn halfway through cooking. Rest 5-10 minutes until cake pulls away from sides. Invert on serving dish. Serves 6-8.
Maxi-Time: Medium (50%) 5 minutes. High 2-3 minutes.

● *Substitute 1⅓ cups prepared fruit pie filling in place of pineapple for variety in* **FRUIT FROSTED CAKES**. *Either blend fillings with brown sugar or omit sugar. Microwave (high) 7-9 minutes, rotating ¼ turn halfway through cooking. (2-layers may be prepared and stacked for a gorgeous dessert.) Rest 10 minutes before inverting. Serves 6-8.*

● *A fall favorite is Apple with Spice Cake or Gingerbread with Mincemeat. In February we serve Cherries with Chocolate. Lemon, Peach, and Blueberry are good with yellow cake, any time!*

● *Lightly* **sprinkle fruit Jello over warm cake** *to form colored glaze.*

● *Keep a mixture of blended sugar and cinnamon on hand for toppings.*

SOMETHING SPECIAL CHEESECAKE — *It is special!*

1 9-inch cooked crumb crust	½ cup sugar
2 eggs	1 tsp. vanilla
4 (3 oz) pkgs. soft cream cheese	⅓ cup chocolate chips

Prepare crumb shell (p. 180). Beat eggs, cream cheese, sugar and vanilla with mixer until smooth and creamy; pour into crumb crust. In a small glass dish, melt chocolate (high) 1-1½ minute. Spoon in drops over pie. Swirl with a fork. Microwave (high) 4-5 minutes, rotating ¼ turn every minute. When pie has cooled to room temperature, chill until serving. Serves 8.

Maxi-Time: Medium (50%) 8-10 minutes.

- *This pie is good in any crumb crust, but chocolate is special.*
- *Double recipe for 8-inch round dish.*
- *Add 1-2 (2 oz) squares chocolate, melted, for* **CHOCOLATE CHEESE CAKE.** *For* **PLAIN CHEESECAKE,** *omit chocolate.*

Notes: _____

FRUIT LAYERED CHEESECAKE — *A deluxe dessert!*

1 9-inch crumb crust	1 egg
1 (8 oz) pkg. cream cheese	1 cup sour cream
⅓ cup sugar	3 Tbsp. sugar
½ tsp. lemon or almond flavoring	½ tsp. almond flavoring
	1 (21 oz) can fruit pie filling

Prepare crumb crust (p. 180). In medium glass bowl soften cream cheese (high) 30 seconds. Blend with sugar, flavoring and egg. Pour into cooked pie crust. Microwave (high) 3-4 minutes, rotating ¼ turn halfway through cooking. In same bowl combine sour cream, sugar and almond. Spread evenly over pie. Microwave (high) 2-3 minutes, rotating ¼ turn halfway through cooking. Pour pie filling evenly on top. Chill until serving. Serves 5-6.

- *Cherry, blueberry and peach fillings are favorites.*

Notes: _____

Magic: Refresh stale cake 10-20 seconds per serving.

Think Time — Not Heat!
Think Microwave!

TWO-LAYER PARTY CUPCAKES

A fun cupcake for children from Barbara Pohlman who teaches microwave cooking in Cedar Rapids, Ia.

1 (18 oz) plain chocolate cake mix	⅓ cup sugar
	1 egg
1 (8 oz) pkg. cream cheese	Pinch salt
	1 (6 oz) pkg. chocolate chips

In medium mixing bowl combine cake mix following package directions. In medium glass mixing bowl soften cream cheese (high) ½-1 minute. Blend cheese with sugar, egg and salt. Stir in chocolate chips. In baking papers in 6 cup muffin pan, drop 2 Tbsp. cake batter in each cup; add 2 tsp. cheese mixture on top (this will sink to bottom). Microwave (high) as follows:

1 cupcake - ½-¾ minute	4 cupcakes - 2-2¼ minutes
2 cupcakes - 1-1½ minute	5 cupcakes - 2½-2¾ minutes
3 cupcakes - 1½-1¾ minute	6 cupcakes - 3-3¼ minutes

Cool slightly. Frost with Easy Chocolate Frosting (p. 161). Makes 30 cupcakes.

- *Eat warm for a special treat.*
- *For extra batter store, tightly covered, in refrigerator up to 1 month.*

MICROWAVE FRUITCAKE—*Takes minutes instead of hours!*

¾ cup soft butter	1 tsp. nutmeg
6 Tbsp. dark brown sugar	1 tsp. allspice
3 Tbsp. corn syrup or honey	⅓ cup brandy or rum
6 eggs	1¾ cups each - red and green
¾ cup flour	candied cherries
¾ tsp. salt	6 cups coarsely chopped
¾ tsp. baking powder	walnuts or pecans

In large mixing bowl, cream butter, brown sugar and corn syrup. Add eggs, one at a time, beating continuously. Blend with flour, salt, baking powder, nutmeg and allspice until smooth. Stir in brandy; fold in cherries and nuts. Pour into 12-cup bundt pan. Microwave (high) 10-14 minutes, rotating ¼ turn every 4 minutes. Rest 15-20 minutes before loosening; invert from pan. Glaze if desired. Makes 1 large cake.

Maxi-Time: Medium-high (70%) 15-18 minutes.

- *Mixed fruit may be substituted for part of the cherries.*
- *Fruitcake may be cooked in 1 qt. milk cartons. Cut off top of clean carton to stand in oven. Fill ¾ full. Microwave (high) 8-12 minutes until toothpick in center comes out clean. Cool completely; peel off carton. Store covered.*

Notes: _____

SHORTCAKE — *Nice with fresh berries and ice cream.*

⅓ cup soft butter
¾ cup sugar
1 egg

¾ cup milk
1¼ cups flour
1½ tsp. baking powder
½ tsp. salt

In medium bowl blend butter, sugar, and egg; stir in milk. Combine with flour, baking powder and salt. Pour into 9-inch round glass dish. Microwave (high) 5-6 minutes, rotating ¼ turn halfway through cooking. Rest 10 minutes. Makes 1 layer.

Maxi-Time: Medium (50%) 4-5 minutes, rotate ¼ turn. High 2-4 minutes.

Frosting

POWDERED SUGAR FROSTING

1 (1 lb) box powdered sugar
¼ cup milk

Pinch salt
1 tsp. vanilla
¼ cup butter

In 1½ qt. glass casserole, blend sugar, milk, salt, and vanilla. Add butter. Microwave (high) 1-1½ minutes. Beat frosting until smooth. Frosting for 2 (8-inch) cakes.

● *Add ¼ cup cocoa for* **CHOCOLATE FROSTING.**

Notes: _____

LEMON SAUCE TOPPING — *Serve warm or cold on cake or dessert.*

½ cup sugar
1 Tbsp. cornstarch
1 cup water

2 Tbsp. butter
½ tsp. grated lemon rind
1½ Tbsp. lemon juice
Dash salt

In 4 cup glass measure, combine sugar and cornstarch; stir in water. Microwave (high) 2-2½ minutes, stirring every 30 seconds. Blend in butter, lemon rind, juice and salt. Makes 1½ cups.

● *For* **ORANGE SAUCE**, *substitute orange for the lemon rind and juice.*

Notes: _____

EASY CHOCOLATE FROSTING — *Special on chocolate cake!*

1⅔ cup sweetened condensed milk (p. 195)
1 (6 oz) pkg. chocolate chips

In 2 cup glass measure combine milk and chips. Microwave (high) 1½-2 minutes. Stir until chips melt. Heat 30 seconds more if needed. Spread on cake or cupcakes. Makes 1½ cup.

● *Store leftover frosting in tightly covered jar in refrigerator. Warm slightly in microwave to spread easily.*

CREAM CHEESE FROSTING

For a flat cake, the frosting spreads evenly. For bundt or uneven, heat a minute and drizzle over cake.

4 oz. softened cream cheese	½ lb. powdered sugar
3 Tbsp. softened butter	1 tsp. vanilla

In small bowl soften cream cheese and butter (high) ½-1 minute. Blend in powdered sugar and vanilla until light and fluffy. Makes 1½ cups.

Notes: _____

Cookies

Bar-type cookies are easy to make with good results. Since there is no browning, frost or cover with chocolate chips or spice mixes. When possible, cook in 6-cup plastic ring mold for best results. Cool 5 minutes before inverting. An extra egg may make batter less crumbly. Start on medium and finish on high to avoid overcooking corners. For **12x8 to 13x9-inch dish** - medium (50%) 8-10 minutes + High 4-8 minutes. Toothpick in center should come out clean. **8-9-inch sq. dish** - medium (50%) 6-8 minutes + High 3-5 minutes. Round or ring dishes eliminate overcooked corners. Shield corners of square dish. They may not look done. Cool 10 minutes on flat surface before adding more time.

There is almost no time saved when making quantities of drop cookies. The dough should be dry (almost crumbling). Mix with an electric mixer. Use an inverted 12x8-inch glass dish or a piece of cardboard, covered with wax paper, for a cookie sheet. The cookie will be soft after cooking. Remove from oven, cool on wax paper while cooking another batch. Avoid overcooking! When the appearance is dry it's done. They don't brown. If cookies burn in the middle, they're overcooked. For even shaping, divide dough into equal portions before shaping. Cooking time depends on volume and size for accurate timing. Fat, sugar and liquid must be reduced to convert conventional recipes.

SNICKER DOODLES — *These are delicious!*

½ cup shortening	1 tsp. cream of tartar
¾ cup sugar	½ tsp. soda
1 egg	Pinch salt
1¾ cup flour	2 Tbsp. sugar
	1 Tbsp. cinnamon

Cream shortening and sugar. Add egg. Combine flour, cream of tartar, soda and salt. Add to creamed mixture. Shape dough into 36 1-inch balls. Blend sugar and cinnamon in plastic bag. Shake balls to coat with mixture. Arrange 10 balls on wax paper covered dish spacing cookies in ring 2-inches apart. Microwave (high) 1¾ to 2 minutes, rotating ¼ turn after 1 minute. (Cookies will puff, then flatten out.) Remove on wax paper and cool. Cook remaining cookies using fresh wax paper for each batch. Makes 36.
Maxi-Time: Medium-high (70%) 2-2½ minutes.

Notes: _____

PEANUT BUTTER COOKIES — *A good microwave cookie.*

½ cup shortening	1 lightly beaten egg
½ cup granulated sugar	1½ cup flour
½ cup brown sugar	¼ tsp. soda
½ cup peanut butter	¼ tsp. salt
	1 tsp. vanilla

Cream shortening and sugars; add peanut butter and egg. Blend with dry ingredients and vanilla, mixing well. Shape into 36 balls. Arrange 15 balls on wax paper covered dish spacing cookies in ring 2-inches apart. Flatten with a fork dipped in flour. Microwave (high) 3-4 minutes, rotating ¼ turn halfway through cooking. Remove on wax paper to cool. Cook remaining cookies using fresh wax paper for each batch. Makes 36.
Maxi-Time: Medium-high (70%) 4-5 minutes.

GRAHAM WAFER SQUARES — *easy and delicious!*

4 oz. pkg. almonds, toasted (p. 196)	Graham crackers, as desired
	1 cup butter
	1 cup brown sugar

Toast almonds (p.196). Line 12x8-inch dish with brown paper. Cover with sectioned cracker squares. In 2 cup glass measure microwave (high) butter and sugar 3-4 minutes until boiling, stirring every minute until boiling. Sprinkle nuts on crackers; cover evenly with hot syrup. Microwave (high) 2½-3 minutes, rotating ¼ turn once. Cool. Cut in individual pieces. Makes 24.

● *Annette Lakefish, Portland, Ore. microwave teacher shared this recipe.*

QUICKIE PEANUT COOKIES — *Rainy-day activity for kids!*

1 (14.5 oz) pkg. chocolate chip Snackin' Cake
½ cup crunchy peanut butter

2 Tbsp. water
1 egg

In medium bowl combine Snackin' Cake, peanut butter, water and egg. Drop by teaspoons (1-inch) in ring on wax paper (12 cookies at once). Flatten. Microwave medium (50%) 3½-4½ minutes, rotating ¼ turn halfway through cooking. Cool. Repeat with remaining mixture reducing time 1 minute. Makes 25-30 cookies.

● *Mix recipes often mean a trip to the store, but with kids at home, you'll probably have this cake mix on hand.*

S'MORES — *No campfire needed!*

Milk chocolate candy bar
Graham cracker squares

Marshmallows

Place 2 squares of candy bar and 1 large marshmallow on graham cracker square. Place on napkin. Microwave (high) as follows:

1 S'mores - 15 seconds
2 S'mores - 25 seconds

3 S'mores - 35 seconds
4 S'mores - 45 seconds

Top with cracker. Rest ½-1 minute to melt chocolate.

● *Overcooking scorches and toughens marshmallow.*
● *Spread peanut butter on soda cracker and cook as above for alternate.*
● *An ideal treat for your many envious friends who want to see something microwaved. Also nice for children, grandchildren, grandmothers, and anyone who remembers going to camp!*

Notes: _____

3 LAYER BAR COOKIES — *An easy, beautiful cookie.*

¼ cup butter
1 cup graham cracker crumbs
1 Tbsp. sugar
½ cup finely chopped walnuts

⅔ cup sweetened condensed milk
1 cup flaked coconut
1½ cup semi-sweet chocolate chips

In 8-inch square dish microwave (high) butter 30 seconds. Stir in crumbs and sugar; pat evenly in dish. Microwave (high) 2 minutes. Cool. In small mixing bowl combine nuts, condensed milk and coconut. Layer mixture evenly over crust. Microwave (high) 3-4 minutes, rotating ¼ turn halfway through cooking. Sprinkle chips evenly on top. Microwave (high) 1-2 minutes. Spread melted chocolate to frost. Cool. Makes 16 squares.

Notes: _____

BUTTERSCOTCH BARS — *Treats in 5 minutes!*

½ cup melted butter	¼ tsp. salt
½ cup brown sugar	1 (6 oz) pkg. chocolate chips
1¼ cup flour	½ cup chopped nuts

Cream butter and sugar. Blend with flour and salt. Press evenly into 8-inch dish. Microwave (high) 3½-4½ minutes, rotating ¼ turn halfway through cooking. In 1 cup glass measure melt chips (high) 1 minute. Frost bars. Sprinkle with nuts. Rest until cool. Makes 25.

Notes: _____

PEANUT BUTTER BARS — *A cooking school favorite!*

½ cup soft butter	1⅓ cup flour
½ cup + 2 Tbsp. chunky peanut butter	½ tsp. baking powder
	¼ tsp. salt
1 cup brown sugar	1 (6 oz) pkg. chocolate chips
2 tsp. vanilla	

In medium bowl cream butter and peanut butter. Blend in brown sugar; add vanilla. Combine with flour, baking powder and salt; stir in chips. Pour into 6-cup plastic ring mold. Microwave (high) 4-6 minutes, rotating ¼ turn every 2 minutes. Cool 10 minutes. Invert. Cut into slices or bars. Makes 20.

● *We use "natural" peanut butter with more oil than national brands. 1-2 eggs may be added for brownie-like texture.*

CREAMY FUDGE SQUARES — *Only 4 ingredients!*

1¾ cups graham cracker crumbs	¾ cup coarsely chopped nuts
1 (6 oz) pkg. chocolate chips	1⅓ cup sweetened condensed milk (p. 195)

In medium bowl combine crumbs, chips and nuts. Stir in milk. Pour into 6-cup plastic ring mold. Microwave (high), covered with paper towel, 4-6 minutes, rotating ¼ turn every 2 minutes. Cool 10 minutes. Invert. Cut in squares or slices. Roll in powdered sugar. Makes 25.

● *Embry Savage places crackers in plastic bag and drives over it with her car to make crumbs! (She cautions — no studded tires!)*

Notes: _____

Magic: To **soften** brown sugar, add a few drops of water to box. Microwave (high) 15 seconds.

CHOCOLATE BROWNIES — *For simple snacking!*

⅔ cup shortening	1 cup flour
1 cup sugar	½ tsp. baking powder
2 eggs	½ tsp. salt
2 Tbsp. water	½ cup cocoa
1 tsp. vanilla	½ cup chopped walnuts

Shield corners of 8-inch sq. glass dish. Add shortening. Microwave (high) 1½-2 minutes. Stir in sugar; cool. Blend in eggs, water and vanilla. Add flour, baking powder, salt and cocoa. Add nuts, either blending or sprinkled on top. Microwave (high) 3½-4½ minutes, rotating ¼ turn twice. Cool before cutting. Makes 16.

Maxi-Time: Medium (50%) 7-9 minutes.

- *Frost with chocolate frosting, or add 1 (6 oz) pkg. chocolate chips (optl.) to batter.*
- *For* **BROWNIE MIX,** *follow package directions. Microwave (high) in 8-inch dish 7-9 minutes, rotating twice. Test with toothpick. Makes 12-16.*

DEEP CHOCOLATE BROWNIES

For Nancy Price, a friend who loves very chocolate brownies.

¼ cup butter	½ cup chopped walnuts
½ cup sugar	½ cup chocolate ice cream
3 eggs	syrup
⅔ cup flour	¼ tsp. salt
	1 tsp. vanilla

In medium glass bowl soften butter (high) 30 seconds. Cream with sugar, add eggs. Combine with flour, nuts, chocolate syrup, salt and vanilla. Pour into 9-inch round dish. Microwave (high) 5-7 minutes, rotating dish ¼ turn halfway through cooking. Cool. Makes 6-8 wedges.

Maxi-Time: Medium-high (70%) 7-9 minutes.

Notes: _____

CHOCOLATE CHIP BARS — *A delicious, easy treat!*

½ cup soft butter	1 tsp. baking powder
⅓ cup sugar	1 egg
⅓ cup dark brown sugar	1 tsp. vanilla
2 Tbsp. water	¾ cup finely chopped nuts
1 cup flour	½ cup flaked coconut
	1 (6 oz) pkg. chocolate chips

In medium bowl combine butter, sugars and water. Stir in flour and baking powder; add egg and vanilla. Blend in nuts, coconut and chips. Pour into 6-cup plastic ring mold. Microwave (high) 4-6 minutes, rotating ¼ turn every 2 minutes. Cool 10 minutes. Invert. Cut into slices or cubes. Makes 20.

SHIRLEY'S DROP COOKIES
A delicious recipe shared by Shirley Howell, Park City, Ut.

½ cup butter	Pinch salt
½ cup milk	1 tsp. vanilla
2 cups sugar	½ cup peanut butter
¼ cup cocoa	3 cups quick oatmeal

In large bowl combine butter and milk. Microwave (high) 45 seconds. Blend with sugar, cocoa, and salt. Microwave (high) 4-6 minutes, stirring once or twice until boiling. Add vanilla and peanut butter until well mixed. Blend in oatmeal. Drop by teaspoons onto wax paper. Chill until firm 1-2 hours. Makes 4 dozen.

Notes: _____

PUMPKIN BARS — *Yummy in the fall.*

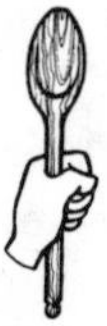

½ cup soft butter	½ tsp. baking soda
1 cup brown sugar	1 tsp. cinnamon
1 egg	1 tsp. pumpkin pie spice
½ cup pumpkin	½ cup raisins
1½ cups flour	¾ cup chopped walnuts

In medium bowl cream butter and sugar; stir in egg and pumpkin. Combine with flour, soda, cinnamon and pie spice. Fold in raisins and nuts. Pour into 12x8-inch glass dish. Microwave (high) 8-10 minutes, rotating ¼ turn halfway through cooking. Rest 10 minutes. Frost with cream cheese icing if desired. Makes 24.

Notes: _____

LEMON SQUARES — *A deluxe, easy cookie*

½ cup butter	1 cup sugar
1 cup flour	3 Tbsp. lemon juice
¼ tsp. salt	¼ tsp. lemon flavoring
¼ cup powdered sugar	2 Tbsp. flour
2 eggs	½ tsp. baking powder

In 1 cup glass measure, melt butter (high) 45 seconds. Stir into flour, salt and powdered sugar in 8-inch square glass dish. Press evenly in dish. Microwave (medium-high 70%) 3-4 minutes, rotating ¼ turn halfway through cooking, until mixture is bubbly on top. Combine remaining ingredients; pour over crust. Microwave (medium-high 70%), 5-7 minutes, rotating ¼ turn once, until lemon becomes fairly firm. Sprinkle with sifted powdered sugar. Cool. Makes 16-20 bars.

Note _____

Puddings

Puddings are the easiest food to microwave! They cook very evenly because energy heats all surfaces. Stirring is necessary to distribute heat to the center of the dish; no scorching because no heat. During the last half of cooking it may be necessary to stir every minute so thickening doesn't settle on the bottom. Glass measuring cups are ideal for cooking or ease when pouring into serving dishes. Small amounts may be cooked in drinking cups (custard). Either high power with water bath or medium (50%) may be used. Use high for stirred puddings.

VANILLA PUDDING — *Simple and quick!*

⅓ cup sugar	¼ tsp. salt
3 Tbsp. cornstarch	2¼ cups milk
	1½ tsp. vanilla

In 4 cup glass measure, mix sugar, cornstarch and salt. Stir in milk. Microwave (high) 5-6 minutes, stirring every minute until mixture boils. Add vanilla. Pour into serving dishes; chill until serving. Serve topped with fruit or whipped cream. Serves 4-6.

●*May be left in dish; chilled and topped with fruit to serve.*
●*An excellent* **VANILLA PUDDING PIE.** *After preparing pudding, pour into 1,9-inch baked pastry or crumb pie shell.*
Notes: _____

FRUITY TAPIOCA

3 medium peeled, cored, sliced apples	¼ tsp. nutmeg
	1 Tbsp. lemon juice
2 Tbsp. butter	⅓ cup quick-cooking tapioca
½ tsp. salt	1 cup light brown sugar
¼ tsp. cinnamon	2¼ cups water

In 2 qt. glass casserole, combine all ingredients. Microwave (high), covered, 8-10 minutes or until apples are crisp-tender, stirring every 2-3 minutes. (Sauce should be boiling.) Rest, uncovered, 10 minutes. Serve warm or cold. Serves 4-6.

●*Substitute other fruits such as 3 cups rhubarb or 3 cups blueberries for apples. Use white sugar.*
Notes: _____

BAKED CUSTARD — *After cooking hundreds — no failures!*

1½ cups milk (or evaporated)	¼ tsp. salt
3 eggs	1 tsp. vanilla
¼ cup sugar	Nutmeg

In a 2 cup glass measure, **scald** milk (high) 3-4 minutes. In 2 qt. glass dish boil 1½ cups water (high) 3 minutes. In 1 qt. glass casserole, beat eggs lightly; add sugar, salt and vanilla. Blend in milk slowly. Place custard mixture in dish with hot water. Sprinkle with nutmeg. Microwave (high) 5-7 minutes, rotating ¼ turn halfway through cooking. (Dish center will "jiggle like Jello" when done.) Rest until cool. Serves 4-6.

Maxi-Time: Medium (50%) 10-12 minutes, rotate every 3 minutes.

- *If hot milk is added to eggs too quickly, eggs will cook and mixture will curdle! Heating milk first reduces cooking time. Avoid overcooking outside edges. Heat transfers to center of dish while cooling. If desired, omit water bath; cover during cooking.*

- *For **INDIVIDUAL CUSTARDS**, divide mixture in 4-5 (6 oz) glass custard or drinking cups. Sprinkle with nutmeg. Place marshmallow in custard cups before filling, if desired. Rearrange during cooking.*

Notes: _____

_____

DARK CARAMEL SAUCE

Mim Leichner served us this delicious dessert.

In 4 cup glass measure, microwave (high) ½ cup sugar and ¼ cup water, 8-10 minutes, stirring once until it darkens and bubbles. Stir; divide into 6 glass custard or drinking cups. Swirl to coat inside. (Mixture hardens as it cools.)

- *For **CUSTARD FLAN**: Pour custard into caramel. Arrange 6 cups in ring on plate. Follow directions above. Invert in champagne glass to serve.*

Notes: _____

_____

PUDDING MIX — *(Not instant)*

Use directions for Pudding Pie (p. 184), omitting pie shell. Pour into serving containers after resting. Serves 4-5.

Notes: _____

_____

OLD-FASHIONED BREAD PUDDING — *Delicious with ice cream.*

¾ cup dark brown sugar
3 slices whole wheat bread
2 Tbsp. butter
½ cup raisins

3 eggs
1¼ cup evaporated milk
¼ tsp. salt
1 tsp. vanilla

In 1 qt. glass casserole, combine brown sugar, bread (buttered and diced in ½-inch cubes), and raisins. In a mixing bowl blend eggs, milk, salt and vanilla. Pour over bread mixture; lightly blend. Microwave (high), covered, 8-10 minutes, rotating dish ¼ turn halfway through cooking. (Edges are firm and center almost *set.*) Brown sugar forms sauce to serve with pudding. Serve warm or cold. Rest 10 minutes, covered. Serves 5-6.

- *A good way to use dry bread. I use whole wheat because it's a favorite (white o.k.) This is a yummy! pudding.*
- *Cover; place in hot water bath; or reduce energy to cook evenly. Milk may also be heated 3-4 minutes to reduce time.*

Notes: _____

_____

QUICK RICE PUDDING — *A quick, easy delicious dessert.*

1 (3½ oz) pkg. vanilla pudding (**not** instant)
2 cups whole or evaporated milk

½ cup quick-cooking rice
½ cup raisins
¼ tsp. cinnamon

In 2 qt. glass dish blend pudding mix, milk and rice. Microwave (high) 6-8 minutes, stirring once or twice until boiling. Add raisins and cinnamon. Cover; rest 5-10 minutes. Stir. Chill. Serves 5-6.

- *Spoon mixture into cups if desired. Delicious with banana pudding mix.*

Notes: _____

_____

Fruit

Fruit softens easily when microwaved with superior flavor and can be used many ways. Cook whole (Baked Apples) or dice and cook longer for a fruit sauce (Applesauce). The delicate shape is retained when combining with other ingredients in Curried Fruit Bake or Spicy Fruit Compote. They are nice accompaniments to the main course. Avoid overcooking! **Heating** only is required, unless cooked fresh. Fresh cooked is best served "crisp-tender." Covering heats more evenly. Defrost frozen fruit easily or combine in recipe while frozen.

APPLESAUCE — *A good healthy dessert!*

4 medium peeled, quartered cooking apples

2 Tbsp. water
¼-½ cup sugar
½ tsp. cinnamon

In 2½ qt. glass casserole, combine apples and water. Microwave (high) covered, 6-8 minutes, until soft but not mushy. Add sugar to taste. If desired, press through colander or whirl in blender. Season with cinnamon. Serves 4-6.

● *For* **RHUBARB SAUCE:** *substitute 2 cups and ingredients above. Follow Applesauce method.*

Notes: _____

BAKED APPLES — *Good variety at breakfast and snacks.*

4 medium baking apples
¼ cup packed brown sugar

2 Tbsp. soft butter
Cinnamon

Core apples; slice skin around the circumference of apple, ½-inch from top. Blend brown sugar and butter. Fill center of each apple; sprinkle with cinnamon. Arrange in ring in 9-inch round glass dish. Microwave (high), covered, 5 minutes, rotating ¼ turn halfway through cooking. Rest, covered, 5 minutes. Test for doneness. Cook 1-2 minutes longer if needed. Serves 4.

● *For* **1 apple**, *use 1 Tbsp. brown sugar and ½ Tbsp. butter; cook 2-2½ minutes. For* **2 apples**, *use 2 Tbsp. brown sugar and 1 Tbsp. butter; cook 3-3½ minutes. Add 1 Tbsp. brown sugar and ½ Tbsp. butter for each extra apple.*

● *If desired, add ½ Tbsp. raisins, chopped nuts, red hots, cranberry sauce, ice cream or mincemeat.*

● *Cooking time may vary with age, variety, and size of apple. For accuracy, weigh and cook 5-6 minutes/lb.*

● *For* **BAKED PEARS**, *substitute in above recipe.*

Notes: _____

BANANA BOATS — *Perfect for kids!*

2 medium bananas	24 miniature marshmallows
	1 (¾ oz) milk chocolate bar

Pull back (but leave attached) upper section of banana peel on inside curve. Slash with knife from end to end; spread open. Fill cavity with 12 marshmallows. Break chocolate bar into squares; place beside marshmallows. Replace peel. Microwave (high) on glass dish 1 minute or until chocolate melts. Makes 2.

- *Substitute chocolate chips for candy bar.*

Notes: _____

_____

EASY FRUIT COBBLER — *Dessert in a jiffy!*

1 (1 lb) can drained fruit	⅓ cup milk
1· cup biscuit mix	1 Tbsp. butter
3 Tbsp. sugar	½ tsp. cinnamon
¼ tsp. almond flavoring	¼ cup chopped nuts

In 8-inch round glass dish spread fruit evenly on bottom. In small mixing bowl blend biscuit mix, 2 Tbsp. sugar, almond and milk; drop evenly over fruit. Dice butter on top. Combine cinnamon, 1 Tbsp. sugar and nuts. Sprinkle on top. Microwave (high) 5-6 minutes, rotating ¼ turn halfway through cooking. Serve warm with whipped or ice cream. Serves 4-5.

- *A little juice may be left with fruit, if desired.*
- *Most fruits (apricots, peaches, cherries, etc.) may be substituted, either fresh or canned.*

Notes: _____

_____

FRUIT IN WINE SAUCE — *Elegant but easy!*

3 Tbsp. butter	¼ cup brown sugar
2 Tbsp. lemon juice	⅓ cup rose wine or cherry
1 (1 lb) can peach halves,	brandy
drained	½ cup cream

In 9-inch glass baking dish melt butter 30-45 seconds; add lemon juice; turn fruit over in juice. Sprinkle with brown sugar and wine. Microwave (high) 2-3 minutes, turning fruit to glaze halfway through cooking. Slowly stir in cream (or it will curdle). Serve warm with sauce. Serves 6-8.

- *Substitute pears for peaches. Cook 5-6 minutes for fresh pears and 2-3 minutes for canned.*
- *Serve with lamb, pork, etc., or as dessert.*

CURRIED FRUIT BAKE — *Complements meat dishes.*

⅓ cup butter	5 maraschino cherries
¾ cup packed brown sugar	1 (1 lb) can peach halves
2-3 tsp. curry powder	1 (1 lb) can apricot halves
1 (1 lb) can pear halves	1 (1 lb) can pineapple chunks

In 1½ qt. glass casserole, melt butter (high) 45 seconds. Blend in sugar and curry. Drain and dry fruit. Arrange well mixed in color and shape. Coat with butter mix. Microwave (high), covered, 3 minutes. Spoon sauce over fruit; rotate dish ¼ turn. Microwave (high), covered, 2-3 minutes. Rest, covered, 5 minutes. Serves 6-8.

Notes: _____

CRANBERRIES — *A Thanksgiving favorite.*

2 cups sugar	1 lb. fresh washed cranberries
1 cup water	

In 3 qt. glass casserole, dissolve sugar in water. Add cranberries; cover. Microwave (high) 8-10 minutes, stirring 2 or 3 times. (Berries should pop and mixture boil.) Rest, covered, 10 minutes.

• *Substitute 1 cup orange juice for water if you prefer orange flavor.*

Notes: _____

MICROWAVED GRAPEFRUIT — *Heat for a new flavor!*

2 grapefruit, halved	Brown sugar
and sectioned	1 Tbsp. butter

Place fruit on glass saucers. Sprinkle each half with 1 tsp. brown sugar. Place ¼ Tbsp. butter in center of each. Microwave (high), covered, 2-3 minutes, rearranging dishes halfway through cooking. Serves 4.

• *One half will heat in ¾-1 minute.*

Notes: _____

STEWED DRIED PRUNES

1 (1 lb) pkg. dried prunes
2 cups water

In 1½ qt. glass dish add prunes and water. Cover 3-4 hours. Microwave (high) 5-6 minutes. Rest, covered, to cool. Serves 8-10.

• *For other dried fruits, follow method above.*

Notes: _____

BAKED RHUBARB

2 cups small rhubarb pieces	Dash salt
2 Tbsp. water	½ cup sugar

In 2 qt. glass dish, combine rhubarb, water, and salt. Microwave (high), covered, 4-6 minutes, stirring halfway through cooking. Add sugar; cook (high) 1 minute. Rest, covered, 10 minutes. Test for doneness. Serves 4.

● *1 tsp. grated orange rind or lemon juice may be added (optl.).*

Notes: _____

SPICY FRUIT COMPOTE — *A salad alternate.*

1 (1 lb) can pears (in eighths)	¼ tsp. cinnamon
2 medium peeled apples (in eighths)	¼ tsp. cloves
½ cup whole cranberry sauce	¼ tsp. allspice

Drain pears, saving 1 Tbsp. syrup. In 1 qt. glass casserole, layer apples and pears. Blend cranberry sauce, cinnamon, cloves, allspice and syrup; spoon over fruit. Microwave (high), covered, 6-8 minutes, rotating ¼ turn halfway through cooking. (Apples should be tender.) Serve warm or chilled. Serves 6-8.

● *An excellent meat accompaniment or dessert.*

Notes: _____

EVERBEST FRUIT COBBLER — *Everyone wants this recipe!*

1 (22 oz) can prepared pie filling	2 Tbsp. brown sugar
½ (9 oz) yellow cake mix	1 tsp. cinnamon
¼ cup melted butter	3 Tbsp. finely chopped walnuts

In 8-inch round glass dish, spoon pie filling evenly. Sprinkle with cake mix. Pour butter over mixture. Combine sugar, cinnamon and nuts; sprinkle on top. Microwave (high) 9-11 minutes, rotating ¼ turn halfway through cooking. Rest 10 minutes. Serves 6-8.

● *One of the easiest, most tasty desserts ever made! Serve warm or cold with whipped cream, cream or ice cream.*

Notes: _____

FRUIT MELBA — *With fruit of your choice.*

In 9-inch round glass dish arrange 4 canned or fresh fruit halves, (peaches, pears, etc.) cut side up. Microwave (high), covered, 3-4 minutes, rotating once. Top with ice cream and strawberry jam. Serves 4.

FRESH APPLE DUMPLING — *Delicious with ice cream.*

¼-½ cup sugar
1 cup biscuit mix
1 egg
⅓ cup milk
2 cups peeled, sliced baking apples

½ tsp. cinnamon
¼ tsp. ground cloves
2 Tbsp. brown sugar
1 tsp. vanilla
3 Tbsp. butter
⅓ cup chopped walnuts

Combine sugar, biscuit mix, egg and milk to form a soft dough. Line 9-inch glass cake pan. Arrange apple slices evenly over top; press into dough. In 1 cup glass measure combine cinnamon, cloves, brown sugar, vanilla and butter. Microwave (high) 30-40 seconds. Stir to combine. Spread evenly over apples in dish. Sprinkle with nuts (optl.). Microwave (high) 6-7 minutes, rotating ¼ turn every 2 minutes. Rest 5 minutes. Serve warm or cold. Serves 6-8.

MOCK APPLE COBBLER — *A delicious fruit dessert*

1 (8 oz) can refrigerated biscuits
4 peeled, sliced baking apples
½ cup dark raisins (optl.)
½ cup chopped walnuts (optl.)

½ cup water
½ cup dark corn syrup
½ cup dark brown sugar
¼ cup butter

Cut each biscuit in half. Arrange evenly over bottom of 12x8-inch glass dish. Sprinkle with apples, raisins and nuts. In 2 cup glass measure, combine water, corn syrup, brown sugar and butter. Microwave (high) 2½-3 minutes stirring every minute until mixture boils. Pour evenly over apples. Microwave (high) covered, 8-9 minutes, rotating ¼ turn halfway through cooking. (Apples should be tender). Rest, covered, 5 minutes. Serve warm topped with whipped or ice cream. Serves 6-8.
● *May be frozen and thawed for serving.*
● *Fresh peaches or pears may be substituted. Reduce cooking time 1-2 minutes.*

Notes: _____

DEFROSTING FROZEN FRUIT: Place frozen fruit in 1 qt. glass casserole. Cover, microwave:

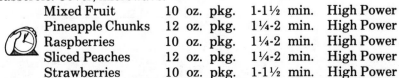

Mixed Fruit	10 oz. pkg.	1-1½ min.	High Power
Pineapple Chunks	12 oz. pkg.	1¼-2 min.	High Power
Raspberries	10 oz. pkg.	1¼-2 min.	High Power
Sliced Peaches	12 oz. pkg.	1¼-2 min.	High Power
Strawberries	10 oz. pkg.	1-1½ min.	High Power

Rest covered, 5 minutes. Separate with fork. (Fruit will not be thawed completely.) Serve slightly frozen or allow another minutes to thaw completely.

FRUIT CRISP

I have been told this recipe is far too easy and delicious, especially for dieters. A cooking school favorite!

4 cups (4 med.) peeled, sliced apples	½ cup rolled oats
⅔ cup brown sugar	¾ tsp. cinnamon
½ cup flour	¾ tsp. nutmeg
	⅓ cup soft butter

In 8-inch round glass dish arrange apples. In mixing bowl blend remaining ingredients until crumbly. Spread on apples. Microwave (high) 5-6 minutes, rotating ¼ turn halfway through cooking. Apples should be tender. Serves 6-8.

- *Red pie cherries, peaches, blueberries, etc. may be substituted for apples. When using canned fruit, cook 4-5 minutes or until fruit is hot. For **RHUBARB CRISP** use ½-1 cup sugar to sweeten fruit or you'll pucker!*
- *Topping becomes more crisp as it cools. Broil if desired.*

Notes: _____

_____

Magic: Don't thaw frozen orange juice in microwave. Vitamin C is very sensitive to heat. It thaws quickly at room temperature or when combined with water.

Jams & Jellies

Jams and jellies are easily made with the *"cook and stir"* method used for sauces and puddings. Make in small quantities especially nice for a last minute *"personalized"* gift. They retain fresh fruit flavor and color. Recipes using powdered pectin require about the same proportion of ingredients as top of the range. An added advantage is never scorching a pan. Cooking time is about the same since mixture must boil for good results. Use medium (50%) for less intense heat after mixture boils.

Select a large container so mixture won't boil over. If it begins to boil over, open door and stir to distribute heat more evenly. During boiling, stir once or twice to blend ingredients and maintain even temperature. Pectin in the recipe assures good *"firming"* without guessing the amount of moisture and natural pectin in the fruit.

Powdered pectin is boiled with fruit so it dissolves before adding sugar. Liquid pectin has been dissolved and is added with sugar. To test for doneness, dip a metal spoon in boiling syrup; remove and tilt until syrup falls from the side. When done, syrup will not flow but will divide into two distinct drops which run together or *"sheet"* from the spoon. Do not double recipe.

APPLE JELLY — *Using juice omits straining pulp.*

¼ cup sugar
3 Tbsp. powdered pectin

2½ cups apple juice
3 cups sugar

In a 3 qt. glass dish, mix sugar and pectin. Slowly add apple juice; bring to boil (high) 6-8 minutes, stirring once or twice. (Covering speeds **cooking**.) Add sugar. Microwave (high), uncovered, 7-9 minutes, stirring once or twice after mixture boils. Test for doneness. Rest 1-2 minutes. Skim foam from surface. Add coloring (optl.). Makes 3 cups.

Notes: _____

APPLE BUTTER — *No worry of scorching pan!*

8 medium quartered apples
   (unpeeled but cored)
1 cup apple cider

1 cup sugar
1 tsp. cinnamon
½ tsp. pumpkin pie spice
¼ tsp. ground cloves

In 2 qt. glass casserole combine apples and cider. Microwave (high), covered, 8-10 minutes, stirring every 3 minutes until apples are soft. Transfer to food mill or blender for smoothing, to even texture. Return to casserole; combine with sugar, cinnamon, pie spice and cloves. Microwave (high) 10-12 minutes, stirring every 3 minutes until mixture thickens. Store in freezer or refrigerator in sterilized jars. Makes 1 quart.

Notes: _____

FROZEN STRAWBERRY JAM — *Make anytime of year*

2 (10 oz) pkgs. frozen
   strawberries

¼ cup powdered pectin
2½ cups sugar
1 Tbsp. lemon juice

In 3 qt. glass dish, thaw strawberries (high) 2 minutes. Mash; add pectin. Microwave (high) 4-6 minutes until mixture boils. Blend with sugar and lemon juice. Microwave (high) 7-9 minutes, stirring every 2 minutes until mixture comes to full boil for 1 minute. Test for doneness. Makes 1 qt.

● *For* **RASPBERRY JAM** *or* **PEACH JAM**, *substitute for straw-berries.*

● *For* **FRESH STRAWBERRY JAM**, *substitute 2 cups sliced fresh berries, 1½ cups sugar and 2 tsp. powdered pectin in recipe above. Store in refrigerator or freezer. Makes 1 qt.*

● *Fresh, frozen strawberries may be used for jam-making. Combine quantities as given in recipe p. 177.*

Notes: _____

FROZEN JUICE GRAPE JELLY — *Mix pectin before cooking.*

1 (6 oz) can frozen grape juice	2 cups hot water
1 (1¾ oz) pkg. powdered pectin	3¾ cups sugar

In 3 qt. glass casserole microwave (high) juice 1 minute to thaw. Stir thoroughly with pectin; combine with water. Microwave (high) covered, 6-8 minutes until mixture boils, stirring halfway through cooking. Add sugar. Microwave (high), covered,. 6-8 minutes, stirring once until boiling. Microwave (high) 1 minute at full boil. Skim off foam. Makes 1 qt.

Notes: _____

UNCOOKED PEACH FREEZER JAM

Uncooked freezer jams have the best flavor of all. Plan space in your freezer for an assortment.

	5½ cups sugar
2 lbs. fresh **ripe** peaches	¾ cup water
2 Tbsp. lemon juice	1 (1¾ oz) pkg. powdered pectin

Peel, pit and puree peaches. (Ascorbic acid prevents darkening.) Measure peaches and water to make 2½ cups. Blend well in large glass bowl with lemon juice and sugar. In 2 cup glass measure combine water and pectin. Microwave (high) 2-2½ minutes to boil. Stir. Boil (high) 1 minute. Combine with peach mixture and stir several minutes until well blended. Pour into sterilized freezer containers. Cover; rest 24 hours at room temperature to set. Freeze. Makes 7 cups.

RASPBERRY FREEZER JAM

Use recipe above, substituting 3 cups berries with water in step 1.
● **Strawberries** may also be substituted.

● **SIMPLE SYRUP** — For freezing fruits prepare in microwave without attention to scorching bottom of the pan.

In 2 qt. glass casserole blend sugar and water as needed for syrup:

Type	Sugar	Water	High Power	Yield
Thin	2 cups	4 cups	12-14 minutes	5 cups
Medium	3 cups	4 cups	13-15 minutes	5½ cups
Heavy	4¾ cups	4 cups	15-17 minutes	6½ cups

Microwave (high) following chart, stirring once or twice to dissolve sugar. Chill before packing with fruit. Thin syrup is used for sweet fruit, heavy for sour and medium for all others.

Pies

Pies, the all-American dessert, are easily microwaved in very little time! Most cook in 10-15 minutes. For one crust pies, cook crust before adding filling, then cook filling in crust. Pour cream filling into cooked pie crust. For a two crust pie, use a combination of microwave and conventional cooking.

Chill pie crust after mixing to tenderize and prevent shrinking. With crumb crusts, melt butter and combine with crumbs. Cook a minute to set; fill. Cook deep dish pie with top crust only. Flavoring crusts will not alter time. The true test of microwave pie crust is after pie is completely cooked — not after crust has been cooked. You will be pleased with the flaky, tender results! High power gives a flakier crust. Use medium high (70%) 7-9 minutes for less scorching if your oven has uneven pattern. My only complaint is they're too easy!

EFFIE'S FOOLPROOF PIE CRUST — *Shared by a student.*

4 cups flour	2 tsp. salt
1¾ cup shortening	1 Tbsp. vinegar
1 Tbsp. sugar	1 beaten egg
	½ cup water

In mixing bowl, combine flour, shortening, sugar and salt. Add vinegar, egg and water mixing lightly with fork or food processor. Form into smooth ball; chill 15 minutes. Divide into 4 equal balls. Roll each on generously floured pastry cloth until 1½ inches larger than 9-inch glass pie plate. Lift bottom crust into plate shaping around rim. Flute edges. Fold an 11-inch piece of wax paper into eighths; cut from center to 1-inch from outside edge. Unfold; place in center of pie crust. Nest 8-inch glass pie dish on paper. Microwave (high) 3 minutes. Remove paper and 8-inch dish; rotate ¼ turn. Microwave (high) 2-3 minutes. Cool. Makes 4, 9-inch pie shells.

- *This excellent recipe was shared by Effie in a microwave class. It's easy to make and can be either frozen as dough, or shaped in pie shells and frozen.*
- **FROZEN PIE SHELLS** *can be cooked in microwave. Transfer from metal pan while frozen. They require 1 minute defrosting.*
- *Rotating is very important or parts of crust will overcook. Covering with second pie dish during cooking distributes steam more evenly for better results.*
- *I've received many letters with ideas for coloring crust. They include instant tea in dough, paint with vanilla, Worcestershire sauce and substituting ½ whole wheat flour for flour in recipe. I've cooked so many I don't object to the natural color.*

- **DEEP DISH CRUST**: Cook separately as above on paper towel with rim turned under (for fluting). (May be sectioned in 6 wedges, if desired.) Sprinkle with sugar and cinnamon (optl.). Microwave (high) 3-4 minutes, rotating ¼ turn halfway through cooking. Cool on rack. Lay on pie during last minute of cooking.
- **LATTICE PIE CRUST**: Prepare dough in lattice strips on paper towel. Flute edges. Microwave (high) as above.
  Maxi-Time: Medium-high (70%) 4-5 minutes.

CRUMB PIE CRUST — *Select flavors to enhance filling.*

1 cup crushed crumbs (graham crackers, vanilla wafers, corn-flake, etc.)	2-3 Tbsp. sugar ¼ cup butter

Combine ingredients in 9-inch glass pie plate. Heat (high) 2 minutes, stirring once. Press evenly onto sides and bottom of dish. Heat (high) 1 minute to "set" crust. Makes 1,9-inch crust.

- *I like to make* **CHOCOLATE CRUMB CRUST** *for Grasshopper Pie (p. 182). Substitute 1½ cup chocolate cookie crumbs, sugar, and butter in recipe above.*
- *Reserve 2-3 spoonfuls of crumbs to sprinkle on top of pie before cooking.*
- *Make in advance and freeze for quick-cooking at a moment's notice.*

Notes: _____

_____

DEEP DISH APPLE PIE — *Pie crust is cooked on top!*

5-6 peeled, sliced cooking apples	¼ tsp. ground cloves
½ cup sugar	1 tsp. lemon juice
2-3 Tbsp. water	1 cup buttermilk biscuit mix
1 Tbsp. flour	2 Tbsp. sugar
½ tsp. cinnamon	½ cup milk
½ tsp. ground allspice	Cinnamon
	Sugar

In 12x8-inch glass dish combine apples, sugar, water, flour, cinnamon, allspice, cloves and lemon juice. Microwave (high), covered, 4-5 minutes until apples are crisp-tender, stirring once. Prepare topping by combining lightly biscuit mix, sugar and milk. Drop by small spoonfuls onto hot mixture. Sprinkle evenly with sugar and cinnamon. Microwave (high), covered, 2-3 minutes. Remove cover, rotate dish ¼ turn. Microwave (high) 2-4 minutes. Rest 5 minutes. Serve with cream. Serves 4-6.

- *Blend ground cinnamon and sugar to sprinkle over light dough for more color.*

Magic: Serve pie warm for added flair! Heat each serving 15 seconds. (Heat ice cream or cheese slice on pie, if desired.)

Notes: _____

_____

STREUSEL TOP APPLE PIE

Mary Engle, Nashville, Tenn. shared this recipe as alternate to crust-topped pie.

1 (9-inch) pastry crust	1 Tbsp. flour
4 cups (4 medium) sliced apples	½ tsp. cinnamon
½ cup sugar	1 Tbsp. lemon juice

Prepare crust (p. 179), adding 1 Tbsp. instant tea to dough for color. Blend apples, sugar, flour, cinnamon and lemon juice. Place in cooked crust. Prepare **Streusel Topping**:

1 cup flour	½ tsp. cinnamon
⅓ cup brown sugar	⅓ cup soft butter

Blend flour, brown sugar and cinnamon. Combine with butter to make crumbs. Sprinkle over apples. Microwave (high) 6-8 minutes, rotating ¼ turn halfway through cooking, until apples are fork tender. Rest 10 minutes. Serve warm or cold. Serves 5-6.

- *Barbara Clark, Gresham, Ore., prepared a similar pie substituting instant tea in pie dough. She makes it in food processor, dough first; Streusel Topping next; slices apples last for continuous use without washing bowl.*

Substitute fresh **PEACHES** *or* **PEARS** *in season. For both cook 1-2 minutes* **less**.

COCONUT CRUSTLESS PIE

One step pie. A good substitute for scrambled eggs at breakfast.

3 eggs	¾ cup flaked coconut
⅓ cup biscuit mix	1½ cups milk
⅓ cup sugar	1 tsp. vanilla
½ tsp. nutmeg	3 Tbsp. soft butter

In mixing bowl or blender combine all ingredients well. Pour into 9-inch glass pie dish. Microwave (high) 7-9 minutes, rotating ¼ turn halfway through cooking. Sprinkle top with nutmeg and toasted coconut. Serves 6-8.

Maxi-Time: Medium-high (70%) 10-12 minutes.

- *Rotate ¼ turn if pie looks like it's going over in dish.*
- *Center "jiggles like Jello" when done.*

Magic: TOAST COCONUT — In pie pan spread 2 to 3 cups coconut evenly on bottom. Microwave (high) 2-3 minutes, stirring every 30 seconds. Less coconut takes less time and more time for more.

PUMPKIN PIE — *Always a perfect pie!*

2 eggs	¼ tsp. nutmeg
¼ cup sugar	½ tsp. allspice
¾ cup firmly packed dark brown sugar	¼ tsp. cloves
	1 (16 oz) can cooked pumpkin
1 Tbsp. flour	1 (13 oz) can evaporated milk
½ tsp. salt	1 baked 9" pastry shell (p.179)
1 tsp. cinnamon	

In large mixing bowl blend all ingredients and pour into baked pastry in 9-inch glass pie dish. Microwave (high) 4-5 minutes until edges begin to *set*. Stir moving cooked edges to center of dish. Microwave (high) 5-6 minutes or until center *jiggles like Jello*. Rest 10 minutes. Knife inserted in center should come out clean. Serves 5-6.

Maxi-Time: Medium (50%) 18-20 minutes.

• *Canned pumpkin pie filling may be substituted for ingredients.*

Notes: _____

GRASSHOPPER PIE — *Elegant for special occasions.*

3 cups miniature marshmallows	1 cup dairy whipped cream
½ cup cream	1 9-inch chocolate crumb crust
3 Tbsp. creme de cocoa	1 dark milk chocolate candy bar
3 Tbsp. green creme de menthe	2 Tbsp. chocolate cookie crumbs

In 2 qt. glass dish combine marshmallows and cream. Microwave (high) 2-2½ minutes until marshmallows puff. Blend evenly; add creme de cocoa and creme de menthe, stirring well. Chill 20-25 minutes until thickened but not set. Fold in whipped cream; pour into prebaked Chocolate Crumb Crust (p.180). Top with shavings from candy bar and cookie crumbs. Chill 4-5 hours until serving. Serves 6-8.

Notes: _____

LEMON PIE FILLING — *Even easier microwaved!*

1⅓ cups sugar	½ cup lemon juice
½ cup cornstarch	1 Tbsp. grated lemon peel
1½ cup boiling water	3 Tbsp. butter
3 lightly beaten egg yolks	1 9-inch baked pastry shell p.179

In 4 cup glass measure blend sugar and cornstarch; stir in boiling water. Microwave (high) 4-5 minutes, stirring several times. When mixture becomes translucent, gradually add a little hot mixture to egg yolks, stirring well. Blend egg yolk mixture into hot mixture. Cook (high) 30-60 seconds more until mixture is thick and even.

Stir in lemon juice, lemon peel and butter. Pour into baked pie shell. Cool before serving. Top with meringue or serve plain. Serves 5-6.
Notes: _____

ALWAYS PERFECT PIE MERINGUE
Vivian Freeman, Portland, Ore., candy expert shares this recipe for a perfect meringue. A mixer is necessary for good results.

1 Tbsp. cornstarch	½ cup water
6 Tbsp. sugar	3 egg whites

In 2 cup glass measure combine cornstarch, sugar, and water. Microwave (high) 1 minute until clear. Cool slightly. Beat egg whites until soft peaks form. Pour in cooked syrup, a little at a time. After well blended, continue beating on medium, 8 minutes. Pour ⅓ mixture onto **hot** pie. Seal around edges. Microwave (high) 3-4 minutes, rotating dish ¼ turn every 45 seconds — or — bake in conventional oven at 400°F., 3-5 minutes; or 300°F., 10-20 minutes. Makes 3 8-inch pies.
- *To cook* **individual meringues:** *drop 6 to 8 spoonfuls in ring on brown paper (not recycled). Microwave medium (50%) 1-2 minutes, rotating if cooking unevenly. Serve on pie or pudding. (May be frozen.)*

Notes: _____

CHERRY PIE — *Combine with convention oven for perfect pie.*

Pastry for 2 crust pie	¼ tsp. almond flavoring
2 (16 oz) cans water-packed, pitted, tart red pie cherries	1 tsp. lemon juice
	Red food coloring
1 cup sugar	2 Tbsp. butter
⅓ cup flour	Water
Pinch salt	Sugar
	Cinnamon

Prepare pie crust pastry for 2 crust pie (p. 179) in 9-inch glass pie plate. Drain cherries, saving ½ cup liquid. In 4 cup glass measure, blend sugar, flour and salt. Stir in cherry liquid until smooth. Microwave (high) 2-3 minutes stirring twice until thick and smooth. Add almond, lemon juice and 2-3 drops red food coloring. Add cherries, mixing gently. Pour into pastry; dot with butter. Prepare remaining crust 1-inch larger than pie plate; cut slashes in center. Moisten edges of bottom crust with water. Arrange top crust over filling and flute edges. Preheat conventional oven to 450°. Brush top with water and sprinkle with sugar and cinnamon. Microwave (high) 7-9 minutes, rotating ¼ turn halfway through cooking. (Pie filling should be bubbling.) Bake conventionally 10-15 minutes, or until top crust is golden brown. Cool to *set* filling before serving. Makes 1,9-inch pie.
- *Substitute other fruits in pies using this technique.*

PUDDING PIE — *Select your own flavor.*

1 (3 oz) pkg. pudding mix	2 cups milk
(**not** instant - flavor desired)	1 9-inch pastry shell

Prepare pie crust for 1-crust pie (p. 179). In 4 cup glass measure, blend pudding mix and milk. Microwave (high) 7-9 minutes, stirring often, until mixture comes to a full boil. Rest 5 minutes. Pour into pie crust. Refrigerate until serving. Serves 6-8.

- *Arrange canned Mandarin orange slices over cooked pie.*
- *Substitute crumb pie crusts for pastry if desired.*
- *For* **BANANA CREAM PIE:** *Slice 2 bananas in pie crust. Pour hot pudding over bananas. Chill.*

Notes: _____

_____

MOCHA JAVA PIE — *A rich pie for a splurge!*

1 crumb crust pie shell	¼ cup powdered sugar
1 (3½ oz) chocolate pudding mix (not instant)	1¼ tsp. instant coffee powder
2 cups milk	½ tsp. vanilla
½ cup whipping cream	2 Tbsp. shaved chocolate

Prepare crumb crust (chocolate is nice) (p. 180). Chill. In 4 cup glass measure combine pudding mix and milk. Microwave (high) 6-8 minutes, stirring every 2 minutes until mixture comes to a boil and thickens. Cool 5 minutes. Pour into chilled pie shell; chill. Whip cream until thick. Fold in powdered sugar, coffee powder and vanilla. Spread evenly over cooled pie. Top with shaved chocolate. Chill. Serves 6-8.

- *Vanilla wafer crumbs may be substituted for chocolate in shell.*
- *Substitute Dream Whip and ½ cup cold milk for whipped cream if desired.*

Notes: _____

_____

- *To cook* **FROZEN FRUIT PIE,** *transfer pie while frozen from foil to glass pie plate. Preheat conventional oven to 450°. Microwave (high) 15-18 minutes, rotating ¼ turn halfway through cooking. Pie filling should be bubbling. Place in conventional oven and bake 10-15 minutes, or until top crust is golden brown.*

Hows? and Whys?

Do all brands cook the same? Most ovens work essentially the same way. Major differences occur with features and include oven wattage which may vary cooking time. Variable power levels give the oven more flexibility. 3-4 speeds will cook almost anything well. Also available are temperature probes, memory controls, and humidity sensors. Individual features include turntables, automatic cooking codes, dual power cooking, built-in units, etc. They are comparable with other home appliances — dishwashers, washers, etc. — which differ by features but perform the same function.

Why does my food cook unevenly? It is impossible to distribute energy in all places in the oven equally — just as it is with the range. Foods accumulate more energy on outer surfaces as microwaves bounce off oven walls. Large foods near the top (energy source) cook faster so must be turned over. Small profile foods like cakes cook faster on outer edges. Elevating the dish may cook more evenly. I consider the **worst problem** of microwaving to be getting the center of food done. We recommend a glass in the center of the dish, a ring or round shaped container or small foods or dishes placed in a ring. "Shielding" corners on large foods or dishes prevents overcooking outer edges where a concentration of energy accumulates. People often refer to "hot spots" where there is more concentration. Stirring mixed or blended foods or rotating dish ¼ turn (½ if dish won't go ¼) overcomes energy concentration and cooks food more evenly. Turntables do this automatically. Many manufacturers claim their ovens to be so even, food doesn't need turning. You will quickly learn whether turning is necessary in your oven. If the pattern is very even — no turning is necessary.

Why is my food tough? Tough or dry food is usually an indication of overcooking. The final cooking occurs during the **carry-over cooking** time. See p. 9-11. Always select the shortest time; add more after carry-over time if additional cooking is needed.

Why do some ovens have variable speeds? They give you more flexibility in the intensity of energy used (p.13-14).Compare these settings with your conventional range settings from high to low. Some foods such as meats or cakes cook better with less intense energy. Adjust the setting as you would conventionally to slow cooking or simmer food. With microwave cooking, you must increase cooking time as you reduce energy.

Is it necessary to have the glass tray on the bottom of the oven in place while cooking? Can I remove it if I need more room? The tray must be in place because it elevates food off the bottom to allow cooking the bottom of your food. Don't remove it. Select smaller foods or dishes.

Do I have to cook small amounts of food? You can cook the amount of food that your oven cavity will hold which is usually ample. As you increase quantities, you also increase cooking time. You may find it more convenient to cook large quantities conventionally. More than 6 baked potatoes would be more practical to cook in the conventional oven. Combine with an oven meal for practical use of time and energy.

How do I cook small portions? They require little cooking time. It may be more practical to place food on a dinner plate and heat 45-75 seconds than to heat each food separately. Cook 1 cup of food (high) 2-3 minutes. (p. 21)

Why does my food boil over? Foods that need to boil have a tendency to boil over if they are not placed in containers large enough for air expansion during boiling action. Use large containers for soups, cereal, rice, noodles, etc. Greasing rim of dish may prevent boilovers. If food is partially warm (such as coffee) heating requires less time than if it's cold.

Does plastic make a good dish cover? Other covers such as glass lids, paper towel, and wax paper make better covers most of the time. Plastic wraps create a very tight seal and have a tendency to melt if exposed to fats, and sugars. I prefer plastic wrap for eggs where a tight seal for a short cooking period is desirable. For some vegetables the tight seal is needed to soften the texture. For using to cover containers, turn back one corner so steam can vent. Plastic lids should **not** be used as the seal may be tight enough to create a vacuum and could cause the dish to burst. The FDA has questioned the use of wraps containing poly-vinyl chlorides such as butcher wrap in the presence of heat since fumes may migrate into the food. Don't overcook covered with plastic wrap — I've seen it bonded to dishes.

Why do rolls get soggy? The porous structure of bread products causes rapid heating. If placed on a flat surface, steam is trapped underneath and bread will be soggy. Elevating on roasting rack for air circulation prevents this. Rolls may be heated in basket, also. When combined with dense foods, sweet rolls, sandwiches, hot dogs, pizza, etc., they absorb moisture from the filling and become soggy if not on a rack. Conventional heat dries the moisture and prevents this from occurring.

Why are breads hard? As with other hard foods, they are over-cooked.

Can I cook popcorn? It's best to follow your manufacturer's recommendations for brands of poppers and whether or not to pop corn. Popcorn can be cooked but shouldn't for several reasons. Popcorn is a dry food and is usually popped in small quantities. When you do not have enough food mass within the cavity, it becomes loaded with energy and may cause microwaves to back into the magnetron tube shortening the life of the oven. This is very similar to operating the oven empty. The oven walls and shelf may become too hot to touch. (They remain cool with other foods.) Popcorn becomes extremely hot during cooking and may transfer heat to the dish, causing it to break. It can ignite grease which could melt the grease shield or damage the door of the oven. In a paper bag it can cause the bag to ignite. Most poppers I've tested leave several kernels unpopped — wasting $. Overcooking is easy to do and may scorch kernels or cause a fire. Even if you keep your popcorn in the refrigerator, cook it with a cup of water, or use fresh popcorn, it will pop with far better results conventionally in the same amount of time with more volume. Popcorn is a major cause of consumer caused service calls on the microwave!

Can foods be home canned in the microwave? No — it is not recommended or safe. Canning in the microwave would be similar to canning in your conventional oven which is very hazardous. There is no way of knowing how much pressure is building inside sealed jars. Can either in a water bath or pressure cooker on range.

Can I cook home-canned vegetables in the microwave? It is best to cook these conventionally. Vegetables must be boiled 10-15 minutes to insure their safety. Boiling action is too intense for this period of time and mutilates the vegetable. Even though they can be brought to boil on high and reduced to medium (50%), the cooking time is so long the range is more practical.

When do I cover my food? Cover foods you wish to steam. Covering will trap heat in the container speeding up cooking time. It usually results in more even cooking.

What foods cannot be cooked in the microwave? Angel food and sponge cakes, deep fried foods, popovers, hard and soft-cooked eggs in the shell, and home canning. Popcorn is not recommended.

Will the Browning Dish damage my oven if I heat it empty? This dish is designed to be heated empty to absorb energy and get hot. A special coating is imbedded in the bottom that absorbs instead of transmitting microwave energy. After the dish is heated, it is suitable for grilling, frying or searing. Use dishes or grills designed for this purpose!

Why do my dishes create sparks? Small pieces of metal act like an antenna reflecting microwaves (very similar to welding or lightning). Do not use dishes that have any metal trim, including the seal on the bottom.

Why do I need hot pads sometime and not other times? Dishes will get hot up to the level of the food because heat in the food transfers to the container. In a half full container or without a lid, you can probably handle the dish without hot pads. To be safe, make a habit of using them except for those foods you specifically know have not transferred heat.

Do I make adjustments for high altitude? Having lived 20 years of my life at altitudes of 5200+ I know how important this is. Make normal adjustments of increasing flour by ¼ cup and water by ⅓ cup. (For cakes, don't reduce liquid but add.) Since boiling is at a lower temperature it may take a little longer (1-2 minutes) to cook foods. This is especially true of dense foods such as potatoes, apples, etc. Always start with recommended times. Add more after resting.

When heating a roll on a napkin, why did sparks fly and the napkin burn? This was probably caused from using a "recycled" napkin which could contain substances that might ignite in the microwave. Napkins are generally o.k. Do not use any **recycled paper** products — napkins, sacks, etc.

Why can't foods be deep-fried? It's difficult to maintain a constant temperature of the fat without a thermometer or thermostat controls.

Can paraffin be melted in the microwave? No — it has no moisture so will not absorb energy to melt. It must be melted by heat transfer from hot water to the wax.

Can jars be sterilized in the microwave? Jars are sterilized by heating with boiling water. A small quantity would be o.k. but a large amount would be very tedious. It takes less time to heat a large amount of water in teakettle on range.

Do microwaves cook foods from the inside out? No — In a low profile food such as a bar or drop cookie it appears to cook this way because more energy concentrates in the center which may cause burning or scorching if overcooked. The same thing occurs on outer corners of large foods where there is more energy concentration. Microwave energy penetrates outer food surfaces about 1-inch. This is the reason for difficulty cooking the center of food.

Microwave Magic

"What else will your speedy 'zapper' do?" is an often asked question with an endless list of answers. There are many uses that don't fit into a recipe category. Some are more than cooking. My husband calls it "magic" when I recommend its use for melting butter, softening shoe polish, heating towels for a hot compress, etc. I feel a handbook like **Let's Cook Microwave!** should have a special chapter to share the many uses with you. It's difficult to be specific with cooking times since the amount of food, the starting temperature and density may vary. Cooking time is proportionate to the amount of food in the oven. In a recipe using preparation times such as scald, boil, soften, melt, thaw, refresh, etc. the micro-wave will do all of these. I've heard of people drying a wet news-paper, panty hose and tennis shoes. I wouldn't do these in the conventional oven or in the microwave! Damage could result if metal is present. If these get too hot, they will ignite. Most non-food uses such as drying flowers are only for very short periods of time.

• *To* **ripen an avocado:** *Microwave medium (50%) 2 minutes. Turn over and cook 1 minute more.*

• **Dry avocado seeds** *for making jewelry and crafts: Fill drinking cup with 1-inch silica gel. Bury seed in cup and fill with gel to i-inch from top. Place 1 cup water in microwave with cup and seed. Microwave (high) 2 minutes. Cool in cup 30 minutes. Check seed for dryness; repeat if needed. If desired, pierce a hole in seed after first heating. Seed turns brown during drying. Air-dry after first heating if desired.*

• **Separate bacon slices** *(high) 15-20 seconds to peel off strips.*

• To **make your baby food,** set aside less-seasoned portions of cooked meat, fish, vegetables, and fruit. Process in blender, food mill or processor to fine desired consistency. Season lightly with salt, pepper, butter and sugar (optl.). Store in covered baby food jars in refrigerator. To heat, remove metal lid and heat in jar, covered, 45-60 seconds (100-110°F.).

—*Meats are especially good because they aren't cooked with added oil.*

—*Junior foods are processed less fine.*

• *Heat* **baby bottle and food,** *(p. 20).*

• **Speed up barbecuing,** (p. 113).

• **When making bread, heat water** to 115°F. for combining with yeast. **Warm flour** 10-20 seconds before adding yeast sponge to speed rising.

- **Speed up bread rising:** Fill 4-cup glass measure with 3 cups water; microwave (high) 6-8 minutes to boil. Place dough in glass bowl. Place dough dish in 12x8-inch glass dish filled with boiling water. Microwave low (10%), covered, 12-15 minutes until double in size. Punch down. Repeat. Transfer dough to glass loaf pan. Repeat until double in size.

- To **speed cooking homemade bread:** Microwave medium-high (70%) 3 minutes, rotating ¼ turn every minute. Transfer to pre-heated 450°F. oven and cook 8-10 minutes until brown. For **nut breads:** Microwave (high) 2 minutes, rotating ½ turn once. Transfer to preheated 450°F. oven and cook 8-10 minutes until brown.

- **Crisp and refresh day old bakery breads,** cookies, crackers, chips, etc. (p. 33). This renews fresh flavor so doesn't take long. Heat (high) 5-15 seconds.

- You'll be spoiled if someone serves you cold **bread or dinner rolls** since they heat in 5-30 seconds (p. 36). Sliced bread takes less time than whole.

- **Warm brandy** *in glass snifter (high) 10-20 seconds to enjoy full bouquet.*

- Make your own **MEAT BROWNING SEASONING** to enhance color of poultry and meats.

¼ cup brown sugar	½ tsp. thyme
1½ tsp. paprika	¼ tsp. marjoram
¼ tsp. garlic powder (optl.)	½ tsp. salt

In glass cup blend all ingredients well. Pour into shaker with semi-large holes. Sprinkle on surface of poultry, meat and fish to improve surface browning. Surface may also be brushed with mixture of Kitchen Bouquet and water; soy sauce; Worcestershire sauce; Teriyaki sauce; or sprinkled with paprika.

- **Soften hard brown sugar** *in paper box by adding a few drops water or a piece of bread or apple. Microwave (high) 10-15 seconds.*
- *To* **soften 1 cube butter** *so it's spreadable, microwave medium-low (30%) 1-2 minutes or (high) 5-10 seconds. If* **frozen,** *add additional 30-60 seconds. To* **melt 1 cube butter** *for combining in a recipe, microwave (high) 45-60 seconds; ¼ cup (½ cube) 30 seconds; 2 Tbsp. 15-30 seconds. To* **clarify butter** *(p. 107).*

- **Soften cheese** *a few seconds (5-15) to serve at room temperature or for blending in a recipe.* **Dips and spreads** *can be softened 15-45 seconds on medium-low (30%) with less danger of melting.* **Soften cream cheese** *(high) ½-1 minute.* **Melt cheese on casserole** *— grated or sliced — (high) 15-30 seconds.*
- **Melt chocolate squares or chips** *for blending or spreading in a recipe medium-high (70%) 1-3 minutes. (Squares can be left in paper wrapper; 1 oz. (high) 1½-2 minutes.)*

- For **CHILDREN'S HOMEMADE CLAY**: In 2 qt. glass dish blend:

  1 (1 lb) box baking soda   1 cup cornstarch
  (about 2 cups)   1¼ cups water

Microwave (high) 4-6 minutes, stirring every 2 minutes until smooth and thick (mixture looks like mashed potatoes and pulls away from dish). Cool on flat plate covered with a damp cloth. When cool, knead on flat surface dusted with cornstarch until smooth and pliable. Use immediately or store in closed plastic bag 1-2 weeks.

—To color clay, add food coloring to water before cooking or blend colors into clay when kneading. For bright colors, mold pieces and harden by microwave or air-dry; paint with water colors or poster paints. To preserve shapes, coat with varnish, shellac, liquid plastic or clear nail polish.

—To make Christmas ornaments or beads, follow directions for Dough Art (below). This dough may be rolled very thin. Your children will enjoy playing with dough for hours!

- **CHILDREN'S PLAY DOUGH**: *A teacher brought this recipe to class one day and I verify it's a real treat for my grandchildren!*

  2 cups flour   1 Tbsp. powdered alum
  1 cup salt   2 cups water
  ½ cup cornstarch   1 Tbsp. oil

In 2 qt. glass dish blend flour, salt, cornstarch, and alum. Whip in water and oil until mixed. Microwave (high) 4-5 minutes, stirring every minute until mixture is thick and lumpy. Cool on flat plate. Knead on floured surface until smooth. Store in covered jar in refrigerator 1-2 weeks.

- *Color when kneading if desired.*

DOUGH ART *for Christmas ornaments, gift tags, baskets and pictures.*

  4 cups flour   1 cup salt
                     1½ cups hot water

In large bowl blend flour, salt and water. Knead on lightly floured surface 6-8 minutes until smooth. Add coloring if desired. Roll ¼-inch thick. Shape with cookie cutters. Pierce several holes in each piece with a needle to release air during cooking. With drinking straw make a hole at the top for hanging. Arrange 5-10 on paper towel covered cardboard (not recycled). Microwave medium-low (30%) 1-1½ minutes/piece rotating ¼ turn and rearranging halfway through cooking. (Ornaments will appear dry; if large pieces are still moist, cook a few seconds longer.) Cool. Brush with shellac before and after painting with water colors.

Mini-time: High, ½ minute/piece with 2 cups water in oven during cooking.

—*Timing varies depending on the number of pieces and their size.*
—*If your oven has a glass tray on the bottom, it may be used in place of cardboard.*
—*Use instant tea or coffee for a toasty colored dough.*
—*Dough may be refrigerated 1-2 weeks in closed plastic bag.*
—*A shellac glaze will preserve ornaments for many years.*
—*Caution: Pieces are very warm when removing from oven. Handle carefully.*
—*Candy Canes and Wreaths may be made by twisting 2 colors of dough rope-style. Moisten pieces lightly with water to join. Red and white are pretty for canes; two green colors for wreaths. Cook as above.*

• **Dough Art Bread Baskets:** *Cover inverted dish of desired size with plastic wrap. Place on cardboard (not recycled) or glass tray. Roll dough 2-inches wider than dish to ¼-inch thick. Cut in ½-inch wide strips (pastry cutter makes edges pretty). Begin at the center and work to outside weaving lattice strips. Trim strips even with top of dish. Roll 2 strips and twist together rope-style. Moisten edges of strips; arrange rope around edge of bowl for rim. Seal edges and overlapping strips with fork and water. Microwave medium-low (30%) 4-6 minutes, rotating ¼ turn every minute until dry. Cool. Remove basket from dish and glaze with shellac or liquid plastic 2-3 times, drying well between each coat.*

Mini-time: High, 2-3 minutes, with 2 cups water in oven, rotating ¼ turn every minute. Air-dry 2-3 minutes. Cook 1-2 minutes more if needed.

• *Prettier when dough is colored with instant coffee or tea.*

• *Microwave (high) a damp towel 15-45 seconds for a* **hot compress.** **Hot finger towels** *(washcloths) may be served with a meal such as barbecued ribs or lobster. Avoid burning yourself if you heat too long.*

• **Convenience and frozen-prepared foods** *often microwave well. Those with breading won't have an oven-crisp texture. Placing on a roasting rack helps preserve crispness. If you object to soft breading, broil 1-2 minutes before serving. Frozen pies need combination (microwave and conventional) cooking to brown crust before serving. Most frozen foods require thawing before cooking. Allow 5-10 minutes resting time before cooking to thaw center of food. The amount of food and density determines cooking time. Thaw and cook using chart (p. 19). Transfer food in foil containers to plastic, paper, or glass for faster, more even thawing and cooking. Select a container approximately the same size as the frozen portion.*

- **Reheat desserts** *generally served warm — pie, cobbler, etc. Soften ice cream or melt sliced cheese on apple pie in 15-20 seconds/piece (high).*

- *Take the chill out of* **dog or cat food.** *Microwave (high) 15-30 seconds in plastic dish.*

- **Hardcook eggs** *for vegetables, salad, and sandwiches (p. 92).*
- **Warm egg whites** *(high) 5-10 seconds to room temperature for more volume when whipping.*
- **Render chicken fat:** *In blender or food processor, finely chop ½-small onion and ½ lb. chicken fat. Add to 9-inch glass dish. Microwave (high), covered, 8-10 minutes, stirring once or twice until fat is crisp. Press through fine sieve. Store, covered, in refrigerator.*
- **Flame spirit or liquor:** *Microwave (high) 2-4 oz. in glass measure 20-30 seconds. Ignite with match and pour flaming over sauce, roast, etc.*

- **DRY FLOWERS:** *Gayle Wiltshire, Lake Oswego, Oregon bought her oven for this purpose. Time and patience give excellent results in minutes. For best results use roses, mums, daisies, asters and pansies or flowers with thick petals. Colors lighten a little and may change. Test dry one flower to judge drying ability. Ingredients needed are: 1 lb. silica gel* (from craft, florist or drug store) to extract moisture from flowers, brush, toothpicks, scissors, florist wire, florist tape, and fresh flowers with leaves if desired. Dry immediately after picking. Leave ½-inch stem on each flower.*
* *Gel may be reused. "Kitty litter" may also be used. Cool between uses.*

In 8x4-inch glass loaf pan or shoe box, layer ½-inch gel on bottom. Arrange with stem down in gel (½-inch apart). Spoon gel around and between petals with toothpick, maintaining natural shape until covered. Microwave (high) with 1 cup water in oven 1-2 minutes. (Time varies with size of flower.) Rest 30 minutes or overnight on flat surface. Remove blossoms with toothpick. Attach florist wire with a hook through top of flower and **carefully** remove gel from buds with brush. Wrap wire with florist tape beginning at flower end. (If not quite dry, hang upside down to dry or arrange right-side-up in slotted roasting rack.) Make flower arrangement. (Plastic spray will help preserve flowers.)
—*Dry leaves separately for 1 minute (high).*
—*Flowers should be about half open and firm. Those with full blossoms lose their petals easily.*
—*Yellow flowers maintain their color beautifully! Try daffodils in the spring.*
—*Do not attempt to dry wet flowers. Cut early in the morning and*

refrigerate for best results.
—Custard drinking cups may be used to dry individual flowers.

• **Soften refrigerated frostings** *(high) 15-30 seconds for easy spreading or blending.*

• **Heated fruit** *has a new flavor, see grapefruit (p. 173), bananas (p. 172), and compotes (p. 174).*

• **Citrus fruits (lemons, limes, oranges and grapefruit) release more juice and flavor** *if heated (high) 15-30 seconds before squeezing.*

• **To peel fruit and tomato skins:** *microwave (high) 10-20 seconds/number. Rest 10 minutes. Strip skins off. Fruit may also be immersed in cup of hot water and heated 30-45 seconds.*

• **Soften dried fruits and "plump" raisins** *by combining 8 oz. (1 cup) with ½ cup water. Microwave (high), covered, 2-4 minutes stirring once.*

• *Make* **garlic spread** *(p. 119).*

• **Dissolve gelatin:** *blend 1 envelope unflavored and ½ cup water. Rest 1 minute. Microwave (high) 45-60 seconds, stirring once.*

• **Gelatin Finger Snacks** *are easy to make and enjoy! (p.153)*

• **Soften soap pieces** *with 1 cup water in microwave (High) 1-2 minutes to utilize "leftovers." Mold into ball when soft.*

• **Ground meats can be browned** *in plastic colander placed in glass casserole. Pour off drippings before mixing with other ingredients. (Onions, celery and green pepper can be softened at the same time.)*

• **Dry fresh herbs** *(p. 61).* **Dry plump, firm mushrooms** *for recipe convenience anytime. Clean; slice and arrange in even layer on paper towel covered cardboard (not recycled). Microwave (high) 6-8 minutes, rearranging slices halfway through cooking.* (**Maxi-Time:** *medium-high (70%) 9-10 minutes, rearranging once.) Air dry until cool. Slices will be semi-leathery and have no moisture when sliced. Store in covered container.* **To rehydrate:** *Combine with liquid in recipe. Rest 5-15 minutes to plump before cooking. (We find these are delicious "nibble food" for snacks when dried!)*

With other foods, drying *may be a very tedious process and will be much more carefree in your oven or food dryer. They can be done in the microwave in small amounts in elevated position on medium-low (30%) to low (10%) but will take about 1½-2 hours in combination with air-drying time.*

• *When* **honey or jam is crystalized,** *return to soft stage by heating (high) 1-2 minutes.*

• **Soften frozen ice cream** *medium (50%) 15-30 seconds for 1 pint; 30-45 seconds for 1 quart; 45-60 seconds for ½ gallon to make serving easier.*

• **Heat hand lotion or baby oil** *(high) 15-45 seconds with lid removed from jar.*
• **Heat leftovers** *without leftover dried-out taste (p. 20).*
• **Soften marshmallows and caramels** *to blend with other ingredients (high) 30-60 seconds.*
• *Cook* **meats and chicken parts** *to use in recipes for main dishes, sandwiches, salads, etc. (high) 6-7 minutes/lb.*

• *Make* **SWEETENED CONDENSED MILK** *with $ savings*

¾ cup sugar	¼ cup butter (½ stick)
⅓ cup water	1 cup dry milk crystals

In 2 cup glass measure add sugar, water, and butter. Microwave (high) 1½-2 minutes until mixture boils, stirring every 30 seconds. Combine in blender with dry milk. Process until smooth. Refrigerate until needed. Makes 1 cup. (Double recipe to substitute for 14-oz. can = 1⅔ cups.)
• **Scald milk:** *1 cup (high) 2-2½ minutes (200°F.).*
• **If nail polish cap is stuck,** *microwave (high) 5-10 seconds.*
• **Shell nuts easier** *by placing 2 cups nuts in 1 cup water. Microwave (high), covered, 1-3 minutes. Nuts may also be frozen for easier shelling.*

ROASTING AND TOASTING NUTS AND SEEDS

Nuts and seeds "roast or toast" very easily when microwaved, saving a great deal of time compared with conventional time. When roasting in the shell, pierce or slash to allow expansion of air during heating. Avoid overcooking. If you aren't sure of doneness, rest 5 minutes; test; then add more time if necessary. Cook nuts uncovered, unless directions say to cover. Glass pie plates make good utensils. Stir often to assure even cooking.

To remove skins from nuts, roll in paper towel or cheesecloth after cooking, or blanch (p. 196). Vegetable oil, butter and salt can be omitted, if you prefer. A good reason for roasting your own nuts is the adjustment you can make in seasonings. Seasoned, onion and garlic salt may be substituted for plain.
—*Place unshelled nuts in freezer 15 minutes for easy shelling.*
CHESTNUTS: Slash crosswise through skin on flat end of chestnut shell. In a glass pie plate, arrange 20-24 chestnuts in even layer. Microwave (high) 3-4 minutes, stirring every minute until nuts are soft when squeezed. Rest 5 minutes. Peel shells; eat warm.
PUMPKIN SEEDS: Rinse seeds in water to clean fibers. Pat lightly dry with paper towel. In a glass pie plate, arrange in an even layer 1 cup seeds. Sprinkle lightly with salt (optl.) Microwave (high) 5-7 minutes or until seeds are crisp, stirring every minute. Rest 5 minutes.
SQUASH SEEDS: Substitute Butternut, Danish, Hubbard, etc.,

seeds; follow directions for Pumpkin seeds.

SUNFLOWER SEEDS: Substitute hulled sunflower seeds; follow directions for Pumpkin seeds. Microwave (high) 4-6 minutes until crisp.

NUTS: In 9-inch glass pie plate arrange nuts evenly. Microwave (high) using chart below, stirring every minute.

Nut	Amount	Microwave High
Almonds	½ cup	5-7 minutes
Cashews	1 cup	10-12 minutes
Filberts	1 cup	8-10 minutes
Peanuts	1 cup	5-7 minutes
Pecans	1 cup	3-4 minutes
Pine Nuts	½ cup	5-7 minutes
Walnuts	1 cup	3-4 minutes

Add 1-2 Tbsp. butter, and salt (optl.) Microwave (high) another ½-1 minute. Rest 5 minutes. Serve warm or cold. To reheat, microwave (high) ½-1 minute, stirring once. Store in tightly-covered container. Freeze, if desired.

● *Cooking times may vary depending on texture and age of nut or seed, and from season to season.*

Notes: _____

_____

BLANCHING NUTS

1 cup water   ½ to ¾ cup nutmeats

In 4 cup glass measure, boil water (high) 2½-3 minutes. Add nuts. Microwave (high) 30 seconds. Drain well. Rub nuts between two pieces of paper towel to slip skins off.

Notes: _____

● **Heat plate of food** *(high) ¾-1½ minute when interrupted by phone call, door bell or late arrival. Refrigerated food requires 30-45 seconds more heating.*

● **Refresh stale rolls** *(high) 10-15 seconds for 2; 20-30 seconds for 4; 30-40 seconds for 6. Wrap in napkin and place in straw basket to retain moisture.* **Crackers, nuts, potato chips, popcorn, etc. may be refreshed** *(high) 15-30 seconds; for full plate, heat 45-60 seconds.*

● **Heat pie slices** *to serve warm and refresh (p. 181).*

● **Soften old and crumbly shoe polish** *(high) 10-15 seconds (no metal).*

● *Make* **STREUSEL TOPPING** *of sugar (white or brown), cinna-*

mon, cloves, dry oats, and nuts. Blend and keep handy to sprinkle on cakes, muffins and doughs.
- **Caramelize sugar** *(p. 169).*
- **Heat 1 cup syrup, honey, or toppings** *for pancakes, rolls and ice cream. Microwave (high) 1-1½ minutes (metal lid removed).* **To remove the last drop from jar,** *microwave (high) 10-20 seconds (no metal).*
- **Thaw frozen bread dough** *in greased 9x5x3-inch glass loaf pan placed in 1 cup boiling water bath in 12x8-inch glass dish. Microwave medium (50%), covered with wax paper, 4-5 minutes, rotating ¼ turn every minute and turning dough over halfway through cooking. Rest 10 minutes in water bath. Bake as desired.*
- **Thaw frozen cakes, brownies and pies** *medium-low (30%) 1-3 minutes rotating ¼ turn halfway through cooking. (If packaged in foil container, transfer to paper or glass before defrosting.)*
- **Soften and heat tortillas** *(p. 43).*
- **Blanch vegetables for freezing** *(p. 70).*

- *To* **test and measure wattage in your microwave:**
  1) In 4 cup glass measure add 2 cups water. Record temperature.
  2) Microwave (high) 1 minute. Record temperature.
  3) Subtract #1 number from #2. Multiply x 17.5=actual wattage.
  Repeat 3 times and figure average of the three.
- **Boil water** *for salads, soups, bouillon, instant mashed potatoes and desserts (high) 2½-3 minutes/cup.*
- **Heat glass of wine** *to bring out aroma and bouquet (high) 15-30 seconds.*

Dieting (Micro-Slimming)

Dieting and the microwave make a perfect marriage. Studies have shown a higher vitamin retention than conventionally cooked foods because of less exposure to air, heat and water. Microwaved foods also have more flavor. Vegetables can be cooked with the water clinging after washing or the addition of 1-2 Tbsp. water for a softer texture. Because of the better flavor, the addition of fats and other high calorie seasonings won't be missed.

The Basic Four Food Groups must be maintained with any sensible diet. Serving requirements are listed with each group:
- 2 servings of milk or dairy foods (2 or more cups for adults, 3 or more for children or special needs).
- 2 servings of meat or protein alternates (2-3 oz. cooked lean meat, poultry or fish; 2 eggs; 1 cup cooked dry beans or peas; or 4 Tbsp. peanut butter).
- 4 servings of fruits and vegetables (1 cup raw or ½ cup cooked

or 1 portion, such as orange, etc.)
— 4 servings of breads and cereals (1 slice bread; 1 oz. ready-to-eat cereal; ½ cup cooked cereal, rice, spaghetti, etc.)

Fats, oils and sugars are used to round out meals and provide calories to meet energy needs.

With the microwave you can reduce added sugar because of the retention of natural flavors in many foods. Steam or poach, covered, in juices from food. Fish, poultry, vegetables and fruit are especially good this way. Fats can be eliminated from some foods and reduced in cooking others. Cooking bacon on a rack (rather than resting it in fat) eliminates calories that would ordinarily be consumed. Butter can be left off toasted cheese sandwiches with excellent cooking results. "Saute" onions, mushrooms and celery without butter. Poultry and fish need no oil to prevent sticking. Cook roasts or large amounts of meat with no flavor loss beginning fat-side-down to eliminate fat that would ordinarily baste the meat. Many vegetables can be "stir-fried." Omit fats and oils and stir-fry with steam from the vegetables for a delicious treat. Even an egg can be cooked without the addition of fat to prevent sticking to the dish. It is important to remember that fat adds flavor to food; however, less flavor is lost because of cooking less time with less water. Avoid adding toppings and sauces high in calories. Season with herbs, spices and sugar substitutes.

Another diet advantage is the ease of preparing foods. Add more variety to your menu when fixing individual foods (even if the rest of your family isn't dieting). There is very little special effort involved in fixing fish for dinner, for instance, when the rest of your family is dining on spareribs or another high calorie food.

Snacking between meals on nutritious low calorie foods is easily accomplished. A baked apple, minus added sugar, can be fixed in 2½ minutes to satisfy your dessert needs in less than 100 calories when your family is dining on German Chocolate cake. All of the following have about **100 calories:**

For These Foods:	Consider These Foods:
20 peanuts	¼ lb. lobster
2 slices bacon	2 cups bean sprouts
1 Tbsp. butter	1 whole cantaloupe
1 (8 oz.) Coke	3 cups raw cauliflower
2 cookies	3 oz. water-packed tuna fish
1 Tbsp. mayonnaise	6 egg whites
1 Tbsp. peanut butter	4½ oz. white fish
9 potato chips	4 cups raw mushrooms
1 oz. steak	1 whole baked potato
¾ cup winter squash	3½ cups summer squash
1 large banana	30 strawberries
½ (7-inch round) waffle	1½ oz. bran flakes

Do you know how long it takes to eat twenty peanuts? Not long. Eating and enjoying a lobster might take an hour. The lobster would be a better choice.

From a simple beginning such as this, you will become more calorie conscious and start a new style of eating. Consult your doctor before going on this low calorie diet for supplements. Below is a sample dinner comparing two styles of eating:

The Old Way		The New Way	
7 oz. oven fried striped bass	388	7 oz. striped bass	192
1 cup brussels sprouts	50	1 cup brussels sprouts	50
2 tsp. butter	60		
baked potato	100	baked potato	100
1 Tbsp. sour cream	30		
salad	10	salad	10
1 Tbsp. dressing	75	low-calorie dressing	20
¼ cantaloupe	25	¼ cantaloupe	25
	738		397

Divide your meal calories by:

	700 cal.	800 cal.	900 cal.	1,000 cal.
Breakfast				
⅓ calories protein or milk	50-60	75-85	95-100	95-100
⅓ calories bread or cereal	60-70	60-70	85-90	85-90
⅓ calories fruit and milk	40-75	65-75	70-80	70-80
	150	200	250	250
Lunch				
⅔ calories protein or milk	100	130	165	165
⅓ calories vegetable or fruit	50	70	85	85
	150	200	250	250
Dinner				
⅔-¾ calories protein & milk	265-300	265-300	300-325	330-375
⅓-¼ calories vegetable & fruit	100-135	100-135	125-150	125-170
TOTALS	700	800	900	1,000

THE SLIM BREAKFAST — 150 calories

¼ cup creamed cottage cheese or ½ cup skimmed milk	50-60 calories
1 slice bread or 1 oz. bran cereal	60-70 calories
⅓ cup drained sliced peaches, or canned fruit, or 1½ fresh peach half	30 calories
Tea or coffee	------
	140-160 calories

- *Allow yourself 20 minutes to eat breakfast. It is as important as any other meal.*

THE KIND AND DELICIOUS LUNCH — 150 calories
At Home

2 oz. water-pack tuna	60 calories
3 hard-cooked egg whites	45 calories
2 cups mixed salad greens	20 calories
2 slices onion or scallion	5 calories
1 Tbsp. Diet salad dressing	20 calories
	150 calories
2 oz. water-pack tuna	60 calories
¼ cup cottage cheese	50 calories
2 slices tomato	20 calories
2 slices onion	5 calories
	135 calories
2 oz. water-pack tuna	60 calories
1 slice tomato	10 calories
2 cups mixed salad greens	20 calories
2 slices onion	5 calories
1 Tbsp. Diet salad dressing	20 calories
1 cup whipped cooked cauliflower, (broccoli, summer squash, gr. beans, etc.)	30 calories
	145 calories
4 egg whites	60 calories
½ cup mushrooms	25 calories
¼ cup cottage cheese	50 calories
2 slices tomato	20 calories
	155 calories

- *Microwave egg whites without butter. Heat mushrooms and stir in cottage cheese. Add paprika and pour mixture into the "omelet." Slide onto your plate and garnish with tomato. Make other omelets with onions and mushrooms; onions, green peppers, and mushrooms; zucchini and tomatoes, etc.*

Lunch at the Office: Take 1 (3½ oz) can water-pack tuna. Order green salad without dressing and blend with low-calorie dressing **or** ¼ cup cottage cheese can be eaten with green salad and low calorie dressing **or** mix ¼ cup cottage cheese with ¼ cup all-bran cereal for a delicious crunchy lunch.

THE LUXURIOUS AND ENVIABLE DINNER — 400 calories
At Home

Breast of chicken (5½ oz)	275 calories
1 cup cauliflower	30 calories
½ cup green beans	15 calories
1 cup tossed green salad	10 calories
1 Tbsp. low calorie dressing	20 calories
1 peach	35 calories
	385 calories
7 oz. sea bass	192 calories
3 stalks broccoli	45 calories
1 cup squash	30 calories
1 cup tossed green salad	10 calories
1 Tbsp. low calorie dressing	20 calories
	297 calories

Dinner Out

Fish (dry, no butter or oil) . . . . 200 calories
Baked potato . . . . 100 calories
1 cup tossed green salad . . . . 10 calories
1 Tbsp. low calorie dressing. . . . . 20 calories
¼ cup spinach (to put in baked potato). . . . . 10 calories
10 fresh strawberries. . . . . 35 calories
                                                                                                    375 calories

• *The basics for dinner include chicken, fish and vegetables. If you want beef, use chopped beef or lean roasts but be sure to estimate the calories. The better the beef, the higher the fat content. Rib steak, for example, can range from 80-125 calories/oz. However, thin-sliced flank or London Broil can be about the same as chicken — 50-60 calories/oz.*

• **Toppings for salads and baked potatoes** *can be the highest calories in the meal depending on amounts used. Low calorie salad dressing is 80 calories less/Tbsp. than mayonnaise. For baked potatoes consider some of the following toppings as a substitute for butter (100 calories/Tbsp.):*
—*Sour cream (26 calories/Tbsb.) In some areas there are low-fat sour dressings (sour half & half) with only a few calories/Tbsp. Heart-smart dieters take note! Most "vegetable oil" sour cream substitutes are made with highly saturated coconut oil and should be avoided by the cholesterol-wary.*
—*Plain yogurt (8 calories/Tbsp.) has a taste and texture similar to sour cream. Try it mixed with parsley or chives.*
—*Low-fat cottage cheese (10-12 calories/Tbsp.) Small curd cottage cheese has a flavor similar to sour cream. Whip in blender with a little onion for more flavor.*
—*Prepare homemade sour cream by whipping equal parts cottage cheese and buttermilk in your blender (10 calories/Tbsp.)* **or** *blend ½ buttermilk and ½ sour cream (18 calories/Tbsp.).*
—*Diet margarine (50 calories/Tbsp.) instead of 100 for butter or margarine. When whipped 1 tsp. (16 calories) may be sufficient.*

For special diets such as **low salt**, the microwave is great since sprinkling salt on foods distorts the cooking pattern. We recommend adding salt only when mixed in foods and it's easy to omit this. If you plan to salt after cooking, omit it for special needs. For the **cholesterol conscious**, low fat and special products such as Second Nature, Egg Beaters, etc. may be substituted for natural foods.

Your imagination will be your best guide in planning meals to meet the special needs of your family, but the microwave will be your best friend in the kitchen to accomplish the results!

Index

(CHECK CATEGORY OR FOOD)

Teachers Kit: **Microwave Cooking in the Classroom,** a kit for teachers includes information about microwaving, use and care, Class Outline, Food & Equipment and Recipe list, Visuals, Microwave Manufacturers list, Features for Selecting, Reference List and other information helpful for planning and teaching a one-week microwave lesson. To order, please send $4.75 check to: Barbara Harris, Microwave Cooking Consulting Service, P.O. Box 2992, Dept. IN, Portland, Ore 97208.

BAKING UTENSILS
American Standard and Metric Units (rounded)

Utensil	American Standard	Metric Units (rounded)
Measuring cups	1 cup	250 ml
	2 cup	500 ml
	4 cup (1 qt.)	1000 ml
Casseroles	10-oz.	310 ml
	8 cup (2 qt.)	2000 ml
	12 cup (3 qt.)	3000 ml
Glass dishes		
Oblong	10x6x2-inch	25x15x5-cm
	12x8x2-inch	30x20x5-cm
	13x9x2-inch	33x20x5-cm
Round or Square	8-inch round or square	20-cm round or square
	9-inch round or square	23-cm round or square
	10-inch round or square	25-cm round or square
Ring Mold	6-cup	1500 ml
Bundt	12-cup	3000 ml
Tube (Angel)	9-inch	23 cm
	10-inch	24 cm
Pie dishes	6-inch	15 cm
	8-inch	20 cm
	9-inch	23 cm
	10-inch	
Cookie Sheet	14x10-inch	36x25-cm
Jelly Roll Pan	15½x10½x1-inch	39x25x3-cm
Loaf Pan	9x5x3-inch	23x13x8-cm

Join the thousands who depend on **Let's Cook Microwave!** for cooking at every meal. It is available by mail-order if you cannot locate it in your local book or microwave store. Please order from the following:

—**spiral wire-bound** — $7.95 plus $1.00 shipping — **$8.95 each**
—**3-ring vinyl notebook binder** — $11.95 plus $1.50 shipping — **$13.45 each**

Payment in U.S. dollars must accompany your order. Allow 3-4 weeks for delivery.

Barbara Harris, Inc.
P.O. Box 2992 - BOF   Portland, Oregon 97208

Please send to: _____

_____

_____ Zip Code

Enclosed find $ _____ for _____ copies of **Let's Cook Microwave!** at _____ each. Make check or money order payable to Barbara Harris, Inc. (US funds, no COD's). Please specify if a gift card is to be enclosed.

Barbara Harris, Inc.
P.O. Box 2992 - BOF   Portland, Oregon 97208

Please send to: _____

_____

_____ Zip Code

Enclosed find $ _____ for _____ copies of **Let's Cook Microwave!** at _____ each. Make check or money order payable to Barbara Harris, Inc. (US funds, no COD's). Please specify if a gift card is to be enclosed.

Barbara Harris, Inc.
P.O. Box 2992 - BOF   Portland, Oregon 97208

Please send to: _____

_____

_____ Zip Code

Enclosed find $ _____ for _____ copies of **Let's Cook Microwave!** at _____ each. Make check or money order payable to Barbara Harris, Inc. (US funds, no COD's). Please specify if a gift card is to be enclosed.